BROADWAY DAY & NIGHT

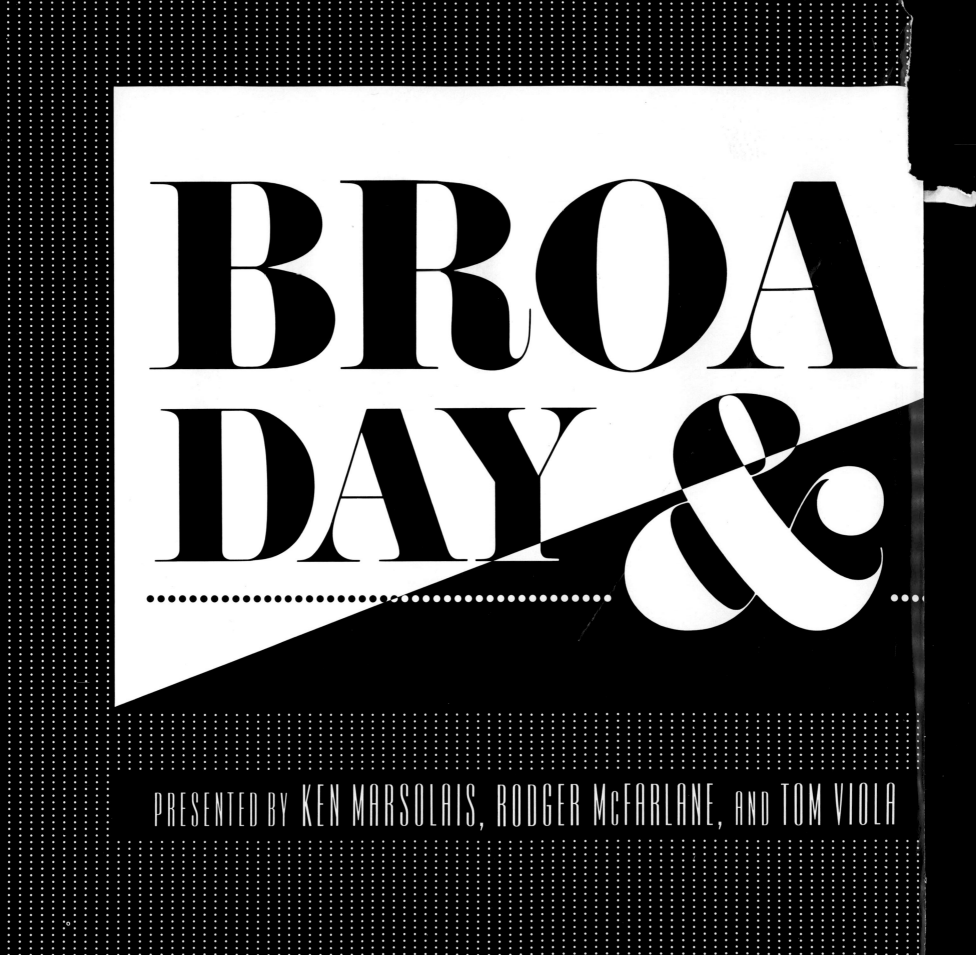

BROA
DAY &

PRESENTED BY KEN MARSOLAIS, RODGER McFARLANE, AND TOM VIOLA

DWAY
NIGHT

DESIGNED BY JOEL AVIROM

A SUE KATZ &
ASSOCIATES, INC. BOOK

POCKET BOOKS
New York London Toronto Sydney Tokyo Singapore

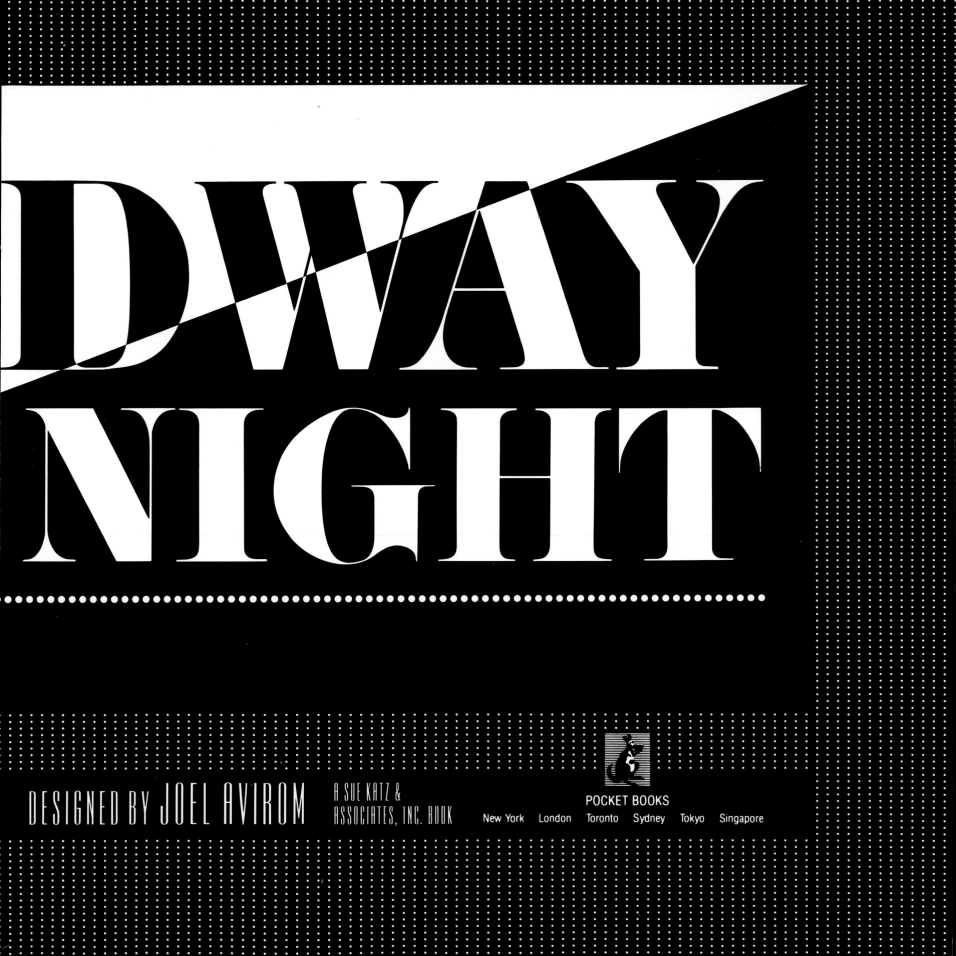

Production Coordinator

Tom Viola

Production Assistants

John V. Fahey and Stefan Fitterman

POCKET BOOKS, a division of Simon & Schuster Inc.
1230 Avenue of the Americas, New York, NY 10020

For information address Pocket Books · 1230 Avenue of the Americas · New York, NY 10020

Broadway ★ day & night / presented by Ken Marsolais, Rodger McFarlane, and Tom Viola.
p. cm.
"A Sue Katz & Associates, Inc. book"—T.p. verso.
Includes bibliographical references and index. ISBN: 0-671-74637-5
1. Theater—New York (N.Y.)—Anecdotes. I. Marsolais, Ken.
II. McFarlane, Rodger. III. Viola, Tom. IV. Title: Broadway ★ day & night.
PN2277.N5B63 1992
792'.09747'1—dc20 92-15288
CIP

First Pocket Books hardcover printing November 1992

10 9 8 7 6 5 4 3 2 1

Printed in the U.S.A.

This book is lovingly dedicated
to all theatrical artists,
but particularly those lost to the plague,
and to every man, woman, and child
living with AIDS today.

The authors' royalties from *Broadway* ★ *Day & Night* will be paid directly to Broadway Cares/Equity Fights AIDS.

BROADWAY ★ DAY & NIGHT could not have been completed without the generous assistance of scores of individuals. Their efforts are not only an invaluable part of this book but also an integral ingredient in the behind-the-scenes theatrical activity that we hope to have captured here.

THANKS TO

Actors' Equity Association, Richard-Jay Alexander, Arista Photo Service, Tobe Arons, The Authors Guild, Inc., Bryan Bantry, John Barlow, Marty Bell, Ms. Binski, Chuck Blasius, Nancy Blechman, Chris Boneau, Mary Lou Brady, Colleen Brown, Adrian Bryan-Brown, Susan Chicoine, Dennis Crowley, Merle Debuskey, Patrick Demarchelier, Maria Di Dia, Erin Dunn, Allen Eichhorn, Joshua Ellis, Gareth Esersky, Bill Evans, Paul Fargis, Bob Fennell, Glenna Freedman, Merle Frimark, Yvonne Ghareeb, Barbara Gold, Jackie Green, Shirley Herz, Manuel Igrejas, Judy Jacksina, Craig Karpel, Larry Katen, Tatiana Kouloumbis, George Lange, Bob Lawkin, Matt Lenz, Cabrini Lepis, David Le Shay, David E. LeVine, David Lotz, Jed Mattes, Robert P. McDonald, Wendy Morris, Fred Nathan, Gilbert Parker, Sid Pinkerton, Susan Potter, Ian Rand, Jim Randolph, Jeffrey Richards, Philip Rinaldi, Emilio Rodriguez, David Rothenberg, Sam Rudy, Pete Sanders, Sandy Schreiber, Shirley Scully, Peter Shaw, Elisa Shevitz, Susan Siegrist, Maria Somma, Martin St. Martin, Marc Thibodeau, Susanne Tighe, David Visser, Paul Walker, Bruce Weber, Barbara Wolfe, Miller Wright . . .

and others too numerous to mention

SPECIAL THANKS TO

Ron Silver for allowing us to annex his office at Equity.

Our friends at Pocket Books: Irene Yuss for keeping us on schedule; Joe Gramm for unflappable administrative assistance and navigating scores of revisions and corrections; Jonathon Brodman for wonderfully even-tempered and expert editing; and especially Bill Grose for his sustained enthusiasm, guidance, and support.

Joel Avirom's design team: Jim Cozza and Barbara Gold.

Joel Avirom for his patience, flexibility, and a steady and unerring artistic vision that showed us how stacks of photos and essays could become a complete book.

Toby Cohen, Tom Conklin, Theresa Desmond, and David Katz at Sue Katz & Associates, Inc.

Our dear friend and colleague, Sue Katz, for her patience, insight, and for being there from idea to finished product.

To the many theatrical artists whose thoughtfully rendered memories had to be deleted in the final page count. The decisions were excruciating and we will most certainly be punished.

And finally . . . Colleen Dewhurst, whose legacy and spirit inform all the work we do, and who, upon seeing the first handful of essays and photographs in the summer of 1991, said, "Oh, bunny, keep going. This will be so wonderful . . ." and who always wanted to see more.

CONTENTS

Photo by Joseph Marzullo

Photo by William Gibson

PRESENTERS' NOTE

This book has been organized into eight chapters that, we hope, will give the reader the ultimate insider's look at the people and crafts that come together to create the two hours or more of live theatrical entertainment that, eight times a week, is Broadway *today*.

The black-and-white photographs (with three exceptions) were all shot especially for this book from March 1991 through the end of May 1992 by a collection of first-rate photographers. Over 130 special shoots were scheduled in dressing rooms and backstage, at various and many auditions, rehearsals, meetings, "put-ins," "load-outs," studios, scene shops, and in many of the places where what you ultimately see onstage is first developed and created. We also shot on the street and in the neighborhood that makes up New York City's theatre district. We are indebted beyond measure to all of these talented photographers for their great artistry, generosity, and enthusiasm for this project.

The essays included here are the catch of a very wide net that was thrown, again and again, over the same time period. The recipients of our many request letters and calls were asked to write about their most "unexpected and/or profound" experience working in or around the neighborhood. What they wrote is that and much more.

A word about "Broadway": the New York theatre district is not found in one neighborhood, produced in a standard house, or represented by a single kind of production. Likewise, this book strays beyond the blocks bound to the south by Forty-second Street and to the north by Fifty-fifth Street, the area that by any tour guide's map makes up the Broadway theatre district. Still—and probably forever—the camaraderie and competition, myth and fantasy, and tales of heartbreak and elation that continue to draw theatrical artists from around the world to New York City are best evoked by the name of the thoroughfare through its heart: Broadway.

This book is not meant, by any means, to be the definitive look at or story of the Broadway of yesterday and today. We do not intend to imply, either by omission or inclusion, that the artists represented here are "the best" or "the only," although they are certainly a remarkable collection of just that. (The best conclusion to be drawn may be that these are only the folks who answer their mail and return phone calls.)

BROADWAY ★ DAY & NIGHT is a subjective representation and reflection of the Broadway stage, its history and its people. A slice of life. A look behind the curtain. Nothing more, nothing less. And if you feel we're being a little defensive here . . . well, welcome to the neighborhood.

We hope you enjoy your stay.

Angela Lansbury in the Broadway production of Stephen Sondheim's *Sweeney Todd.*
Photo by Martha Swope

INTRODUCTION BY ANGELA LANSBURY

As a young child in London, devoted to the movie musicals of the 1930s, I envisioned Broadway as a street that had very broad sidewalks, probably paved in gold, lit by the incredible glow of a hundred theatre marquees, peopled with tap-dancing girls clad in satin shorts and polka-dot blouses shuffling off to Buffalo—a dream world, yes, but one perhaps shared by millions everywhere.

A very few years passed and I found myself—lo and behold—in New York City at the age of fourteen, an English kid and drama student evacuated from war-torn Europe through the good auspices of The American Theatre Wing, the recipient of a scholarship to a first-class drama school. Suddenly Broadway became a reality for me.

I learned about the world of agents and producers, doing the "rounds," being seen at Sardi's, freebies, chicken croquettes at Child's, hat-checking at Schrafft's, eating at the AP Cafeteria at Rockefeller Center for a nickel (buying a cup of coffee and brown-bagging a sandwich from under the counter), and all the while barely able to breathe from the excitement that made my head spin just walking down those fabled streets of the theatre district.

Even with the success I enjoyed as a young character actress in motion pictures, I yearned to work on Broadway. I knew I had not really arrived professionally until I had faced those Broadway critics and audiences.

When the opportunity arose to play opposite Bert Lahr in *Hotel Paradiso,* I jumped at it and learned more about comedy from Bert in six months than I could have learned in six years any other way. From that time on, the die was cast; whenever the opportunity presented itself, I was on that plane to New York.

My first Broadway musical was a desperate, colossal, and now classic flop, Stephen Sondheim's *Anyone Can Whistle* at the Majestic Theatre. It ran for only nine performances, but (thank God!) it led to *Mame,* a glorious experience that lit up the Winter Garden Theatre. A few years later, I played the Madwoman of Chaillot in Jerry Herman's lovely, albeit short-lived, musical *Dear World.* Then came a dream come true—the revival of *Gypsy* and the chance to play one of the great roles in the musical theatre, Mama Rose. My most recent Broadway outing was in the brilliant Sondheim musical *Sweeney Todd.*

People who make a life in the theatre are an extraordinary lot. The passion, discipline, and hard-knocks schooling necessary to succeed place them among the most compassionate and committed people I have known.

The images and words in this book—from the unique viewpoints of just a few of the folks who have devoted their lives to the theatre—provide a rare glimpse of the hard work, serendipity, humor, love, and heroism that make Broadway the stuff of legends.

Welcome to a little piece of our world.

Angela Lansbury

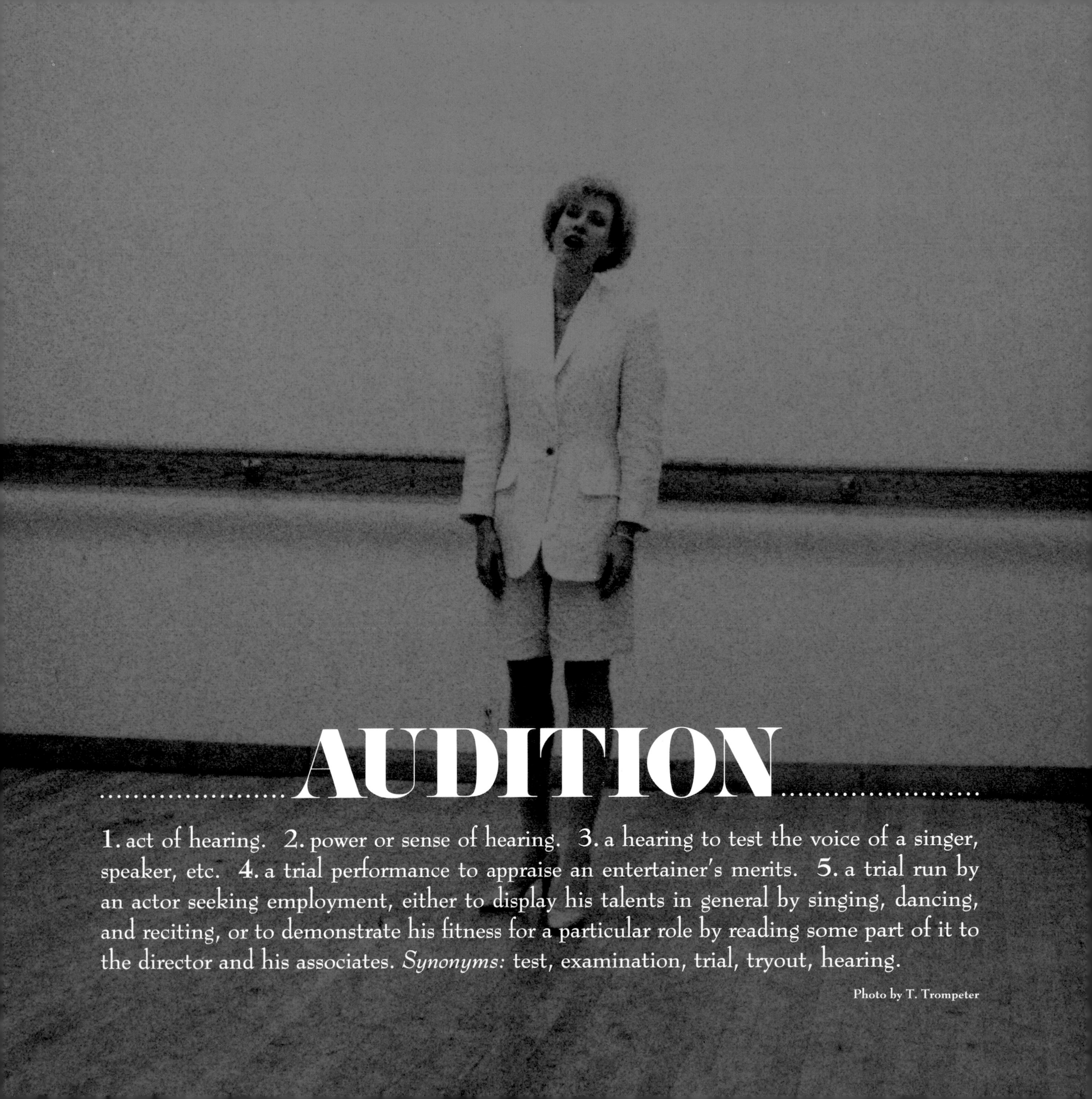

AUDITION

1. act of hearing. 2. power or sense of hearing. 3. a hearing to test the voice of a singer, speaker, etc. 4. a trial performance to appraise an entertainer's merits. 5. a trial run by an actor seeking employment, either to display his talents in general by singing, dancing, and reciting, or to demonstrate his fitness for a particular role by reading some part of it to the director and his associates. *Synonyms:* test, examination, trial, tryout, hearing.

Photo by T. Trompeter

CAROL CHANNING

Whenever I am asked, "Carol, would you ever audition for a part?" I enter into a lengthy dissertation because I do so dearly love to hear my own answer. I would like to say now that I would never take a job unless "the powers that be" *let* me audition. Allow me to explain.

My parents wouldn't let me go near the theatre until I first, like so many of us, went to college. So I decided to go to Bennington, which is in the lower left-hand corner of Vermont. On the map it's always purple, you know. Anyway, I should explain to you that Bennington is a progressive college for young women, although I understand they do allow some men to attend now, but the ratio is thirty to one, so girls have to be really progressive.

I am very grateful to Bennington, though, because every winter each of us girls was expected to leave school and go out and get a job at whatever it was she was majoring in. Since I was a drama-dance major, I naturally hot-footed it to New York to get a job performing.

The biggest theatrical booking agency was—I guess it still is—the William Morris Agency. So I went straightaway there and asked to speak to the president, a Mr. Abe Lastfogel. He was a man who was known as having a touch of genius. And so, of course, as a result he never saw anyone. Excepting occasionally John Wayne . . . or Katharine Hepburn, or Mrs. Lastfogel. He saw a lot of her. Well, somehow, through some mistake of his secretary's, there I was face-to-face with the great man himself. He was a rugged tycoon. He could make or break anyone's career with a single bite of his cigar.

I swung right into my first number, something I was sure of because it was a big hit with the girls at Bennington—a simple ancient Gallic dirge in obsolete French. The French was so obsolete and so ancient that it was spoken before all Gaul was hauled together. The dirge was adapted for the original Greek tragedy *Orestes* . . . and this was the most thrilling part of the whole thing—"The Orestes Funeral Chant." I remember how Mr. Lastfogel's eyes filled with wonderment as I showed him how the women of the Greek chorus lamented the ravages of war and the shortage of men. I had a little drum to accompany myself. The dirge was in 9/5 time. Very difficult. I sang, *"Premier le massacre des enfants et la mère . . . ,"* and so on.

When I finished the dirge, Mr. Lastfogel said that he thought I should do someone better known than Orestes, like Sophie Tucker. I sensed that I was losing the great man's attention. I switched to another song that the girls at Bennington just loved—a Haitian corn-grinding song rendered by the natives as they stomp on the kernels with their feet. I explained that they sing of their lost youth and pray for rain.

When I finished the chant, Mr. Lastfogel thought he could see some signs of improvement but that perhaps it would be wiser for me to get out of ethnic music and into the straight classics . . . like Ethel Merman. As I say, the man had a touch of genius. As he was ushering me to the door, I said, "No, please, Mr. Lastfogel, I have a beautiful song here that I ran across in my studies on Mittel-European cultures," and before he could close the door in my face, I began it:

"Moishe Chaim Boruch Schmil
Chapt a kitzl in der schtil."

"Wait," Mr. Lastfogel said, "I think I see a glimmer of talent in this girl." He said that his grandmother used to sing songs like this to him when he was a very little boy. Well, do you know, Abe Lastfogel and I wound up singing this song together! That was my first audition. He sent me over to Marc Blitzstein, who wrote modern American operas. The title of this one was *No for an Answer.* Blitzstein was casting his one big comedy song, "I'm Simply Fraught with You." I got the part, my first part on Broadway. And that's how I got into the theatre!

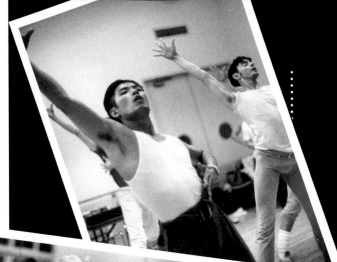

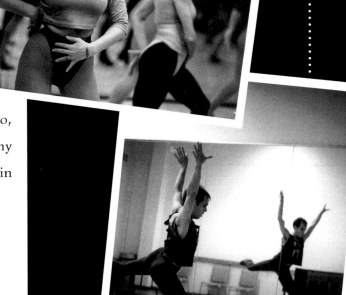

Open dance call for the international tour of *A Chorus Line*.

Photos *(opposite, and above)* by John Huba

Callbacks for the international tour of *A Chorus Line*.
Photos *(above, and opposite)* by John Huba

I have lost count of how many times I've auditioned since then, and just as often I did not get the job. Of course, I was as broken up as everyone is when she fails, but what could be worse than finding out in rehearsals that you couldn't help being wrong for the part as far as the director's idea of the role is concerned so you had to be fired or, worse yet, if you end up reading what critics had to say about your work in a disjointed production.

You see, auditioning is a two-way street. It's one thing to get the job, but another to make sure the boss knows what he's getting. If I had auditioned for my big flop, *The Vamp,* the whole tragedy would have been circumvented. The creative forces could have seen I had another whole character in mind from theirs. Auditions clear the air and set everyone on the same track or eliminate those who aren't able to be on it—maybe me.

I will never forget after David Merrick had settled on me as Mrs. Levi in *Hello, Dolly!* Mr. Merrick asked, "Who do you think we should have as a director?" I suggested Gower Champion. You see, I had had success with Gower as director-choreographer in a little revue called *Lend an Ear,* but there was a problem. Gower didn't want me. He thought I was still Lorelei Lee in *Gentlemen Prefer Blondes.* I said, "Gower, please let me audition for you. I'll read the character for you from *The Matchmaker* [the Thornton Wilder play on which *Hello, Dolly!* was based]." I remember I was playing at the time in Shaw's *The Millionairess.* It was late at night in my hotel, but I was so in love with Dolly that it didn't bother me at all. We finished reading the role at dawn. Gower, listening intently all this time, finally said, "I'll buy that."

Many of us know that most every show in its formation goes through a baptism of fire. Once Gower said "I'll buy that" we stood together like a ship's rudder in a storm. He made tremendous changes in the show, but he never questioned my concept of Dolly. By the way, it was a great relief to Jerry Herman and Mike Stewart that we were all one creative family.

When the motion picture producer Ross Hunter, the director George Roy Hill, and Julie Andrews asked me to play in *Thoroughly Modern Millie,* I told them I loved the character and agreed to do it then and there—provided I could audition. This perplexed George Roy Hill, who said, "But Carol, the part was always yours." I said, "Please tell me this after you see me do it." Well, as it turned out, everybody was happy. I, of course, was happiest.

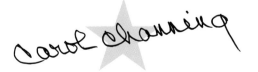

The same thing happened with my lifelong friend Mary Martin. She called and said, "I have a script here, and if you think so, it could be a play in which we could work together," as we had always wanted to. It was called *Legends* by James Kirkwood and was about two ex–movie stars. Once I had read the script I found that Mary and I both thought it was funny, we could play the characters, and the play needed work. I called Mary and asked to come to Palm Springs to read my part for her. Mary said, "You don't have to audition for me." But I was on the next plane and stayed with her in Palm Springs until the first day of rehearsal. In a way it was a long audition, but Mary and I never had a problem with our characters. We wished we could have said the same for the script. We broke box office records and the audiences were happy.

Why are auditions so agonizing? We actors have got to learn to embrace them. Does it help to know that not only you are seeking the role, but those who are casting are hoping that you are the one for the role? You are there to aid and abet *them*.

No, this doesn't help because you haven't had the exercise yet of flexing the particular muscles used uniquely by this character. You have only the character in *mind* and you hope your thoughts somehow come through. That's one reason why auditions are agonizing—you are not ready.

Right now, I am asked to do a television series, but first I must audition for the role. Auditions! I find, regarding them, that I am absolutely beside myself, but then beside myself has always been my favorite position.

Carol Channing

Callbacks and onstage with the international tour of *A Chorus Line*.

Color photo by Martha Swope

Black-and-white photo by John Huba

Photo by John Huba

PETER LAWRENCE

I have been a stage manager for twenty years, and perhaps because of my survivor status people often ask me for my advice.

Here is the advice I gave a young performer once.

In 1982 I stage-managed a new musical called *Rock 'n' Roll! The First 5000 Years*—an unfortunate title for a very innovative musical. The idea was that eleven singer/musicians would sing, dance, and play most of the major rock-and-roll songs of the past thirty-five years.

The show, directed by Joe Layton, was difficult to cast. Each performer had to be able to imitate convincingly ten different singers and play the instruments that those performers used. But even more difficult was finding the two understudies—one man and one woman who could sing and play every rock-and-roll song ever written. We said we were looking for two "jukeboxes."

Vinnie Liff and I auditioned over 2,500 non-Equity hopefuls, came up with a cast that Joe Layton approved, and proceeded to issue contracts.

Everyone signed gratefully except the woman understudy, who, instead of signing her contract, told me that she had decided to go to California and try to begin a recording career.

"You're nuts," I told her. "You're going to give up a job understudying on Broadway to move to California for a nonexistent recording career!"

But Madonna Ciccone ignored my sage advice and went to California. A couple of years later I saw her first album at a record store. She had dropped her last name and become just Madonna.

Advice doesn't count. Only desire.

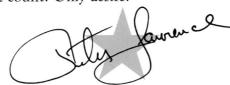

EMANUEL AZENBERG

As I get older, I find I am asked more and more frequently: "How do you get started in the theatre? How do you get a foot in the door? How do you begin?" (Sometimes I even find I am asking myself these questions!)

The truth is, it is a cumulative process: you make a phone call, you have a friend, you get some sort of a job, you meet a stage manager, you get a better job (now you are sweeping out an off-off-off-Broadway theatre), you meet a producer, you become an assistant company manager, etc., etc., etc. This is a difficult process to explain to a twenty-two-year-old fresh out of drama school and full of ambition, enthusiasm—and information. This is an even more difficult process to explain to the *parents* of a twenty-two-year-old. "Congratulations! You have just paid a jillion dollars to put your child through school, and if he is lucky, he will get a job sweeping out a theatre and maybe meet someone."

Well, it was true in my case. I started out as an assistant to a company manager in an off-Broadway theatre called The Renata (until recently the Bleecker Street Cinema). It was 1959. My magic moment came later on—in 1961 when I was the company manager for a not-well-remembered Broadway play called *Sunday in New York,* which starred Conrad Janis, Pat Stanley, Sondra Lee, Pat Harrington, Sr., and featured a new blond twenty-four-year-old named Robert Redford. We played on the same softball team—of course. . . .

In 1963, when Redford was starring in *Barefoot in the Park,* I got a phone call from him saying, very confidentially, that Mildred Natwick and Kurt Kasznar were not very good softball players and he needed a team. Redford played first base. I played shortstop. Carmine Caridi played third base. Lou Tiano was the catcher. In truth, that is all I can remember about that team, except the second baseman. He was a pretty good hitter, he didn't have a lot of range at second, and he had a strange name—Doc. That is how I met Neil Simon.

Nine years later I luckily and gratefully became Neil's producer. Since I cannot believe—nor does anyone else in the theatre—that producers do anything special, I am convinced that whatever position I have achieved and sustained over the years has to do with my ability to pick up a ground ball or hit a softball—*that* is what I had confidence in. The producing part is still a mystery.

Manny Azenberg

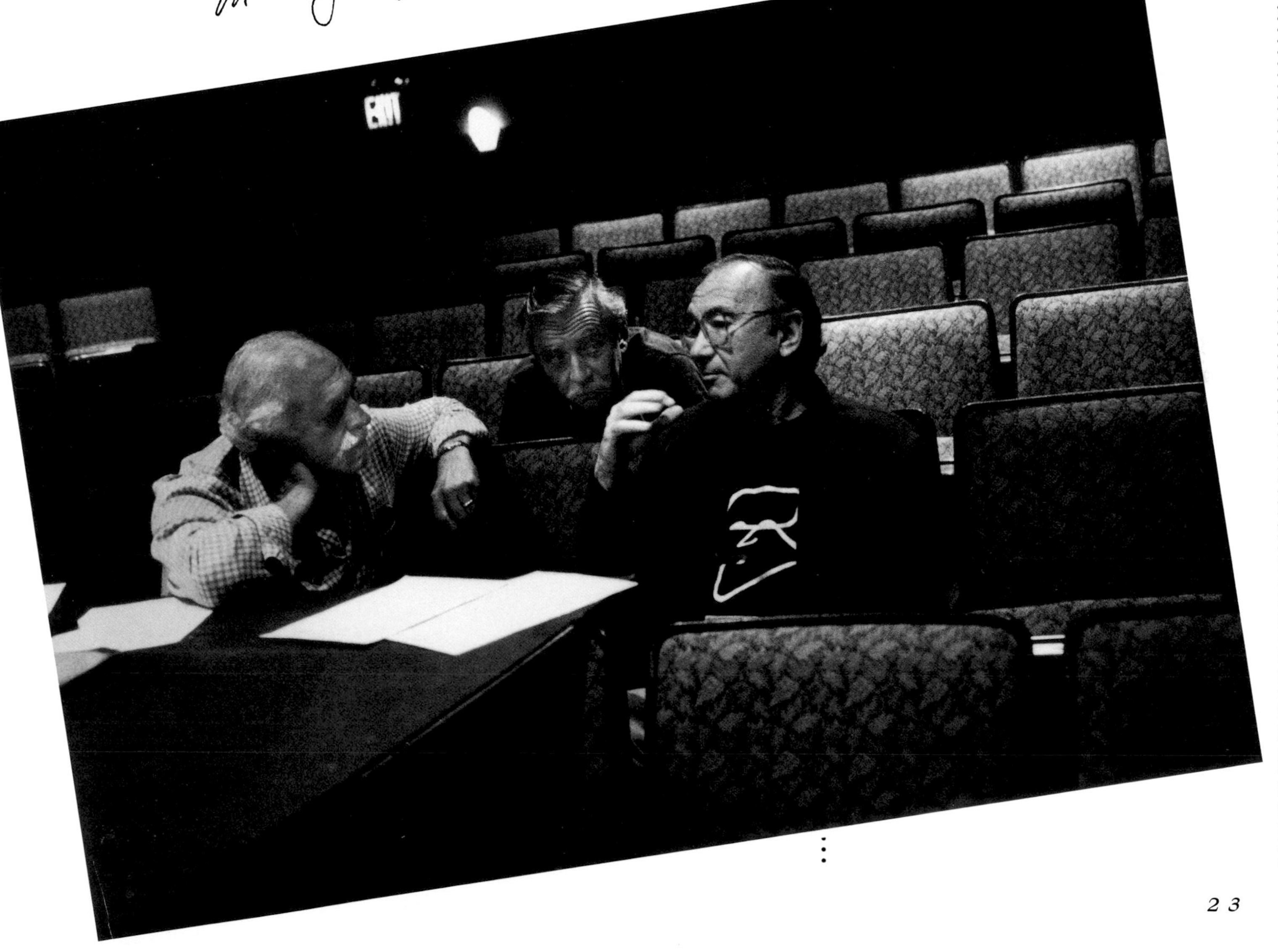

Gene Saks, Manny Azenberg, and Neil Simon at the auditions for *Jake's Women*.
Photo by Allen Frame

ELI WALLACH

Josh Logan asked me to audition for the upcoming new musical *South Pacific.* "I can't sing," I said. All through school, teachers would wince when I tried a song. "Someone is flat," they'd say, and they always looked directly at me. "Never mind," said Logan with a great smile of assurance. "All you have to do is read. We just want you to read a scene from the play."

So on the appointed day I walked into the Majestic Theatre, out on the stage, looked into the darkened auditorium where Logan, Hammerstein, and Rodgers were sitting, gulped, and then read the lines handed me by the stage manager. "That was fine," said a voice out of the blackened void. "Now sing!"

Again I gulped and then remembered my wife Anne Jackson's sage advice: "If they ask you to sing, just act it; improvise something." At this point the pianist ran up to me and asked, "What key?" That's like asking a blind man to open a lock. "Key, key?" I asked. Then I whispered to him. He returned to the piano and waited. I then improvised—put an imaginary coin in an imaginary phone, dialed an imaginary number, nodded to the pianist, and sang, "I'll be down to get you in a taxi, honey. Better be ready by half past eight. Now, honey, don't be late—" Then I hung up the phone and spoke to the trio out there in the dark. "Sorry, sorry. I can't sing, I've got butterflies in my stomach." "It's all right, it's all right," said Logan with aplomb. "We'll get you a real phone next time."

P.S. I didn't get the job, but Logan put me into *Mr. Roberts* with Henry Fonda, where I spent two happy years—without singing a song.

Eli Wallach

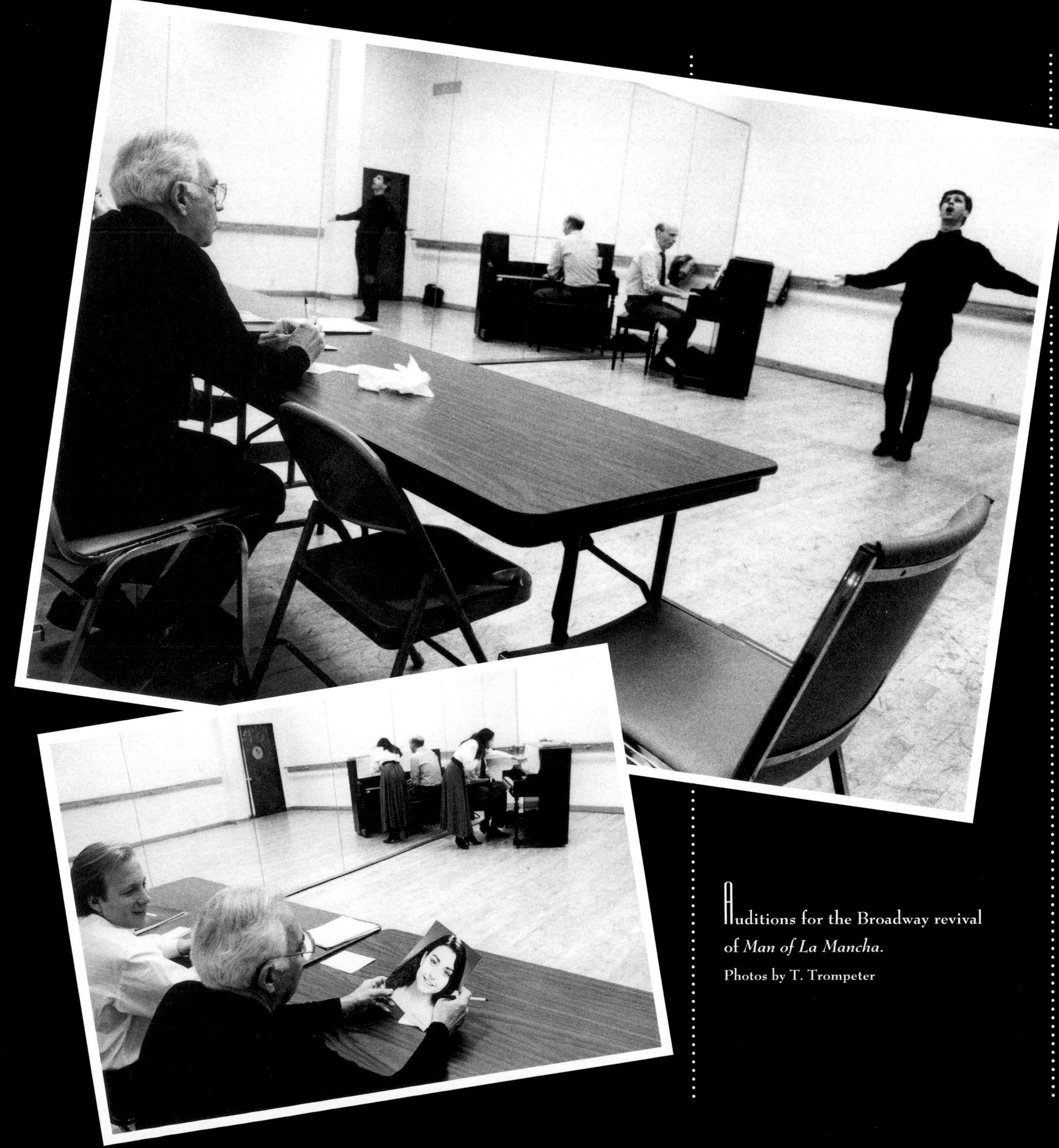

Auditions for the Broadway revival of *Man of La Mancha*.
Photos by T. Trompeter

BARRY BROWN

"Find a property, raise the money, and bring it in."

That's the advice I got from Ron Field when I told him I wanted to be a producer and that I was looking for a job (any job) on his upcoming production of *On the Town*.

It was a lunch that ultimately cost us two years and a few thousand dollars.

When my late partner, Fritz Holt, and I decided to become producers and produce *Gypsy* in London, our only thought was to get Angela Lansbury to star as Rose. *Gypsy* had never been done in London because, as Arthur Laurents later told us, "No one there ever wanted to attempt it without Ethel [Merman]."

Both Fritz and I knew Steve Sondheim personally, Fritz as production stage manager of both *Company* and *Follies,* and I since my father had been an employee of the music publishing company that published Steve's catalogue. We went to Steve with our idea, which he liked, and he suggested that, in order to proceed, we should meet Jule Styne and Arthur Laurents and talk it through with them. They both responded very positively, and Arthur agreed to direct.

Fritz and I decided to go to London to explore coproducers and general managers, and as luck would have it, Angela Lansbury was going to be there at the same time—on a press tour for *Bedknobs and Broomsticks*.

Through Angela's agent, an appointment was set up for us to have lunch with Angela and her husband, Peter Shaw. We met them in the lobby of the Connaught Hotel, Angie coming down the stairs with her arm in a cast and looking none too hungry. We said our hellos, looked at her arm, and I asked, "What happened?" She gave me a look that said, "What *are* you, blind *and* stupid?" and answered simply, "Broke it." Not a good beginning.

We ate, told them of our hopes and plans, and were answered with, "No, thank you, not interested, thanks anyway." So we said our good-byes and let them pick up the check. Mistake.

But by this time, Fritz and I were really into *Gypsy*. So for the next year and a half we pursued other actresses, continued to raise money, and, happily, developed a close relationship with Arthur, Jule, and Steve. By late 1972 we'd raised $185,000 of the $275,000 capitalization (that's right, $275,000!), but still had no star.

Then one day, out of the blue, the phone rang and it was Angie. "Is the offer still open to do *Gypsy?*"

"Yes, yes, yes!" we shouted.

We wondered what had happened to make her change her mind almost two years later. Well, a journalist friend of theirs was visiting them at their farm in Ireland over the Thanksgiving holidays, and Angie happened to be reading aloud from one of the London papers that a certain actress had been signed (not true) to play Rose in the London premiere of *Gypsy*.

"Oh, they asked me to do that two years ago," Angie said.

"What!" the journalist friend shrieked. "You turned down the chance to make your London debut in the greatest role ever written for a woman in the history of the American musical theatre? Call them right now and tell them you'll do it."

And she did. And we did. Four months later we were in rehearsal, and one month after that we opened. And the press hailed it as "the most exciting thing to happen in London since V-E Day."

After running in London for a year, *Gypsy* transferred to America and began a six-month national tour, culminating in its arrival on Broadway at the Winter Garden Theatre. The show was a huge hit, and Angie won her third (out of four, to date) Tony Award for playing Mama Rose.

"Find a property, raise the money, and bring it in." Sounds simple, no?

Open call for the national tour of *Bye Bye, Birdie*.
Photos by John Huba

HAROLD PRINCE

Paraphrasing Arthur Laurents in his libretto for *Gypsy:* "Everyone in the theatre listens to everyone."

To best illustrate, the following anecdote:

In 1949 I was casting director of *Call Me Madam,* a musical written by Irving Berlin and Lindsay and Crouse for Ethel Merman, to be directed by George Abbott, choreographed by Jerome Robbins, and produced by Leland Hayward, the most prestigious producer on Broadway. Chorus auditions were held in the Imperial Theatre where thousands of singers sang for fourteen jobs. They waited outside the stage entrance behind police stanchions, and we fed them into the theatre a hundred at a time, where they were initially screened for "type."

In the midst of the chaos, the stage doorman called me to the phone. "Irving Berlin," he whispered. I picked up the phone.

"Who is this speaking?" asked Berlin.

"Harold Prince, sir. I'm stage-managing the auditions."

"Is George Abbott around?"

"No, I'm afraid not, Mr. Berlin. He came in and saw one thousand people auditioning and left. He won't be back until the end of the day."

"Well, is Lindsay or Crouse around?"

"No, I'm afraid not, Mr. Berlin. I heard Mr. Abbott phone and tell them to stay away."

"I don't suppose Ethel is around?"

"No, Mr. Berlin, Miss Merman wouldn't be expected at a chorus call."

"Is Jerry Robbins anywhere in the theatre?"

"No, Mr. Berlin, this is a singing audition. He won't be here until we audition dancers next week."

"Well, is Leland in the place?"

"No, sir, Mr. Hayward came for the start of the day and left."

Long pause. "Who did you say you were?"

"Harold Prince, Mr. Berlin."

"What exactly do you do?"

"I'm casting director, and I'm stage-managing this audition."

After a shorter pause: "I see. Well, you'll do. . . ." Whereupon he sang an entire chorus of a new song he had written for the show. When he finished . . .

"What do you think of it?"

"I like it, Mr. Berlin."

"So do I!" And he hung up.

Principal auditions and dance call for the national tour of *Bye Bye, Birdie*.
Photos by John Huba

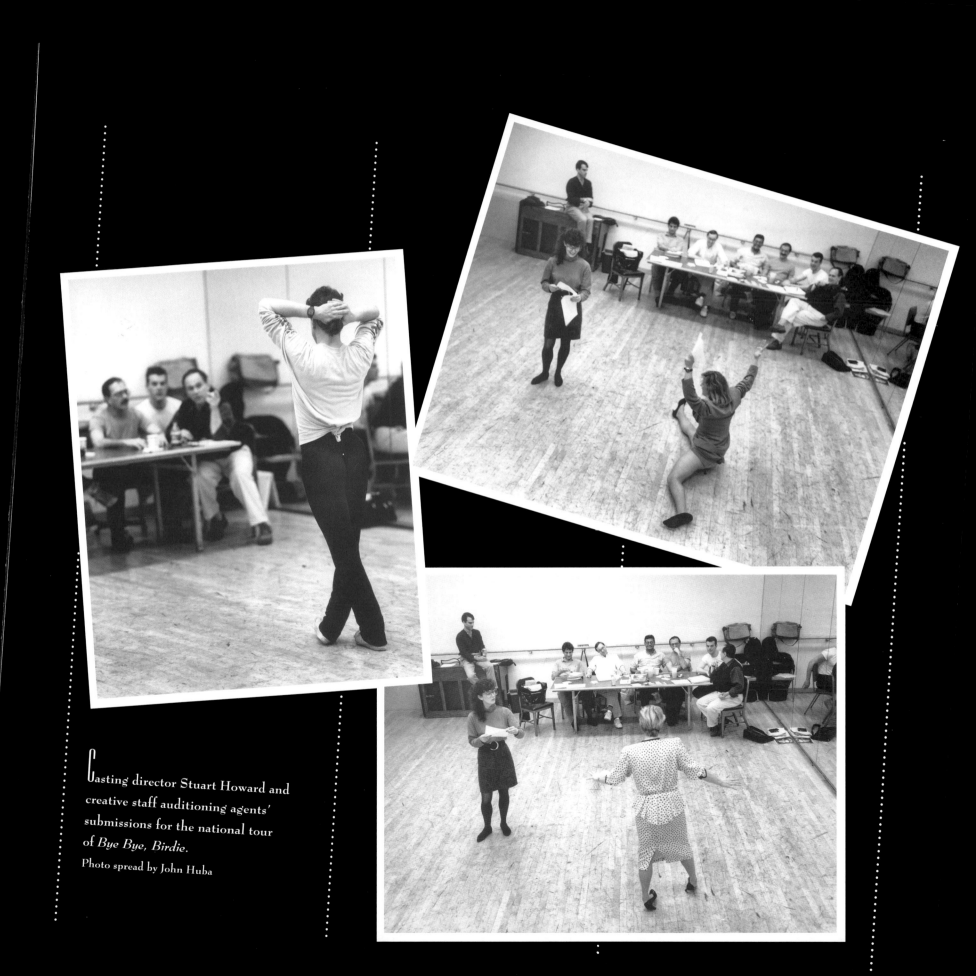

Casting director Stuart Howard and creative staff auditioning agents' submissions for the national tour of *Bye Bye, Birdie*.

Photo spread by John Huba

STUART HOWARD

How could I not be thrilled to meet the legendary Arthur Laurents for whom I was to cast *La Cage aux Folles?* Well, I was thrilled . . . but I was also scared to death because of his reputation for being, shall we say, "difficult." To make matters worse, on the first day of auditions, Arthur decided to quit smoking cold turkey . . . he was not a happy man . . . and as I quickly learned, when Arthur is not happy, the world around him quakes. *La Cage* was the first Broadway musical I cast, and I was literally feeling my way in the dark supported by the executive producers, Barry Brown and Fritz Holt, who continually reminded me to watch my step in front of the formidable Arthur. My steps, as you can well imagine, were taken gingerly.

For some reason I've never understood, I was instructed by the show's producer that certain actors were not to be auditioned . . . among them was George Hearn.

My heart in my mouth, I scheduled an audition for George, feeling that he was the man most right to play Albin. George was the first actor to audition for *La Cage* on the stage of the Belasco Theatre, gowned by Theoni V. Aldredge, wigged and made up by Teddy Azar, and gamely supported by his friend Colleen Dewhurst. My heart was beating as loudly as George's as he sat on the piano, sang "Where or When," and dazzled everyone. When he finished, Arthur turned to all assembled and congratulated me for finding the man who would eventually play Albin in New York and London, and win a Tony Award. Fade out.

Fade in after eight more shows with Arthur, the perfect director for whom to cast: he not only cares passionately about the show but about the people who work with him . . . and trusts them to do their jobs.

Stuart Howard

CAMERON MACKINTOSH

Nothing in my theatrical memory has, or I suspect ever will, eclipse the opening night of David Merrick's production of *42nd Street.* No scriptwriter could ever come up with a more extraordinary mix of musical comedy, melodrama, and real-life histrionics than *42nd Street*'s first night and Merrick's onstage announcement of the untimely death of the show's great director, Gower Champion.

To put the impact of the evening into perspective one has to go back to the show's original announcement. Merrick had been away from Broadway for almost a decade, disillusioned by a series of noble failures in the midseventies and unsatisfactory flirtations with Hollywood. *42nd Street* was to be America's greatest producer's comeback. The project's announcement was met by considerable industry cynicism and lack of investment. Merrick was so incensed he decided to ignore everyone's opinion and put up the entire enormous $2 million capital himself (oh, glorious days!). He opened the show at the Kennedy Center's Opera House in Washington where it played to pretty good business and encouraging reviews, but was by no means a racing certainty. I was in New York at the time and, being very anxious to see the show, went down to Washington to see a fairly full Saturday matinee. The show was still being worked on, but I was bowled over by a fabulously exhilarating piece of consummate showmanship that by sheer staging talent and performance spun the old yellow corniness of the plot into true musical-comedy gold. After the show, I went backstage to see Michael Stewart, the show's author, whom I knew from London. Brimming with enthusiasm, I asked him if Merrick had any plans for London, and he said why didn't I ask him myself as he was staying next door at the Watergate Hotel. So round I went, rang his room—filled with trepidation because of the great man's legendary reputation—and a few minutes later we started what for me was an extraordinary two-hour talk about the show, the theatre, and the art of creating musicals. He didn't know me, our paths had crossed only once back in 1973 when he attended a preview

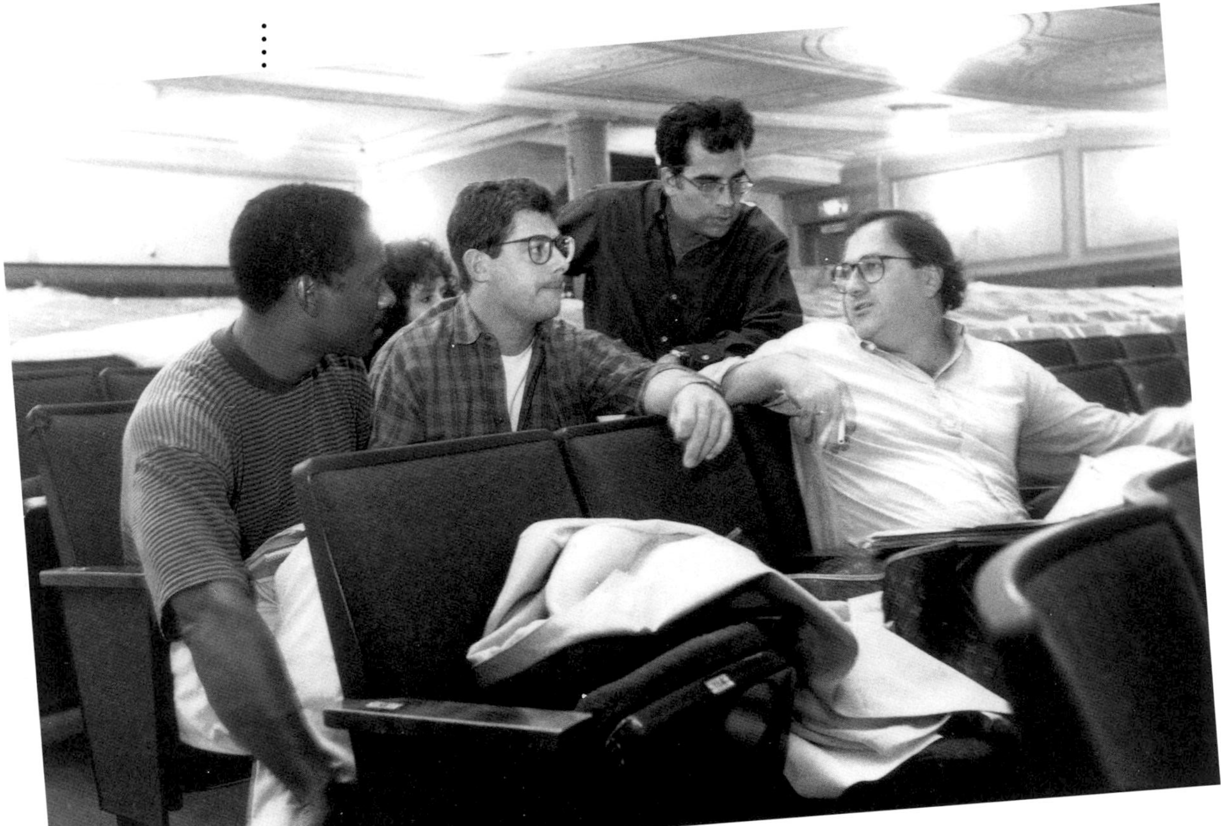

Author Clarke Peters, publicist Merle Frimark, producers Cameron Mackintosh and Richard Jay-Alexander, and casting director Vinnie Liff at the Broadway auditions for *Five Guys Named Moe.*

Photo by Joan Marcus

of a musical I was doing in London, but he most charmingly poured out his tremendous knowledge and enthusiasm to me without a trace of condescension or self-importance. It will always be one of the most treasured conversations of my life.

We discussed my possible involvement in the London production, and he invited me to be his guest at the upcoming Broadway opening night. During the period between the closing in Washington and the Broadway opening, Merrick played every trick in the book with the media. Refusing to schedule previews, opening the show for a night then closing it again. Building up a dizzying ''Is it on or is it off?'' campaign. No one does this better than Merrick, and everyone relished the great showman's ruling the roost once more.

As we expectantly took our seats in the star-studded auditorium of the Winter Garden Theatre, on August 25, 1980, nobody knew that the drama we were about to witness two and a half hours later had already started early that day. Gower Champion was already dead. He had died in a hospital earlier that morning, but only a few people knew, and Merrick was determined to keep it that way. One person in particular couldn't know: *42nd Street*'s leading lady, Wanda Richert, who was also Gower Champion's girlfriend. The company was kept in rehearsals at the theatre all afternoon, and all telephone communications to the theatre were cut. Merrick did everything in his power to stop the news from getting on the wires, and the hospital was sworn to secrecy. Miraculously, considering the gossip-driven industry we are in, the secret was kept, and the curtain went up on what was to be the finest epitaph anyone in the theatre could ever have—a brilliant, copper-bottomed smash hit showing the talent of one of America's greatest director/choreographers in peak form.

At the end of the show, the audience went wild; the little girl from Allentown, Wanda Richert, had done as Jerry Orbach, playing the fictional director, had ordered—she'd gone out there a chorus girl and come back a star. At the height of the cheering and standing ovation, on came Merrick, hand up to his chin gazing at the stage floor; the audience went even wilder. Merrick had done it again, reversed his fortunes and delivered a triumphant evening that had his personal stamp all over it. As he shook his head at the approbation, he said quietly, "This is a very tragic moment." The audience laughed and roared more. He was playing them, they thought—the irrepressible showman was having a game, pretending the show hadn't gone down well—they loved it and laughed louder. He tried to stop them, and eventually, waving his arms around, he managed to quiet the audience enough to be heard to say, "No, no, no, you don't understand. I have to tell you Gower Champion is dead." The bombshell dropped. The cast, arranged behind him, gasped and screamed. The cheers and hurrahs froze in the audience's throat. The cries of the cast were pierced by the sound of the distraught horror and disbelief of

Wanda Richert. Pandemonium reigned until several minutes later, Jerry Orbach, just as he had done playing the director not long before onstage during the show, took command of the situation, calmly ordering the curtain down, the cast off the stage, and the audience to leave. Life was imitating art. This was a fusion of fact and fiction we were witnessing. A numbed hush fell over everyone as we filed out of the theatre, only to be pierced, so I believe, by the voice of Ethel Merman saying, "I'm glad he managed to get all the changes in in time."

As we all went out onto Broadway, we were dazzled by the razzmatazz of numerous floodlights sweeping in from the theatre and the sky. This was a great old-fashioned opening, with police on horseback, press photographers, and huge crowds waiting to see their favorite stars. Well, they saw them all right, but they didn't hear them, as the surrealism of the evening continued with the crowd walking out to the glamorous party that was waiting for them in the ballroom of the Waldorf-Astoria. Everything was as it should be except for the ghostly murmur of fifteen hundred people in black tie and evening gowns walking across Manhattan.

No press agent could ever have dreamt up a story to get more coverage, and the following day the media propelled Gower Champion, David Merrick, and *42nd Street* to legend. Despite the press frenzy Merrick had to deal with, he still kept his appointment with me, but sadly this meeting was to turn out to be the end of my dream of working with David Merrick. Thereafter, I found the road to *42nd Street* diverted to a dead end. With hindsight I think that the advice and encouragement that were so willingly given to me by David Merrick were worth infinitely more than anything I might have tried to painstakingly negotiate out of him by doing the show. Thank you, David.

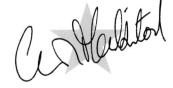

.. PREPRODUCTION ..

1. theatre term that suggests creation before creation, constructed by use of prefix *pre,* meaning before in place, time, order, or rank, and *production,* n. 1. act of producing; creation; manufacture. 2. something that is produced. 3. a literary or artistic work. 4. a work presented on the stage or screen or over the air. 5. the act or process of producing. No known synonyms.

Photo by T. L. Boston

KEN BILLINGTON

In over twenty years of lighting Broadway, Las Vegas, and Radio City Music Hall, one of my most memorable projects was the legendary concert Ethel Merman and Mary Martin gave at the Broadway Theatre on Sunday, May 15, 1977.

On the first day of rehearsal I went to the old Nola Studios on Fifty-seventh Street to meet the ladies. I was introduced to Mary first. She was most gracious, and as we talked, she told me how excited she was to be working again after a ten-year retirement. Although her eyes never left mine, I could not help but notice that she was rummaging through her purse. Out of the blue in midconversation she slapped a large piece of fabric down on the table and said, "This is what *my* first gown will be. I don't know what *she'll* be wearing," gesturing to Ethel. I thanked her and then crossed the room to talk to Miss Merman.

"Miss Merman, I'm Ken Billington."

"Are you doing the sound?" she bellowed.

I explained that I was the lighting designer, but she was much more interested in her sound than the lighting. I mentioned that she had performed *Gypsy* at this same theatre, and I was sure no one had ever complained about not hearing Ethel Merman. She then told me that the microphones in the footlights were no good, and she refused to use a hand-held mike. With a large gesture she said, "My hands, my hands, I sing with my hands," saying what she really wanted was a radio microphone. "They're great. . . . You put the mike between your tits, slap the amplifier on your leg, and you can sing all night!" After that first harrowing ten minutes I didn't know what the next two weeks would bring.

As lighting designer I always see rehearsals to familiarize myself with staging and music so I'll be prepared to set light cues when the show moves into the theatre. About a week later I asked to see a run-through of part of the show. At three P.M., when I arrived, Donald Saddler, the director, asked the ladies if they would run the finale for me. This was a medley they had performed in the early fifties on a TV special celebrating the fiftieth anniversary of the Ford Motor Company. Ethel didn't know why they had to run the number: "Can't you just listen to the record?" Mary chimed in, "Merm, if Ken needs to see this, then let's do it for him." Ethel's protests continued, but Mary finally won.

The stage manager set up one lone folding chair for me facing the ladies' two stools in the center of the small rehearsal hall. After taking their places, Ethel parked her famous chewing gum in her cheek, and the show began.

The medley intertwined popular songs with songs associated with each lady. While Mary was singing out in full voice selling a great show, Ethel was laying back since she didn't want to do this rehearsal anyway; that is, until she heard Mary sing "My Heart Belongs to Daddy." Ethel realized she was being shown up, so she now began "I Got Rhythm" in full voice. The competition had begun . . . for an audience of one sitting eight feet in front of them. As they broke into the last number, "There's No Business Like Show Business," they stood up, walked closer to me, and belted out as if they were in Carnegie Hall. As two of the greatest musical-theatre stars ever sang the show business anthem to me, my eyes filled with tears of joy, and I realized that *this* is the reason I went into the theatre. After the huge musical-comedy ending, the room was silent except for the quiet sobs of the lighting designer. Ethel slid her chewing gum back and said, "Hope you got it!" And did I ever.

And ever since, when I have a demanding day working in the theatre, I think about that afternoon and know how lucky I am to be doing what I love.

Ken Billington

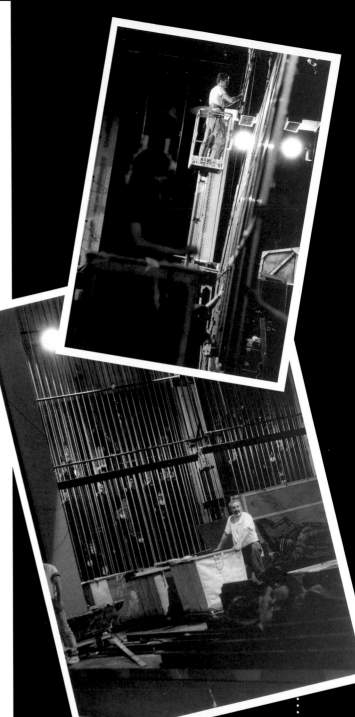

Load-in for *Gypsy* at the Marquis Theatre.

Photos *(above, and opposite)* by Paulo Netto

ROBIN WAGNER

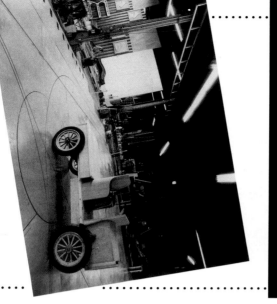

Construction of Robin Wagner's sets for *Crazy for You.*

Black-and-white photos by T. L. Boston

Color photo *(opposite)* by Joan Marcus

It was March of 1976 and we were part of the first Chinese-American Arts Exchange. Each day in Peking the twenty-four of us would set off for another amazing destination: the Great Wall, the Summer Palace, the Ming Tombs, etc. Each morning, we would coerce Michael into coming along, although it was clear that his interest was minimal. What interested him more than any monument were the long evenings in the bar of the hotel, a bridge table in the lobby with bottles of Chinese spirits on it, talking until the wee hours with the students who would man the so-called "bar" . . . that is, until the morning we visited the Peking School of Dance. Every morning thereafter, four days in all as I remember, he would be up at dawn with his dance bag, waiting for the government taxi to drive him there. We went on with our official tourist duties until the fourth morning, when he said as he left, "Come over to the school around noon. I want to show you something."

We arrived at noon and there, outside, were dozens of dance students standing bundled on the frozen ground, staring through the windows of the academy, seemingly impervious to the weather. In the building, more students were pressed against the glass doors to the classroom, while inside, dancers hugged the walls around the room like a human baseboard. Michael, with his most gracious smile, welcomed us into the space, offering us the few collapsible wooden chairs directly behind a single firepot, which was the only source of heat in the room. As we sat down, he turned on the portable cassette deck he had brought with him from home, and the music of the Hustle filled the room. Three men and three women dancers began an exquisitely choreographed ballet that for the next eleven minutes transported us across those boundaries of language, culture, and geography that had separated our worlds for so long. It was not the same Hustle that we knew from Studio 54, and yet it was still American. The movement was gentler, lyrical and lovely, without the hard edge we were used to seeing. It was a vision of another sensibility. This kind of music had never been heard on this part of the earth. The expression on Michael's face was pure joy. And most joyous of all was his pride in having done something, or maybe having left something, in Peking.

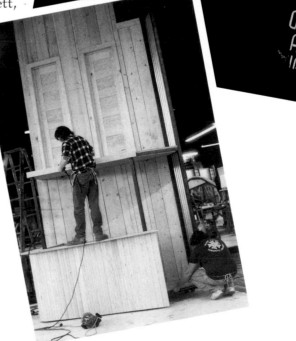

Later that night, at the monolithic Peking Train Station, we boarded the sleeper cars that we were to take to Soochow; bicycles began arriving outside our window, not just a few, but what seemed like hundreds. It appeared that the entire School of Dance had biked some six miles across the city to say good-bye to Michael. Two of the dancers who had performed presented him with a few small gifts wrapped in white tissue with red ribbons. One of them apologized for the meagerness of the gifts and for the absence of a few students who could not come to say good-bye, saying that they were very sorry and would he please forgive them. Michael, realizing that virtually the entire school had shown up, and being deeply moved, replied, "Let me do something, let me send you something. There's got to be something I can do for you!" The two dancers conferred, and then one of them said, "Well, there is one thing that you could do, Mr. Bennett." Michael's reaction was instantaneous: "Anything, I'll do anything you ask me." Then they replied, "Please, Mr. Bennett, please, don't dance in Shanghai."

Michael told me later that evening that if he ever wrote an autobiography, it would be called *Please, Don't Dance in Shanghai.*

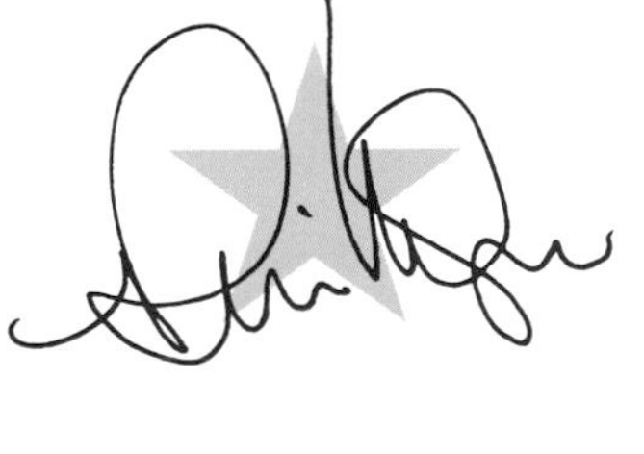

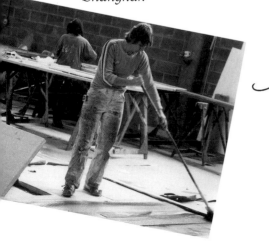

Backstage at the put-in for *Gypsy* at the Marquis Theatre.
Photos by Paulo Netto

TONY WALTON

I miss Bob Fosse terribly—and mostly I miss his mischief.

There were times under stress when his moods could get famously dark, but more often than not, his passion for the work at hand was infectious and sometimes exhilarating. And sometimes not.

When we were getting ready to try out *Pippin* at Washington's Kennedy Center, we spent patient hours fine-tuning the sequences following the opening number: "Magic to Do." The entire deck split open and slid imperceptibly upstage in order for a Medieval Palace Setting of Silk, Rope, and Scrim to be whisked upward into place by Ben Vereen—the Leading Player. A little while later it unexpectedly rose even farther to become Charlemagne's Campaign Tent for "War Is a Science." Various practical pieces completed each stage picture, and Bob more or less patiently organized the handling and timing of all this along with some pretty tricky Jules Fisher lighting cues.

Pat Zipprodt's costumes were flamboyant and subtly sophisticated (and involved some nifty formfitting scraps of armor for the always-gorgeous Fosse dancers), and all of these Bob integrated fluidly into the scenic and lighting shifts while we watched in delight. A delight mingled with relief that our risky design plan seemed to be working . . . and from Bob's mood, it even seemed in the cards that there might be a compliment or two in the offing.

Bob's Cheshire-cat smile grew wider as our complex visual scheme gave way to a completely black and bare stage for Ben Vereen's solo introduction to a seductive slither of a dance.

Vereen, dressed entirely in black—in our black void—posed in a tiny pool of white light as a Straw Hat and Cane sailed out to him from the wings.

And as Ben started his dance, Bob leaned over to me in the darkness and sighed:

"Aah . . . now *that's* what I call a set!"

JOEL GREY

When Hal Prince first spoke to me about the way he envisioned the MC in *Cabaret,* he recalled a heavily made-up man in a German nightclub he had seen when he was stationed there during the war. He remembered this performer with lipstick, rouge, lashes—a garish and gaudy spectacle.

Makeup had always held a great fascination for me, being brought up as I was as a child actor at the highly esteemed Cleveland Playhouse. At nine years old, I would sit in the dressing room, rapt, as I watched the older actors put on beards and mustaches made of crepe hair, wigs, shading, putty, etc., to create their characters. I never missed an Olivier performance, for in addition to his brilliant acting, one could look for inspired makeup ideas that said so much about and added such mystery and magic to the particular part he would be playing. He, along with Chaplin, Cagney, Lorre, and Astaire, would become my role models as I grew up in the theatre.

But back to the MC. One day after rehearsal, we went about experimenting. Hal and I found that using women's traditional makeup—base, rouge, lipstick, lashes, etc.—certainly was unusual, but *something* was missing. The MC was androgynous—not female. He also had to exist on different levels—as the symbol of decadence and as a real "flesh and blood" second-rate performer in a tacky cabaret. My wife had been an actress and had a makeup case full of goodies. I remember the excitement as my fingers searched out each of the colors and textures, the way I imagine a painter does with a blank canvas, then watching this character come to life: beginning with a base called juvenile pink (this creep would want to look younger), followed by Johnson's baby powder. Then thick, dark brown, slightly arched eyebrows, dark orange liner under the brows, blue lids, and my wife's ancient throwaway lashes, so thick with mascara that they looked like black construction paper. Not fussy or fluttery, but more like a ventriloquist's dummy—opening and closing. A raspberry rouge, and for the lips, *not* lipstick (no shade of lipstick looked quite right), but an age-old German shading stick called Leichner's Lake. Under the bottom lip, brown shading indicating a lurking beard. Dippity-Do flattened the hair—a center part to indicate the period (late 1920s)—tight against the skull, and (drumroll) . . . there in the mirror (cymbal crash) . . . "*Willkommen, bienvenue,* welcome."

Joel Grey

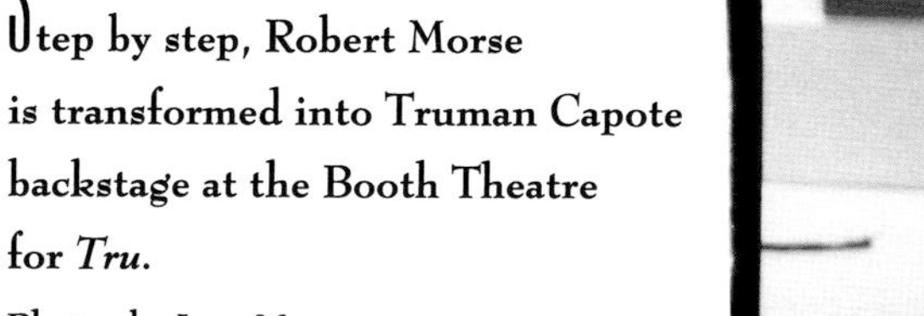

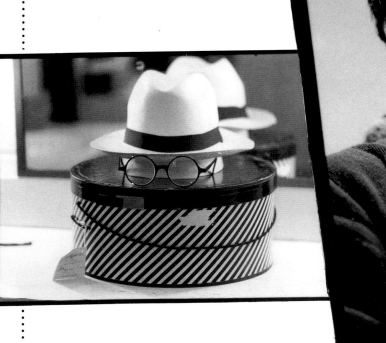

Step by step, Robert Morse is transformed into Truman Capote backstage at the Booth Theatre for *Tru.*

Photos by Joan Marcus

ROBERT MORSE

Iconoclastic memories . . . hard to believe. While doing *Take Me Along* at a very young age, can you imagine the pleasure I received sharing the stage with the dear man Walter Pidgeon? Walter Pidgeon . . . didn't he discover radium? Didn't he help the boys return from Dunkirk? *Madame Curie.* Walter Pidgeon . . . tall . . . always wearing a beautiful suit. I can still see him strolling down Fifth Avenue with a foulard in his breast pocket, a walking cane, a croquet cap, and an impeccable suit to match.

I played Richard in *Take Me Along.* Walter Pidgeon was my father. This was class. This was distinction. It was always "Mr. Pidgeon" this and "Mr. Pidgeon" that, and he'd say, "Oh, Bobby, call me Walter." I held him in sure reverence. I still do today.

The Shubert Theatre. Forty-fourth Street. Opening night. Before the show I was informed that Mr. Pidgeon wished to see me in his dressing room to present a "small opening-night gift."

Walter Pidgeon giving me an opening-night gift! I whisked across the stage, ran up the stairs, and knocked on his dressing room door. "Who is it?" boomed the stentorian voice of the most dignified gentleman in all of show business.

"It is I. Bobby. Bobby Morse. Richard [my character's name]." I waited.

"It's Richard!" I repeated. "Bobby Morse, you sent for me!"

The voice boomed: "Come in, come in. Open the door!"

I turned the knob, opened the door. I stood there in shocked silence, my eyes bulging. The sight I saw was Mr. Pidgeon, the paragon of elegance and refinement, casually peeing in the sink.

"Don't be so alarmed, boy. Aye, actors have been doing this in the dressing rooms ever since I can remember."

"Oh, I see."

Show business . . . another lesson learned. I'll never forget Walter Pidgeon doin' his thing in the sink. I pass this story on with love and wonderment. Tradition!

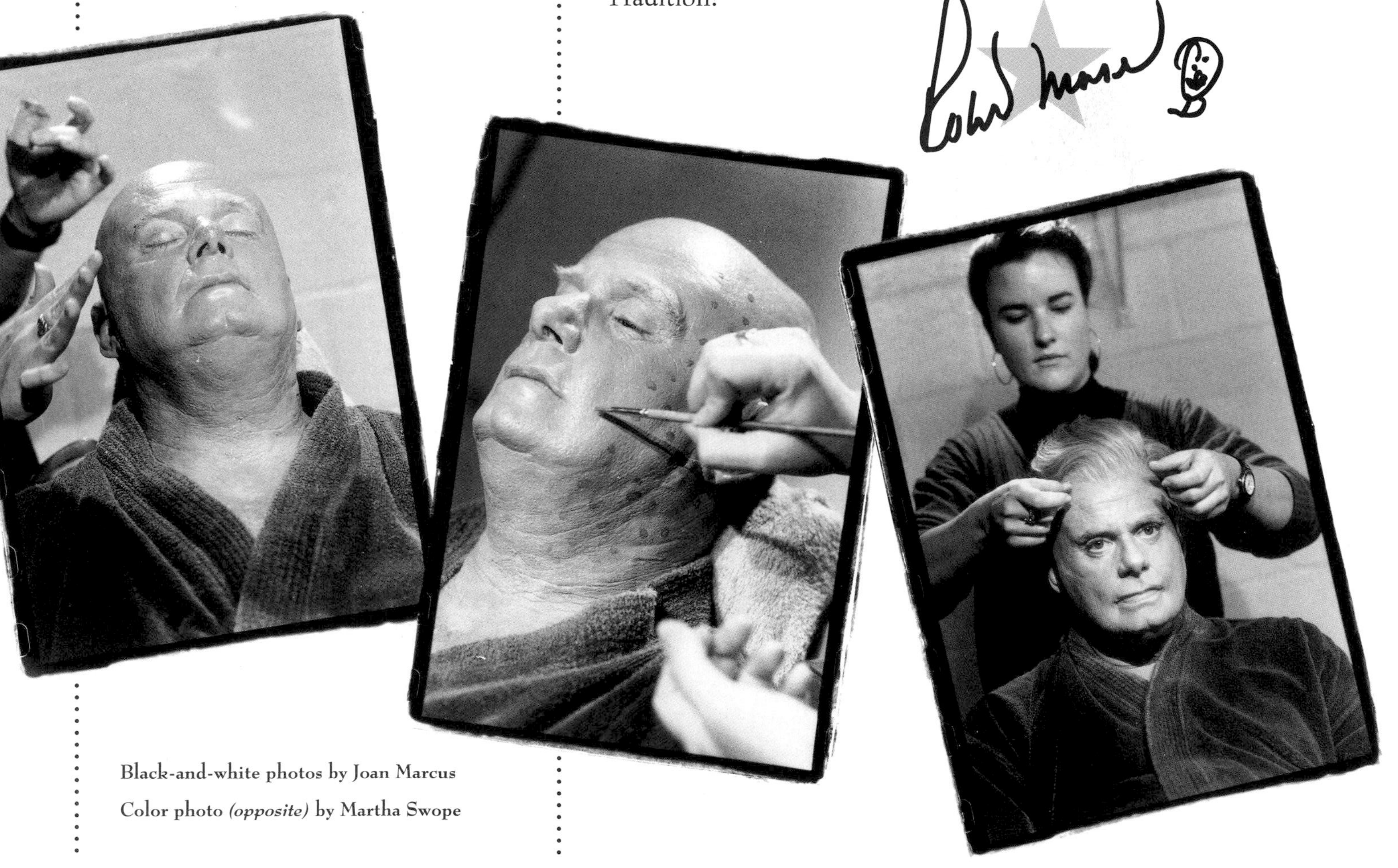

Black-and-white photos by Joan Marcus
Color photo *(opposite)* by Martha Swope

BARBARA MATERA

In the twenty-five years that I have been executing the costumes from the drawings of designers, I have worked on scores of shows, with designers such as Irene Sharaff, Raoul Pene DuBois, Miles White, Theoni Aldredge, Florence Klotz, Patricia Zipprodt, Robert Mackintosh, Willa Kim, William Ivey Long, and Santo Loquasto; all have created costumes for many hits and some misses. The memories I have are not only about clothing and designers, actors and actresses, but also about the wizards who assist me in this execution. These memories always come to mind under the title of a show, in this case *Mame, Legends, Evita,* and *On Your Toes.*

While we were working on the original production of Jerry Herman's *Mame,* we had a lovely orange-and-white cat named George who made his home in the workroom. George was a street cat, but like so many of us, he adapted to his new environment beautifully. Unfortunately, George developed a taste for tulle and one day was found contentedly munching his way through Angela Lansbury's "Peckerwood Dress." Everyone is forgiven one moment of madness. But not long after, George was discovered dining on a wedding dress that Ms. Lansbury was to wear in Hal Prince's film *Something for Everyone* and was permanently dispatched from the workroom. While no one could dispute his taste in leading ladies, tulle and lace were definitely not on the menu.

During rehearsals for *Legends,* which had a Western setting, Elizabeth Ashley, the show's star, called me backstage to say that "although this character is tough and brawny, I think it would be useful if I had a fan. And, darling, I really need one to work with during this afternoon's rehearsal."

I hurriedly called my assistant Allison and asked her to bring a fan, any fan, from the shop. After a while, I saw Allison come into the theatre. I called her over and whispered frantically, "Where is the fan?"

"In her dressing room," she replied.

"What kind of fan is it?" I asked. A puzzled look came across Allison's face. I asked again, "Is it feather, is it lace, or what?"

Barbara Matera and staff create the Theoni V. Aldredge costumes for *Nick & Nora (above,* and *opposite).*
Photos by T. L. Boston

She answered hesitantly, "Electric . . . with a cord."

This explained the rather long sideward glance I had received from Ms. Ashley upon her first entrance at that afternoon's run-through.

On the occasion of making the clothes for *Evita,* we were busy embroidering the famous white sequin dress that Patti LuPone was to wear when she sang "Don't Cry for Me, Argentina." Now, some of our beaders, although their fingers work magically, are getting along in years and a little hard of hearing. One of them, Teresa, asked, "Who is this dress for?"

"It's for *Evita,*" I replied.

There was a pause. "A beadah? A beadah? If she's a *beadah,* why can't she bead her own dress?"

Soon after she won the Tony Award for Best Actress in a Musical in the hit revival of Rodgers and Hart's *On Your Toes,* Natalia Makarova came into the studio for a fitting. She arrived and walked across the reception area, literally dragging a long, red-fox coat, looking a bit tired, but glamorous. As I stood waiting for her, someone called out, "Oh, here comes Broadway's newest star!" Natalia stopped, rolled her eyes and quietly uttered, "Tvinkle . . . tvinkle . . . tvinkle."

Frantic schedules, fittings, refittings, directors' needs, and star personalities are all part of the execution of the costumes for every production. Designs change, stars come and go, shows open and close. What is constant is my love for my work and the very talented people with whom I share the workroom. But to continue as I have for over twenty-five years, I must endeavor to find the moments of fun in each project. These are what I remember, and without them, what I indeed love would be just a job.

Barbara Matera

ALYCE GILBERT

It all began with a phone call on the pay phone in the basement of the Shubert Theatre:

"Michael Bennett wants to speak to you."

"Hello, Alyce . . . how many finale costumes do we have anyway?"

"Since the two tours and the bus and truck closed, about three hundred. . . . I'd have to count them . . . there wouldn't be that many top hats and shoes."

"Great, thanks . . . bye."

Thus began a process that would end with rivers of gold and silver, filling the aisles of the Shubert Theatre in the most memorable day and night for me, and many others . . . the performance that made *A Chorus Line* the longest-running show in Broadway history: number 3389. From the time Michael Bennett and Joe Papp decided to make a big celebration of the event, the New York Shakespeare Festival staff, led by Bob Kamlot, Bob McDonald, Steve Cohen, and many noble assistants, joined with production stage manager Tom Porter and his assistants to produce a combination of class reunion, preproduction of a new musical, homecoming, publicity stunt, and family therapy, while continuing to perform *A Chorus Line* eight times a week.

That week in September 1983 began with 332 former and current cast members being sorted into six companies—arousing all the old "use me, choose me" emotions—and marshaled through a parade of rehearsals, parties, interviews, and costume fittings while each found his or her own place in the line again.

While the Shubert wardrobe crew, including Ted August and Bee Sherman, who had been dressing *A Chorus Line* since the Broadway opening, and Harry Eno, who had joined the crew in 1978, held the fort with the current New York cast in the Shubert dressing rooms, I set up a giant dressing room–wardrobe room onstage at the Booth Theatre, which adjoins the Shubert and was empty at the time and generously lent by the Shubert Organization.

Together with Karen Lloyd, who had supervised one of the early road companies, and Bobbie Sue Albrecht and Charles Auburn of the original dressing staff and a fabulous crew of dressers, many with histories with *A Chorus Line* in New York and on the road, some of whom were on the crew in 1990 when *A Chorus Line* finally closed, we dressed all 336 of them in Theoni V. Aldredge's mighty achievement, the *Chorus Line* finale costumes, and Woody Shelp's glowing top hats, which reappeared from trunks, parents' attics, and closets for one more time. One hundred and twenty performers were also fitted in Theoni's audition clothes, with much help from Milo Morrow and the NYSF costume shop. Of course, we didn't know that *A Chorus Line* would continue for so long and that we would have the last performance without Michael, or Jimmy Kirkwood or Ed Kleban, and that Nick Dante would be barely strong enough to attend the closing.

In 1983, only one person who had been in *A Chorus Line* had died: Danny Ruvolo, who had been killed in a car crash, the way that you used to assume young men died in peacetime.

I didn't know, standing on the stage of the Booth, surrounded by finale costumes, with ranks of improvised dressing tables on the stage and in the mezzanine . . . dressing rooms filled with Cassies, Zachs, and the original cast . . . that so many young men who danced that night would not see *A Chorus Line* close.

Performance 3389 was astonishing. . . . Michael and Bob Avian with the massed dance captains, Baayork Lee, Troy Garza, T. Michael Reed, Alex Mckay, and Roy Smith, had engineered a miracle.

The current New York cast opened the show until the selection of the line, when the original cast . . . to mad applause . . . appeared behind their photographs and performed "At the Ballet," when after Kay Cole's high note, another company appeared—the companies came and went invisibly as if they turned into a mist—all a part of Michael's black-box magic and the extraor-

Wardrobe supervisor Alyce Gilbert backstage at *The Will Rogers Follies*.
Black-and-white photos by Frank Franca
Color photo by Martha Swope

dinary bond that existed among designers Robin Wagner, Tharon Musser, Theoni V. Aldredge, and Michael to make the magic.

There were three adorable Vals, nine Pauls, and heart-stoppingly, Donna McKechnie, facing her mirrors, which rose to reveal her successors suddenly, the stage full of red skirts . . . "Nothing" sung in Japanese, Priscilla Lopez singing "What I Did for Love" surrounded by the original cast and ghosts from many companies for each character melting away to leave the original company on the line for the elimination and the amazing finale: first the original cast from stage right and the New York cast from stage left, then another cast upstage and another beyond that until there were six lines, all bowing at once.

Then, by wizardry that has always been attributed to Bob Avian, they all vanished except for the nineteen originals, who were linked in a circle, to be joined by everyone as the mirrors turned into a sunburst, and the houselights came up, and every aisle from orchestra to balcony was filled with top-hatted, high-kicking dancers . . . some with happy memories, some with painful ones . . . all suddenly realizing that they could do it, could be a part of it, and that just to do it was a joy, however brief.

Alyce Gilbert

REHEARSAL

1. something recounted or told again. **2.** (a) a private performance or practice session preparatory to a public appearance; (b) a practice exercise. **3.** practice for public performance. **4.** drill or train by repetition. *Synonyms:* play, perform, preparation, preparatory, making ready, perfection, maturation, evolution, gestation, incubation, practice.

Photo by Martha Swope

JOHN CULLUM

Camelot was in trouble. Opening night in Toronto, the second act barely managed to get under way before midnight. Moss Hart, our director, was in the hospital from a heart attack, and Alan Jay Lerner, bookwriter/lyricist, soon joined him with stomach ulcers. The show was foundering and nobody was at the helm.

Boston reviews were not good. That had a dampening effect on everybody, but it was his foster father's, Philip Burton's, criticisms that made the strongest impression on Richard. Alan, barely out of the hospital, was trying to direct the show, but nothing was really happening—piddling changes in the script, a couple of new songs that went in one day and out the next.

On a Wednesday after two dreary performances before noticeably hostile audiences, a rehearsal was called for eleven the next morning to go over song-and-dance numbers. Burton blew up: "Asinine! The bloody show's too long. You want me to dance around all day and sing my head off. That's not going to help anything." And off he stormed to the nearest bar, followed by half the company. Later, we adjourned to Richard's hotel room. By three-thirty A.M. all were gone but me. Richard was still boiling mad. "Phil Burton is a marvelous director. He has the know-how and guts to make major cuts and changes, but Moss and Alan are afraid of him," he snarled. "*Camelot*'s a good show, dammit! It's incredible that it's being pissed away."

With Richard still pacing like an angry lion, I fell asleep on the sofa. Around six A.M. I heard on the phone, "Julie, darling, it's me. . . . Yes, of course, *me,* Richard! Who the bloody else would be calling you at this hour?"

He's talking to Julie Andrews, I thought.

"Darling," Richard growled, "I'm lonely and very sad. I want to come down and be with you." There was a pause. Then Richard rasped out, "You don't love me!" He slammed the phone down. "Cullum, are you awake?"

I froze. The phone rang. Richard grabbed it and said, "No, no, now! You don't love me the way I love you, that's all!" He slammed the phone down.

I jumped up, looking at my watch. "Hey, Rich, have I been asleep? It's almost seven o'clock; we've got rehearsal in a few hours. You okay?" Richard said nothing, just smiled.

Those who knew Burton know how meticulously punctual he was about rehearsals, but Richard didn't appear that morning at eleven and was nowhere to be found for the rest of the day. I was his understudy, and it didn't take long to establish that I was the last to see him. "I left his place at four-thirty A.M.," I lied. I was depending on Julie Andrews to be my alibi, and sure enough, Julie told everybody, "Richard called me around six."

As I frantically went over songs, dances, and lines, I thought, "How could Richard do this to me?" Precisely at "half hour," as I was being pinned into King Arthur's first-act costume, Richard calmly walked through the stage door. He apologized to the company, "I'm dreadfully sorry, dearhearts. It shan't happen again." Richard had made his point. Next day, Philip Burton took over as our director.

When the show opened in New York City, Phil Burton's name was not in the program. So far as I know, he never got credit for any of the work he'd done. Maybe he preferred it that way, maybe he didn't want to upstage Richard —that would certainly have been like Phil. But because of Phil, we were a hit, and *Camelot* earned a place in the annals of great American musicals.

Things might have turned out differently. That fateful morning when Richard disappeared, an anxious Alan Jay complained, "For heaven's sake, Julie, if Richard wanted to come to your room, why didn't you let him?"

With bell-like tones in oh-so-proper English, Julie answered, "Well, I simply couldn't do that, could I? After all, I am a married woman." And then in a way I'll never forget, she added sweetly, "But of course, you know, I did leave my door *unlocked.*"

John Cullum

LARRY GELBART

Who says Broadway doesn't care?

Who says the only heart on Broadway is the one you eat out when your best friend has a hit?

March of '63. I hail a taxi outside of Sardi's to take me to a run-through of *A Funny Thing Happened on the Way to the Forum*. The run-through is for an invited audience before the show goes on the road prior to its New York opening in May. No costumes, no scenery. A "gypsy" run-through.

The cabdriver correctly guesses—my glasses, my beat-up manila envelope, enough anxiety to fill the empty seat beside me—that I have something to do with the theatre. I tell him I'm involved with a new musical.

"Good luck," he says. "I'd like to see a success come out of this cab."

After the run-through, the first reaction comes from Arthur Laurents. He pronounces the show sensational. Things are looking good for the cabdriver.

The show opens in New Haven. It's not very good. Not really. Not yet. Arthur comes to see it and says it's absolutely marvelous.

We do a lot of work on it before our next stop, Washington. The reviews are terrible. Arthur travels to see a performance and says the show is terrific.

The work continues. We play a week of previews in New York. Arthur catches one and says the show is wonderful.

The changes go on.

Opening night. The curtain comes down. The audience response is electric, enthusiastic.

I'm standing at the back of the house, numbed by it all, when Arthur Laurents comes up the aisle to tell me that the show is fabulous.

I thank him for how supportive he's been, for always saying how much he liked the show.

Arthur's reply? "And *this* time I mean it."

NATHAN LANE

Being cast in the revival of Noël Coward's *Present Laughter* directed by and starring the one and only George C. Scott was probably the biggest break of my career. I had just signed with a new agent, Jeff Hunter, who asked if I would be interested in doing a small part in a play on Broadway. I had just costarred with Mickey Rooney in an NBC series and was what they call "hot" for about twenty minutes. I had been dying to get back to the theatre so this was great news. He said, "George C. Scott is doing an old Noël Coward play at Circle in the Square and there's this would-be playwright named Roland Maule. I think you'd be just right for it."

"A Broadway show with George C. Scott? I think I could squeeze that in," I said jokingly.

Well, I read the play, and it turned out to be a terrific part. I thought for sure they would want a star or someone with more credits than I had at the time. Anyway, the appointment was set up, but I didn't know whether Mr. Scott would be there for the first audition. They called my name, and as I walked down the steps of the theatre, I heard that unmistakable voice. My heart started pounding. I was introduced to the stage manager, Michael Ritchie, the casting director, Lynn Kressel, and Mr. Scott. He was extremely gracious and friendly, chatted a moment, and then asked me to read the first scene with Michael.

Now, I had been a part of a comedy team for about three years. One of the sketches I had done with my partner was about what happened to Christopher Robin, the whimsical little boy in A. A. Milne's Winnie the Pooh stories. He was now thirty-five and his father wanted him to leave home and get a job. All Christopher wanted to do was have tea parties in the forest with Pooh and his friends. I used this character as a basis for Roland.

On my second line George laughed uproariously, which shocked me. This continued throughout the reading. I thought he was being extremely kind. I finished, he thanked me, and two days later I was offered the part. I was

George C. Scott, Bette Henritze, and company at the first rehearsal of Circle in the Square's revival of *On Borrowed Time*.

Photos by Marcia Lippman

ecstatic. I bounced off the walls for an hour and felt very lucky. Never had a job come so easily.

That show turned out to be a big break for many people, including Kate Burton, Dana Ivey, and Christine Lahti. It was a wonderful rehearsal period.

However, during the first two weeks George somehow got it into his head that my name was Norman. He would say, "Norman, try this," or, "Hey, Norm, go with that." Norman, Norman, Norman! Now, George is a charming, intelligent, and very funny man, but a formidable figure nonetheless. Especially to me. He had always been one of my acting heroes, so I was too intimidated to tell him he had my name wrong. In fact I thought of legally changing my name to Norman rather than contradicting him. When the cast started to giggle quietly whenever he called my name, I knew it was time to say something. So I said, "George, I hate to be the one to break this to you, but my name is Nathan, not Norman, Nathan. And by the way, big guy, I loved you in that movie *MacArthur.*" Fortunately everyone laughed, including George, who looked at me and said, "Okay, kid, from now on you can call me Greg." The show became a big hit and I will never forget the laughter of that opening-night audience. Every actor should be lucky enough to make a Broadway debut under the leadership of a general.

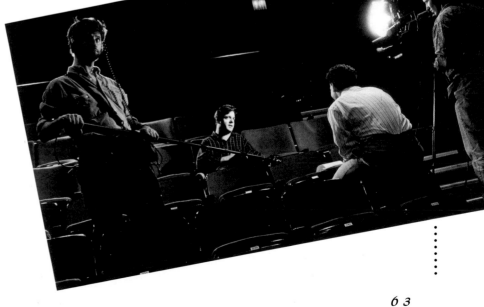

Nathan Lane at a press rehearsal for *On Borrowed Time.*

Photo by Marcia Lippman

Rehearsing the company of *Five Guys Named Moe.*
Photos by Joan Marcus

FRANK D. GILROY

TIME: *now.*

PLACE: *a Broadway bar.*

AT RISE: *a* PLAYWRIGHT *and a* DIRECTOR, *both midforties, have just been served drinks.*

DIRECTOR

One week to previews.

PLAYWRIGHT

And all is well.

DIRECTOR

You mean that?

PLAYWRIGHT

Of course.

DIRECTOR

I'm relieved.

PLAYWRIGHT

You don't think we're in good shape?

DIRECTOR

Yes. But I wasn't sure how *you* felt.

PLAYWRIGHT

I couldn't be happier.

DIRECTOR

Then why . . .

PLAYWRIGHT

Why what?

DIRECTOR

Nothing.

(*Raising his glass.*)

Cheers.

PLAYWRIGHT

(*Staying the* DIRECTOR'*s hand.*)

Not till you tell me what you were going to say.

DIRECTOR

You haven't missed a minute of rehearsal.

PLAYWRIGHT

What about it?

DIRECTOR

You're entitled to a day off.

PLAYWRIGHT

You don't want me at rehearsal?

DIRECTOR

Just for a day.

PLAYWRIGHT

I'm in the way.

DIRECTOR

Not in the least.

PLAYWRIGHT

Why then?

DIRECTOR

It would advertise you feel I'm doing a good job.

PLAYWRIGHT

A public vote of confidence?

DIRECTOR

Yes.

PLAYWRIGHT

Consider it done.

DIRECTOR

Now I feel like an ass. Forget it.

PLAYWRIGHT

I insist. There are things I've been neglecting a day off would let me attend to.

DIRECTOR

Really?

PLAYWRIGHT

Really.

DIRECTOR

Nothing like a day off to freshen the eye.

PLAYWRIGHT

No need to sell me.

DIRECTOR

In your heart of hearts you don't want to do it, do you? . . . Well?

PLAYWRIGHT

No.

DIRECTOR

Besides being your right, you feel it's your duty to attend all rehearsals.

PLAYWRIGHT

That's not it.

DIRECTOR

What then?

PLAYWRIGHT

Remember Lindsay and Crouse?

DIRECTOR

They wrote *Life with Father.*

PLAYWRIGHT

There's a photo of them on the wall of The Dramatists Guild. A candid shot in an empty theatre. Crouse, feet perched on the seat in front of him. Lindsay in the row behind. Their expressions blissful, rapturous, sublime. Know why?

DIRECTOR

No.

PLAYWRIGHT

It's a rehearsal.

DIRECTOR

The point eludes.

PLAYWRIGHT

How many plays have you directed?

DIRECTOR

Counting this one, forty-four.

PLAYWRIGHT

Counting this one, I've had five plays produced and we're the same age.

DIRECTOR

What's the punch line?

PLAYWRIGHT

(Doing math in the air.)

Four weeks rehearsal multiplied by forty-four . . . four times four is sixteen . . . carry one . . . times four is one seventy-six.

(Regarding the DIRECTOR.)

You've spent one hundred and seventy-six weeks in rehearsal while I—four times five—have spent but twenty weeks in that magic environment which directors and actors take for granted but playwrights mostly dream about.

DIRECTOR

I never thought about it like that.

PLAYWRIGHT

Few people do.

DIRECTOR

(Raising his glass.)

To Lindsay and Crouse.

PLAYWRIGHT

To Lindsay and Crouse.

(They touch glasses—freeze.)

The End

Frank D. Gilroy

SUSAN STROMAN

In answer to the question "What is my favorite form of dance?"—to everyone's "tapping" surprise I am quick to reply "slow dancing."

Ever since that first slow dance in high school I've always loved the feel, the look, the whole experience of a man and a woman dancing close together.

I was fortunate enough to have a dance partner for four glorious years. We met every day in a studio. We danced for hours—challenging each other with difficult tap steps, partnering, and of course, slow dancing.

When Jeff passed away three years ago, it was a great emotional loss for me. I carry what we discovered together through all my work today. I will always cherish how he stimulated me choreographically.

While working late one night creating steps in my living room, I was stumped on a section of the big tap duet between Karen Ziemba and Jim Walton in *And the World Goes 'Round.* It was around three in the morning and I decided to call it quits. Dejected, I went to bed knowing I had to teach the dance at ten A.M.

I had a dream that night of Jeff and me working out in the studio. He was being very hard on me with one particular step—making me do it over and over again! The dream ended with the dance developing into a staged extravaganza. Full costumes, orchestra, and even a star field behind us!

The next morning, while I was putting on my makeup, I thought back on the dream and smiled at the memory of us dancing together. I then realized that the step Jeff was drilling into me was the step I was searching for the night before. That morning I taught K.Z. and Jim Jeff's step, and it remains as an applause-getter in the tap duet in *And the World Goes 'Round.* (And to take advantage of a good thing—the same step is in disguise in *Crazy for You* every night.)

It was the only dream I've ever had about Jeff, and as I'm not prone to remembering dreams, I doubt it will happen again. The last year between *And the World Goes 'Round, Liza Minnelli—Stepping Out at Radio City Music Hall* and *Crazy for You,* I feel as if I have been on the "musical comedy ride of my life." How lucky can you get? Even luckier to have had Jeff Veazey in my life and in my dreams.

Susan Stroman

Choreographer Susan Stroman, Fred Ebb, and staff *(opposite)* in rehearsal with Liza Minnelli for the Radio City Music Hall presentation of *Stepping Out*.

Black-and-white photos by John Huba

Color photo by Frank Micelotta

Behind the scenes at "half-hour" and onstage at the Gershwin Theatre for the revival of *Fiddler on the Roof*.
Black-and-white photo by William Gibson
Color photo by
Carol Rosegg/Martha Swope Assoc.

ARTHUR LAURENTS

I have memories of New Haven when it was the first stop on the tryout circuit, but they are of other people's plays and musicals, not mine. I had two plays and a musical begin there. The musical was called *Do I Hear a Waltz?* with a score by Richard Rodgers and Stephen Sondheim. Dick behaved very badly to Steve, and the director never came to the theatre. He stayed in the hotel and smoked dope while each new hustler he imported from New York watched the show. I think the director had the better time. How it was after the show when the trick went back to the hotel, I don't know. Certainly livelier than anything that went on at the theatre.

The first play I wrote, *Home of the Brave,* didn't play New Haven, never went o.o.t. (out of town) as *Variety* puts it, but opened in New York after only three previews. That was fine with me: I was in my twenties and believed in success and immortality.

My second play was my first New Haven experience. Called *Heartsong,* it was about abortion (oh, I was ahead of my time!). Produced by Irene Mayer Selznick, it had a new script, a new director, and except for Shirley Booth, a new cast for each of its three tryout towns: New Haven, Boston, and Philadelphia. I began to age. The experience was devastating and lonely and sent me to Hollywood to write myself out of debt via *The Snake Pit* and *Rope.* I then came back to where I so wanted to belong. I was thirty-one and counting.

My second play to start in New Haven was *The Bird Cage,* directed by Harold Clurman and starring Melvyn Douglas, a lovely man and a lovely actor. I suspect part of the reason Mel did the play was that he and his wife, Helen Gahagan Douglas, were being hounded by the congressional witch-hunters in Hollywood, and Mel felt his desirability waning. I was also among the hunted, and that makes a firm bond.

Harold surrounded Mel with a bevy of attractive actresses, some of whom were talented, headed by Stella Adler. At the first morning's reading, Stella swept in, looking dazzling (even in beige and a hat). She read like royalty visiting a hospital, left for lunch, and never came back. She was feuding with her husband, the director.

Maureen Stapleton replaced her in the role of an alcoholic Social Register matron. Maureen was then twenty-three years old and fresh out of Buffalo. She was dazzling and had such elegance that the audience thought the Persian-lamb coat she wore was the mink it should have been. Among the other actresses were the wife of Zero Mostel and the wife of Tony Canzoneri—both wives had terrific legs and dangerous mouths. Well, all the ladies in the company had dangerous mouths—this was 1950, when women were called ladies—and the stagehands in New Haven complained about their language. In the midst of one very spirited game of charades during the long tech, one of the ladies yelled: "Will you cocksuckers be quiet so we can get on with the

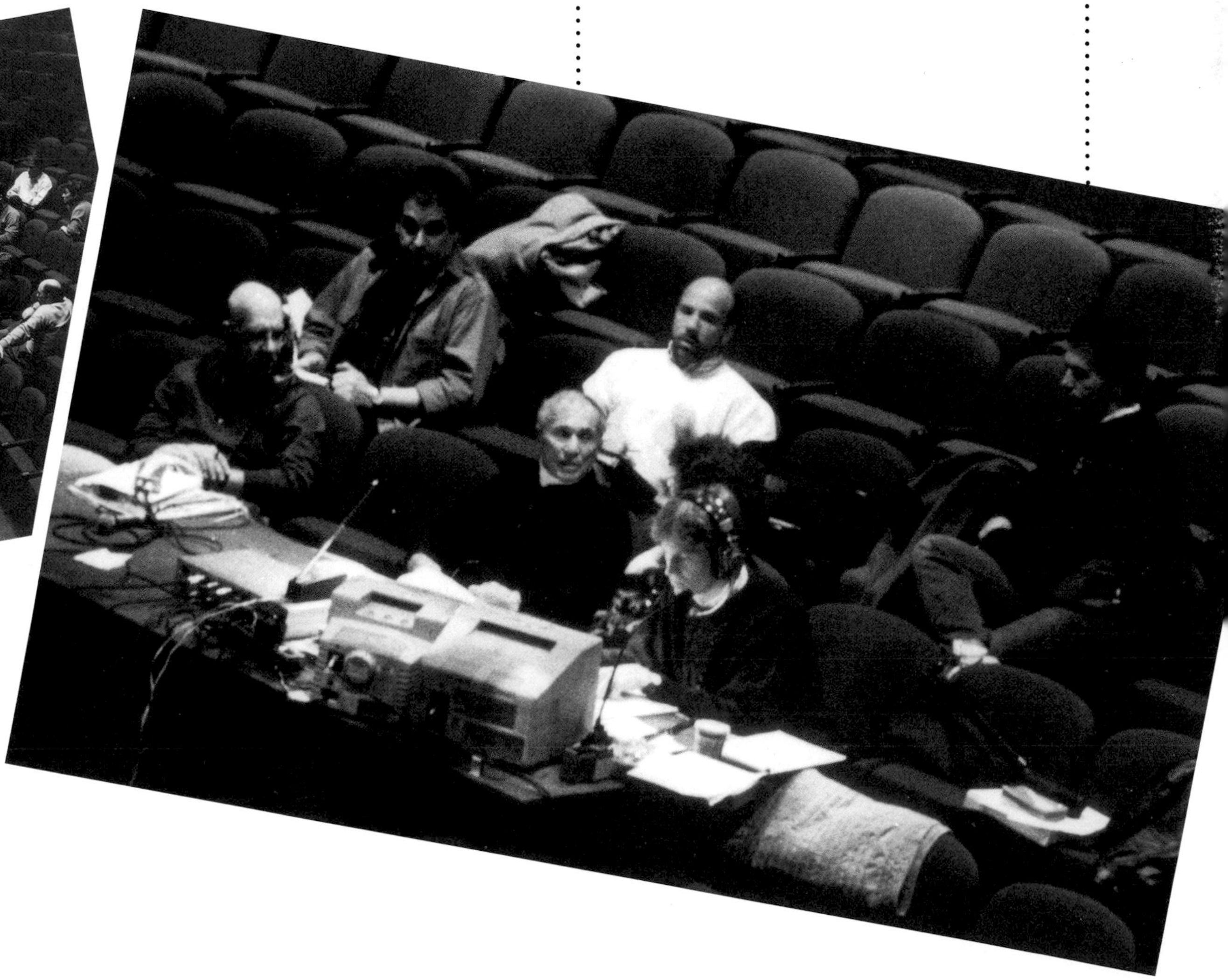

Production stage manager Craig Jacobs *(left)* giving notes to the company of *Gypsy* during final rehearsal before opening at the Marquis Theatre. Director Arthur Laurents *(below)* and *Gypsy* creative staff at final dress rehearsal.

Photos by William Gibson

game?" To which another retorted: "But that cunt called me a peasant!" I think that's what caused the stagehands to complain.

Harold was an enjoyer, he even enjoyed the stagehands. And always, always, he talked: blowing his cheeks out like Triton working to make waves, rubbing his hands like a genie over a bottle. He was gorgeous, I thought he was a genie. He had sent me a five-page, single-spaced analysis of the play, and I had rewritten with those pages as a biblical blueprint. He was wonderful on themes, talked wonderfully on inner, under, and outer meanings. He had the cast enthralled as he explained character, the complexities of the play, the socioeconomic background, foreground, underground. I was a bit impressed with myself myself. He was not always so clear with the actors. Once he said to Maureen: "Darling, I don't think you know what you're doing in that scene." "I don't know what the fuck I'm doing in the whole fucking play," she answered. (Maybe *that's* what got to the stagehands.)

Jonathan Hadary and Tyne Daly in rehearsal for *Gypsy*.

Photo by William Gibson

Color photos *(opposite)* by Martha Swope

The set also confused her—to be fair, it confused the whole company, the ushers, and the audience as well. The play took place in a nightclub. Designed by Boris Aronson, it was two-tiered, entirely in black, white, and gray. Stunning, very atmospheric—but confusing. Once, during a rehearsal in Philadelphia, Boris jumped on the stage with a shriek and placed a high-heeled orange shoe on the top of an upright black piano. "*Now,* Harold?" Boris pleaded. "Now it's art!" Harold confirmed. He wasn't kidding. I was quite old by then.

The stairway posed an interesting problem. "When I go up these stairs, where the fuck am I going?" Maureen asked one day. (That was in Philadelphia and the stagehands didn't complain. Maybe they had been warned.) Harold said, "To the street outside, darling." "No, dear," Boris corrected, "you're going to Melvyn's office." The text said the stairway took her to the main floor of the club, but I was fine, aging well. I had already had my Big Birthday.

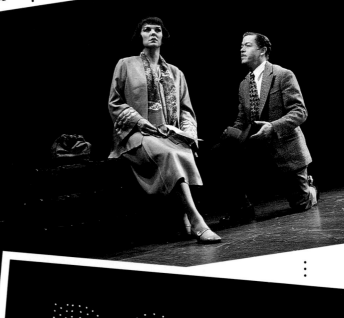

That had occurred opening night in New Haven. There was a gala party at the Taft Hotel where we all stayed. Harold was adorable to watch, talking nonstop, rubbing his hands genielike, in his particular heaven because he was surrounded by his actresses, each elbowing the other, the better to hear the sermon directly from the Mount. I envied his joy, his ebullience, his enthusiasm. He and everyone else were celebrating. I was trying to drown an inner voice that was worming me, scaring me. I sneaked between actresses and tugged at his sleeve.

Very softly, "Harold."

"Enjoy success, my boy! It's a hit!" The magic word.

"Harold, can we please talk?"

"Enjoy yourself!"

"Harold, I think there's something wrong with the play."

Sharply now: "You worry too much. Enjoy yourself!"

Did he know or didn't he? Harold Clurman wasn't much good at blocking, at staging, but he was very good on plays. Harold Clurman knew plays. Was there anyone who knew more? Kazan said Harold should direct the first three days of any play and then go home. I think now Harold must have known; I think perhaps he was as frightened as I was and was covering up. But was he? I never found out.

I went back to my cell, lay down on my narrow, metal plank, and broke out in a frightening sweat. There *was* something wrong with the play; Daddy didn't know, Daddy couldn't help me. *If anything could be done, I would have to do it myself, by myself.* That was when I became one hundred years old, when I had the Playwright's Birthday. It's that or remain the adolescent victim. To this day, I am governed by the conviction that if I don't do it, it won't really get done.

In the morning, I told Harold—he was busy on the phone listening to Stella—that I was going back to New York and would meet him in Philadelphia with a rewrite (I hoped). Even now, so many years later, I can see myself riding alone on the train back to New York from New Haven, numb with that terror particular to the theatre.

But by the time we got to New York, I had figured it out: the play was schizophrenic. Not only did it have *two* heroes, but the protagonist (Mel) was the antihero. In the middle of frantic rewriting, I had another epiphany. (They come fast to a playwright after he hits a hundred.) *What I was doing would make the play better but would never make it good.* When there is a basic flaw, a cancer, you can never make it good without going back and starting again. That you can always make anything better is why so many hearts start beating again o.o.t. But then the result comes to Bway and it's heart failure. It was too late for *Bird Cage,* there wasn't time.

I did the best, I think, that could be done and handed the rewrite to Harold when I got to Philadelphia. Without comment, he put it into rehearsal, started talking, blew his cheeks out like Triton, rubbed his hands like a genie. But nothing was in the bottle.

The Bird Cage got mixed reviews, which, then as now, meant failure. Harold reviewed it himself for a magazine. He said he had done the play to encourage its young author. I sent a note: "Dear Harold, the ship went down with all hands on board, including you."

Years later, Harold told me Clifford Odets felt Harold incurred resentment by setting himself up as an impossibly omniscient father figure. And then he asked: Had he done that to me? It was the only time I had ever seen Clurman wistful. I said yes, he had, but it didn't matter because he had given me my one hundredth birthday.

DOROTHY LOUDON

When I was a kid, I wanted to be two people—Eleanor Powell and Fats Waller. I wore turbans and hurled through flaming hoops singing "Rosalie." It is difficult to do that without catching fire. I know. I tried it in my backyard. And when other kids were singing "Jesus Wants Me for a Sunbeam," I was singing "Your Feets Too Big."

One day my mother took me on the train to Boston (probably to get me out of the backyard). We saw *Life with Father* at the Wilbur Theatre—and I came home on the train clutching my first Playbill.

From that day on I never wanted to be anything but an actor on the stage. I pored over that little Playbill until it began to crumble. It was my only connection to the reality of that magical trip to Boston. . . . Many years later, and a lot of life's flaming hoops in between, someone slipped a Playbill under my dressing room door. There it was again, my only connection with yet another magical trip. This time it was New York City . . . 1962 . . . the Winter Garden Theatre . . . the opening night of *Nowhere to Go but Up*. I read my first "bio" over and over. Especially that last line, "This is her first Broadway show." It had to be true. I read it in Playbill. I was, at last, an actor on the stage—in the sweet arms of the theatre. I'd found a pal for life.

Eleanor would have been proud. And as good old Fats used to say, "One never knows, do one?" Dorothy do.

Dorothy Loudon

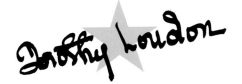

Dorothy Loudon in rehearsal for the Roundabout Theatre's revival of *The Matchmaker*.
Photo by T. Trompeter

Male chorus and dancers *(opposite)* rehearse "Luck Be a Lady" in the Broadway revival of *Guys and Dolls*. Director Jerry Zaks *(right, center)* confers with J. K. Simmons and Walter Bobbie of *Guys and Dolls*.

All black-and-white photos by Joan Marcus

Color photo by Martha Swope

FAITH PRINCE

Jerry Zaks, Faith Prince, and Jay David Saks at the recording session for the cast album of *Guys and Dolls*.
Photo by Nick Sangiamo

It was February 1980. I had arrived in New York City just two weeks before and was fortunate enough to find an apartment on West Ninety-eighth Street right away. Upon hearing the news, my mother promptly scheduled a visit to make certain I was going to be okay and that the stories she heard about the neighborhood were not true. Some were. Some weren't.

Jim Walton, with whom I had gone to school a couple of years before, was understudy for a new show, *Scrambled Feet,* a revue that was playing at the Village Gate on Bleecker Street. While my mom was in town, Jimmy called to tell me that he would be going on. Mom and I rushed down to the theatre to see him in the show. *Scrambled Feet* consisted of one woman, three men, a piano, and a duck. Jimmy was covering one of the men. Just before the end of the first act, Mom leaned over to me and whispered, "You would be wonderful in this show!"

During the second act, I began to watch the show thinking that maybe she was right. Yeah, I could do this show. We were to meet Jimmy afterward but had to sit through a seminar that the company was giving for a group of college students from Colorado before he could leave. During the presentation, which was actually quite interesting, my hand just shot up, almost of its own will. I still couldn't get what my mother had said to me out of my mind. I could do this show. I *should* do this show.

Jeffrey Haddow, one of the writers of the revue, who was leading the seminar, called on me, thinking, I'm sure, that I was part of the group from the Rockies. "Do you have a question?" he asked.

"Yes," I replied. "Do you need another girl?" By this time, Jimmy was nearly under his chair.

"As a matter of fact, we do," he said. "Do you play the piano?"

"Absolutely."

"Do you sing?" he continued.

"Of course."

"You should talk with our stage manager after the seminar," he said, before turning to another question from the students.

I spoke to her before we left and scheduled an audition for the next day. A week later I got the job, my first in New York. That was twelve years ago. To this day, every job I've had since—in *Jerome Robbins' Broadway, Falsettoland, Nick & Nora,* and the revival of *Guys and Dolls*—can all be traced back to that first chance, that first job that set me on track to having a career on the Broadway stage. If there is a moral here, it's this: Listen to your mother and when your hand goes up—let it.

Faith Prince

In rehearsal and onstage with Faith Prince and "the Hot Box girls" from *Guys and Dolls.*

Color photo by Martha Swope

Black-and-white photo by Nick Sangiamo

SHELDON HARNICK

Sooner or later every theatre professional learns that to work in the theatre is to know disappointment. That is why, as a writer, I cherish a conviction acquired slowly and painfully, that quality work will eventually find its audience. The history of the musical *She Loves Me* helped formulate that conviction more than any other theatrical experience I've undergone.

The creation of *She Loves Me* was a joy. Those of us who worked on it had fallen in love with its characters and with the wry and poignant situations. Joe Masteroff's book was the fertile soil from which sprouted a bumper crop of songs by Jerry Bock and myself. Don Walker's orchestrations were unusually fresh and buoyant. Harold Prince and Carol Haney brought this material to charming life through a superb cast headed by Barbara Cook. And we had the additional joy of receiving good notices when we opened on Broadway in 1963. We settled in for a run of two to three years.

Our joy was short-lived. After an initial surge at the box office, we soon realized that word of mouth was, apparently, not good. Was the show too gentle? Too literate? We had no idea. All we knew was that this was a show we dearly loved, and that, for reasons which mystified us all, business was falling off. In my despair, I asked my dear friend (now my wife) Margery Gray to look into the future and tell me how long the show would run. After a brief meditation, she told me that we'd run at least three hundred performances but not much more, a prediction that proved to be astonishingly accurate.

To deepen my dejection, our score did not even receive a Tony Award nomination. Had we all been totally mistaken about the quality of *She Loves Me*? The lack of a Tony nomination was such an unexpected disappointment that when the score was nominated for a Grammy Award, I couldn't bring myself to attend the ceremony. I felt I had my fill of disappointments and didn't want to subject myself to yet one more. Our score won the Grammy Award. In retrospect, I suppose this should have been the sign I needed to restore my faith in the show's quality. But the success of the cast album was overbalanced by a total absence of stock and amateur activity.

Our first stock production didn't occur until more than a year after our Broadway closing, a *long* year, during which the show seemed stone-cold dead. To our delight, audience response was warm and business was excellent. An added bonus was a letter we received from the cast. They wrote to tell us that they loved the show, thoroughly enjoyed performing it, and couldn't understand why it hadn't run longer. But productions over the ensuing years were few and far between.

Ten years or more later, Joe Masteroff, Jerry Bock, and I made the startling discovery that *She Loves Me* had attained the status of a "cult show," i.e., it had become one of the favorite musicals of a small circle of dedicated theatre buffs. Revival productions increased and, ever so gradually, the circle widened as *She Loves Me* entered the ranks of musicals that are performed regularly (if not as frequently as, say, *Annie*).

Now, after all these years, we *still* don't know why *She Loves Me*'s Broadway run lasted only eight and a half months. Was it ahead of its time? Was it caviar? Does it matter? No. What matters is that it has found its audience or its audience has found *it.* And to me what matters as much, if not more, is that the experience helped form the conviction I now cling to: that work of quality will ultimately transcend unperceptive reviews, and/or initially unreceptive audiences, and go on to win understanding, recognition, and acceptance. Thin-skinned as I am, this belief has enabled me to face critical rejection and mixed audience response with some degree of equanimity and confidence.

For me, this conviction is an invaluable weapon in the never-ending battle with the disappointment and heartbreak that lie in wait to ambush every theatre professional.

Sheldon Harnick

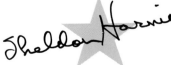

BARBARA COOK

Let me tell you about Jule Styne. You know he wrote all those terrific scores—*Gypsy, Funny Girl, Bells Are Ringing.* But did you know he's the last great reminder that Damon Runyon once passed this way—and did you know he speaks in "isms" that make Sam Goldwyn look like a piker?

After the first concert performance of *Follies* at Lincoln Center in 1985, he sidled over to me, put a friendly arm around me, leaned close—as he usually does—and said, "Barbara, baby, you're lookin' great. You walked onstage tonight—you sang eight bars before you opened your mouth."

In 1964 he asked Arthur Hill and me to play the leading roles in a show he was doing with Lester Osterman—*Something More,* based on the novel *Portofino P.T.A.* with music by Sammy Fain, lyrics by Marilyn and Alan Bergman, and book by Nate Monaster. Jule was to direct for the first time. Unfortunately we lasted only a couple of weeks. It was disappointing at the time, of course, but in retrospect it was worth it just to watch Jule in all his glory.

One day toward the end of the rehearsals an unusual air of excitement was in the rooms. "The Sisters"—his assistants—told me this was the day. The day he would give his notes and instructions to Ralph Burns, the orchestrator. I still didn't get it. But by the time Ralph arrived, I had been told Jule was famous for these performances. You see, Jule didn't just explain to Ralph how he wanted the songs to sound. Sitting at the piano, he became the orchestra, and by turns, all the instruments—the whole company surrounding him, beaming, thrilled to be sharing all this with him and with one another.

And it was really "something more" watching Jule direct. He reveled in it. I expected jodhpurs and a riding crop any day. One afternoon during a break he called Arthur over—calling him by his character's name. "Bill—uh, Bill—I've just asked them to set up for act two, scene two." (Jule's rocking up and down on his toes with his hands clasped behind his back—gazing up toward the ceiling.) "Bill—now, Bill—I've been thinking—in this next scene—twenty-two—in this next scene—you're offstage."

It wasn't long after that he had an attack of the "vapors" one day and said he wouldn't be able to continue as director. It seemed pretty clear he felt the directing idea hadn't been such a good one, and by the time we arrived in Philadelphia, Joe Layton was there to help us.

But Jule had a great eye. He always wanted the genuine stuff. One evening before we opened out of town during the technical dress rehearsal, an actor who had a minor role—ten or fifteen lines—was really tearing up the scenery. There we are onstage watching this guy onstage carrying on when from the darkness out front came Jule's unmistakable voice: "No, George, no! Don't act, just rehearse."

Jule, this is one Doll who thinks you're an okay Guy.

Barbara Cook

Musical director Wally Harper and Barbara Cook.

Photo by Arturo E. Porazzi

WILLIAM FINN

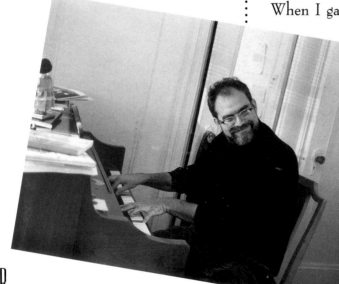

I was sixteen. Earlier that evening I had flown into New York from Paris, returning from my first trip to Europe, and was picked up at the airport by my parents and grandparents, who had driven in from Boston to meet me. It was late, we were cranky (especially me), so my father gave me fifty bucks and told me to go make a friend. A minute later I am out on the street, looking to my left, looking to my right, when I see the lights of Broadway and decide that the only friend I want to make is my old friend Musical Comedy. Intermission was over everywhere. So I went from theatre to theatre, where I would explain to anyone who would listen, "I know the show is almost over, but I just got back from Paris and I am leaving tomorrow for Boston, and I love this show"—whatever show it happened to be—"and could you maybe find it in your heart . . . ?"

Each person said, "Sorry, sorry, your story warms me, but not tonight."

Except one lady, guarding the door at the Winter Garden, where *Mame* was playing late in its run, who had obviously taken her happy pills that day. When I gave my appeal, she laughed and said, "Sure, come on in." Just in time for the best finale in the world. What a welcome home!

Only a short time later—I can't believe they were almost simultaneous—I heard Larry Kert sing "Being Alive" from *Company,* and they had to scrape me off the ceiling. It was that good. Life is seldom as good as the best of musical theatre.

Bill Finn at the piano in his studio.
Photo by Arturo E. Porazzi

Photo call for the company of *Falsettos* at the Golden Theatre *(left)*.
Black-and-white photo by William Gibson
Color photo by
Carol Rosegg/Martha Swope Assoc.

FRANCIS RUIVIVAR

In August 1991 I replaced Jonathan Pryce as the Engineer in *Miss Saigon* during his two-week vacation and was excited about getting a chance to perform the role. The rehearsals went smoothly, but nothing could've prepared me for my encounter with the Cadillac during "American Dream."

For some strange reason the past shows I've been involved with have been huge, complex technical marvels. I survived *Chess* on Broadway, *Cats* on the road, and of course the mother of all spectacles, *Shogun, the Musical* at the Kennedy Center and on Broadway. But with *Miss Saigon*'s raked stage, jumping on the Cadillac took on a life of its own.

My put-in rehearsal was the first time I encountered this obstacle. I had done about four run-throughs (without the car) and had discovered the Engineer would be a physically demanding role. At that put-in rehearsal, as I neared the end of "American Dream," I realized that I had to jump up and over the front of the Cadillac, which was about four and a half feet high (due to the rake), from a standing position! My legs were so tired by that point I literally had to pull myself up by the windshield wipers! The hell with humping the car—I couldn't even get on top of it! It was a great laugh; thank God it was a rehearsal.

On my opening night I was nervous about two things: remembering all the words and getting on the Cadillac. Fortunately everything went well, and that Cadillac and I became more and more intimate every night!

Francis Ruivivar and the company of *Miss Saigon* in rehearsal onstage at the Broadway Theatre.
Photo by Marcia Lippman

ELAINE STRITCH

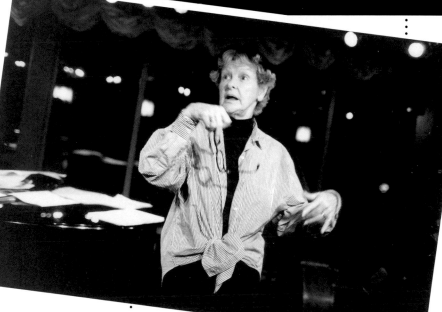

I love this particular experience because it is both an example of creative good acting—concentration and so on—*and* because it is also very funny.

During a performance of *Virginia Woolf* (*Who's Afraid of,* that is) in the fight scene—or one of the fight scenes, I should say—the sofa caught on fire from Nick's (Bill Berger's) cigarette in the previous scene. In the next scene, the actor playing George, Donald Davies, said to me, "The sofa is on fire." I said, "So?" To which he replied, "Well, you run everything else around here, so put it out!" I marched over to the bar, picked up my bottle of vodka (water, of course) and went to pour it on the now smoldering sofa. Then, on second thought, I went back to the bar, grabbed *his* bourbon (iced tea, of course), and doused the sofa with his—not *hers*—booze! The audience fell about. We, of course, being good little actors, went on as if nothing whatsoever had gone wrong.

I loved the humor and most of all the concentration on both our parts. Now, we all know that Jack Daniel's bourbon or Smirnoff vodka poured onto a fire would cause mayhem. So in addition to the concentration and discipline of both Donald and myself, I find it fascinating that the audience was able to suspend their disbelief. Granted, Donald was sensational—but I had to top him. I don't know whether that was my character or me! Maybe a little of both.

Elaine Stritch rehearsing a Rodgers and Hart revue at Rainbow and Stars.
Photo by Robin Platzer

Tommy Tune, Keith Carradine, and the company of *The Will Rogers Follies* in "tech" rehearsal at the Palace Theatre.

Black-and-white photos by Linda Alaniz

Color photo by Martha Swope

JULIE WILSON

It was 1949. I had been working at La Maisonette, a nightclub in the St. Regis Hotel on Fifth Avenue in New York City. One afternoon, during the run, I received a call from my agent, Barron Polan. "Julie," he said, "I want you to come to Arnold Weissberger's cocktail party." (Mr. Weissberger was a famous showbiz lawyer.) I was reluctant. I am not much at cocktail parties or meeting a lot of strangers. But Barron thought that it was important as there would be people there he wanted me to meet. "I definitely think you should go," he said, hanging up the phone. And that was that.

So I went. When I arrived, Barron met me at the door and immediately took me over to Bella Spewack, the playwright. Bella took one look at me and said, "Julie, you'd be a perfect Bianca!" Cole Porter's now-legendary *Kiss Me Kate* had opened just months before at the New Century Theatre and was a great hit. I had heard that the producers were now looking to cast the national tour. Patricia Morison, the show's original Kate and star, was also at the party. Bella grabbed my hand and dragged me over to meet her. "Pat," Bella said, "wouldn't Julie be perfect for *Kiss Me Kate*?" Patricia was very sweet. "Ideal," she said. "What are you doing now?" I told her, and the next week, Bella Spewack, Patricia Morison, and a whole crowd from the company of *Kate* all came to see me at La Maisonette.

Afterward, they came backstage and were wonderful about telling me how much they enjoyed the show. But just before she left, Pat pulled me aside and said she'd call Cole Porter and tell him that Bella was right. "We've found our Bianca."

After I finished out the season at La Maisonette, I went out to do a gig in Los Angeles at the Mocambo on the Sunset Strip, owned by a handsome white-haired gentleman, Charlie Morison (no relation to Patricia). One night after the show Charlie said, "Julie, somebody very important is here who came to see you. He's in my office downstairs. Julie," he added as I turned toward his office, "it's Cole Porter."

I nearly dropped dead. All my life, I'd been in such awe of him. I adored his music. Now I could barely move. (Only one person since then has affected me in that same way—Stephen Sondheim.) Taking a very deep breath, I walked into the office. Charlie introduced me. Cole Porter was standing alone very quietly. He looked me over and smiled. "I enjoyed you enormously," he said. I knew then I would never forget that moment. Then he gave me an added and absolutely wonderful gift: "I think you'll make a wonderful Bianca in the national tour." You can imagine how thrilled I was.

Julie Wilson

Julie Wilson rehearsing
Cole and Coward
at the Kaufman Theatre.
Photos by Arturo E. Porazzi

In rehearsal with the company of *Jelly's Last Jam.*
All photos by Martha Swope

GREGORY HINES

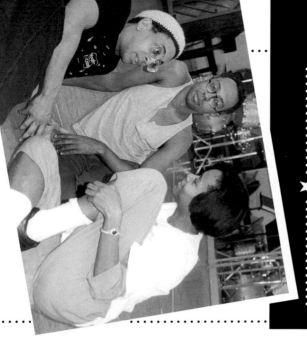

Gregory Hines, director George C. Wolfe, and Tonya Pinkins take a break from rehearsal for *Jelly's Last Jam*.
Photo by William Gibson/Martha Swope Assoc.

I was born on One Hundred Fiftieth Street and St. Nicholas Avenue in Harlem and raised in Brooklyn. As a teenager, it was always a big thrill for me to come into Manhattan and go to the theatre. One of the most exciting performances I saw at that time was Sammy Davis in the musical *Golden Boy* at the Imperial Theatre. I saw that show four times. In those days, I had a couple of girl friends. I took each of them. But the last time, I went by myself. The show was that kind of experience for me. I didn't have to be—didn't want to be—with anyone else. I could sit in that theatre and, with Sammy onstage, feel connected to everything going on.

By "number four," I knew the show pretty well. I was ready to go on. Now, Sammy had a laugh that wasn't a real laugh. It was a phony laugh that was all part of his persona. Somebody would say something—on a talk show or in his nightclub act—and he would laugh and stamp his feet. Everybody knew it was phony, but it was all a part of his thing.

So this time Sammy comes onstage with Al Freeman, Jr., who's playing his manager. Sammy's just done some sparring offstage and he's to have a rubdown. It's a serious scene. But as he came out, Sammy's laughing. I could tell even then that this was the genuine thing. The more he tried not to laugh, the worse he broke himself up. Now, Al Freeman, Jr., he wasn't cracking a smile. He was composed and looking at Sammy as if nothing is wrong, although the look also lets you know that he knows everything is. This is making Sammy laugh all the more. I figure out that Al has said something to Sammy just before they stepped out onstage. That's the only thing explaining why Al's holding it together and having to ad-lib while Sammy's howling. But I loved seeing Sammy break up like this. I felt like I was in on something.

Since then, I've had a number of times myself onstage where something breaks me up. And I'm really in a jam because now when I start to laugh I immediately remember Sammy going up and I lose it a bit more. I idolized Sammy Davis, Jr., but never more than when he laughed . . . for real.

Gregory Hines

Onstage at the Virginia Theatre with Gregory Hines and the company of *Jelly's Last Jam*.

Photos by Martha Swope

JUDITH IVEY

During the run of a revival on Broadway of *Blithe Spirit* (I was playing Ruth), one of those wonderful disasters occurred that forces an actor to think on her feet, or in my case, my knees. I was seated at the time waiting for the curtain to rise on the "tea scene" with Madame Arcati. Our curtain was a masterfully painted drop of an English country scene. A long, heavy pole weighted the drop at the bottom. We also had a gorgeous tea table with silver trays that held cucumber sandwiches, teapot, cups and saucers, silver spoons, and sugar cubes in a beautiful china bowl.

During this matinee as the drop/curtain rose, I discovered the tea table had been placed too far downstage as I watched it rise in the air along with the drop, then fall with a resounding crash, which sent tea, china, sandwiches, and in particular, sugar cubes everywhere.

I sat staring. I waited for the air to clear of gasps and whispers, then called for our maid, Edith. The actress ran onstage, her eyes as big as the saucers on the Oriental rug. I directed her, "Please, bring more tea, sandwiches, and unbroken china." Feeling very cocky with my cleverness, I began crawling about collecting sugar cubes and putting them back in the pristine sugar bowl. I was on my hands and knees when it struck me that ever-so-proper Ruth would never be crawling about, much less recycling her sugar cubes. So, as the maid returned with the replacements, I turned to her on my knees, with my "dirty" sugar cubes, and with great conspiracy said, "Make sure you mention this to no one, Edith." The audience roared with laughter and applauded our recovery. I hope Mr. Coward was pleased. . . .

Judith Ivey

JASON ROBARDS

My first New York appearance was in the Children's World theatre production of *Jack and the Beanstalk* in 1946 as the rear end of the cow that is bartered for a bean by Jack's father. If one can call it an appearance. I don't think they trusted me to operate the head of the cow . . . it spoke. This might have been ingenious casting as I have been known to speak eloquently from the rear. The cow is sold by Jack's father for the famous bean because it is not producing enough milk to keep the family from starving. Paige Johnson, in a masterful interpretation, was playing the role of the father, and it was for him to utter the immortal line, "I'm afraid we'll have to sell you, Bossie." And the front end of the cow, played by Dorothy Surkont . . . a strict taskmistress . . . and the hind end (me) waddled bovinely offstage right. I then proceeded to my other task of stage-managing the show . . . a strange kind of double duty theatre people are asked to perform.

Forty years later I was playing the part of Grampa in a memorable revival of *You Can't Take It with You* with Colleen Dewhurst, Elizabeth Wilson, James Coco, and the masterly Paige Johnson . . . among others. At the end of the second act the entire household is arrested by the FBI for setting off fireworks in the basement. Paige Johnson, Jack's erstwhile father, was playing the part of the FBI's fearless leader and order giver, and as he arrested me, he shouted above the onstage pandemonium not the line that the playwrights had given him, but a line that had not been heard on the New York stage in forty years . . . "I'm afraid we'll have to sell you, Bossie" . . . and showed me not his badge but an ugly snapshot of the front end of the cow from the rear view.

Jason Robards

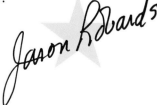

Director Zoe Caldwell, Judith Ivey, and Jason Robards at a read-through for *Park Your Car in Harvard Yard.*
Photo by Joan Marcus

ZOE CALDWELL

Lighting designer Tom Skelton and Zoe Caldwell confer at a rehearsal for *Park Your Car in Harvard Yard.*

Photo by Joan Marcus

Some years ago I was playing in *Medea* with Dame Judith Anderson in the Eisenhower Theatre at the Kennedy Center when it was announced that Vladimir Horowitz was to give one of his rare recitals in the concert hall at the Kennedy Center on a Sunday afternoon at, of course, four o'clock. Sunday was our day off. Dame Judith had often mentioned Horowitz when explaining to me how amateur I was at taking curtain calls. "A true artist's curtain call is part of the performance," she explained, "not some slapdash piece of modesty at the end."

So now she could show me the real thing, and on that glorious Sunday, she sat next to me in a high state of excitement. She had told me that she knew Horowitz. She had been at a party in Charlie Chaplin's suite at the Savoy Hotel when World War II had been declared. And Horowitz had suddenly said, "May I play?" And did, and quelled everyone's fear.

"I shall take you back to meet him," she declaimed.

The recital, the audience's rapt attention and adoration were thrilling, but the curtain call was a university course in curtain calls.

Dame Judith, who was tiny, got smaller and smaller as we battled our way backstage and shuffled along in the queue to greet the master. Suddenly, she said, "I don't think he'll remember me; let's not bother." But too late; we were there at the door of his grand room facing a phalanx of his wife, his manager, the manager of the concert hall, and other important folk, and, at the apex, Horowitz. Tiny Judith was unable to speak until a startled Horowitz held out his hands to her and said, "Oh! Do you remember me?"

ROBERT WHITEHEAD

It was a dilapidated nightclub in Detroit where I first met Ethel Waters. I was trying to get her to do a new play *(The Member of the Wedding,* by Carson McCullers.) In spite of *Stormy Weather, Cabin in the Sky,* etc., Ethel had become slightly forgotten during the war years.

After she sang a couple of numbers, we sat at a dark table and I tried to push her into signing a contract with me. She told me that my play didn't have God in it and explained her special relationship to *her* God. I took her home to a rather shabby room.

She said, "I gotta tell you, Mr. Whitehead, that I have been on my knees by that bed praying, 'Oh! Lord, dear Lord, when are You gonna get me a good bookin'?' "

I said, "I'm coming to you now with that good booking." But I returned to New York without a contract.

Awhile later, when she was through in Detroit, I got her to come to dinner at my apartment. Carson McCullers was there. It was a spring night and after dinner there was a shattering electric storm. Ethel said not to worry, because of her special connection with the Almighty—and she proceeded, as she sat in an armchair, to sing in a kind of bluesy way, "His Eye Is on the Sparrow . . . and I know He watches me."

It was very beautiful . . . and we suggested, at that moment, that we put that song into the play. Now, *The Member of the Wedding* had God in it. And Ethel signed a contract.

Robert Whitehead

Advertising executive Jim Weiner and producers Roger L. Stevens and Robert Whitehead at rehearsal for *Park Your Car in Harvard Yard.*

Photo by Joan Marcus

JOANNA GLEASON

They say that it's the worst. It's what they wished on Hitler. That he may be forced to preview a musical out of town (dictators beware, previewing in town runs neck and neck as a nightmare). But here we were: the company of *Into the Woods,* James Lapine, Stephen Sondheim, and a tantrum of New York actors ripped away from the city at Christmastime now repotted temporarily at the Old Globe Theatre in San Diego, California, December 1986. Actually, we had already spent Thanksgiving here in rehearsals, and spirits were on the high side. The staff and crew of this first-class theatre were warm, highly skilled, and best of all, theatre minded. Business, budget, politics, and ego trips were, if they even existed, never brought into the workplace.

But I was blue. It wasn't the play, I loved it. And the score was a marvel, a challenge for an actor, all the right things. But it was Christmas and I was not with my son. I was doing a show that might or might not have a future in New York. I was having my thirty-something crisis . . . I was blue. Blue, but happy to be working.

Steve had completed the last song for act two, a quartet called "No One Is Alone," and wanted James and the four actors to stay after the run-through to hear it before working it into the previews the next night. I was asked to stay because I had the car and was driving people home. We entered a tiny rehearsal room lit only by a bare forty-watt bulb and took chairs as Steve sat down at the world's oldest piano. He rolled over the first two chords with the dexterity of a bear in an overcoat. But the mood was established in an instant. Here was Sondheim, eyes half-closed, singing in a raspy half-whisper: "Mother cannot guide you, now you're on your own . . . only me beside you, still you're not alone."

I'm sure Steve was more intent on us hearing the message for what it was: the notion that each man's actions impact on every other man eventually and ultimately. But that's not what I heard. . . . As I tried to see James, Chip,

Barry Bostwick, Joanna Gleason, and director/author Arthur Laurents *(left)* in rehearsal during the previews of *Nick & Nora*.

Black-and-white photo by T. Trompeter

Color photo by Nathaniel Kramer

Louann, Kim, or Ben through my tears, I saw that they too were awash. This song, being sung by its creator, was at once an anthem, a carol, a hymn, and a love song for us at that moment in our lives. We spanned five decades in that room that night. Since that time we have all entered the next one up . . . marriages have come and gone, babies have been born, and loved ones have died. The song would be sung the following Christmas on Broadway, and to my great joy, I would sing it, as well. I still sing it to myself, and each time I do, it feels like I am unwrapping a gift. A gift from Steve, a gift from the theatre.

Joanna Gleason

PETER NEUFELD

It was 1968 and as the assistant company manager I was sent by myself to the Shubert Theatre in Philadelphia. There I was to take care of the management end of *Here's Where I Belong,* a musical version of John Steinbeck's novel *East of Eden,* which was trying out prior to an opening at the Billy Rose Theatre in New York.

And I fell in love.

Forget about the book and score; they had already taken my virginity in rehearsals. But out of town I fell in love with the show curtain, the dimming houselights, the opening dissolve, the underscoring—even rehearsals that went into overtime. It was the first show I worked on where, now that I knew the basics of my own job, I could additionally concentrate on the evolution of the material and focus even further on the personal dreams and goals of everyone connected with the show. I existed for nothing except this musical and every individual connected with it—and lost 17 pounds during the tryout.

At the Philadelphia opening, one of my bosses, Gene Wolsk, came up to me and very matter-of-factly informed me that I was returning to New York to go into rehearsals for *George M!* and take it to Detroit. I paled and said, "I can't, I'm doing this show." Gene acknowledged that situation, but was emphatic that the situation was changing. I stood my ground. He looked at me and said, "What if I tell you you're fired and no longer *have* a job with this show?" I started to perspire and said that I would keep my hotel room in Philly and come back to New York when the show moved back. In response to Gene's question as to how I intended to pay for the hotel, I told him I'd borrow the money from my parents. He looked at me for a real long moment, grinned, hugged me, and said, "Okay, kid, you win."

At five forty-five in the afternoon the day following the Broadway opening of *my* musical (you see it belonged to me now), the producers, in the face of disastrous reviews, made the decision not only that they would have to close the show, but that in fact last night's opening had *been* the closing. For reasons

Madeleine Potter, Fritz Weaver, Martin Sheen, Tony Randall, and the company of the National Actors' Theatre rehearsing their premiere production, *The Crucible*.

Photos by Joan Marcus

I no longer recall, I was the representative sent to the theatre to let everyone know. I walked the length of a very quiet alley to the stage door of the Billy Rose and waited. As each member of the cast, crew, and orchestra walked in for that evening's performance, I let each of them know we had already closed and our show would never be performed again.

It was a very quiet group who packed up makeup and instruments, gathered up opening-night flowers and unpinned telegrams from the walls, and left their theatre for the last time. I walked onstage and was acutely aware of the worklight spilling onto the orchestra parts as each lay opened on the music stands in the pit, seemingly prepared to sneak into the opening bars of the prologue.

A week later Gene and Manny Azenberg found me a job working for another management firm taking over as manager on *I Never Sang for My Father,* which had already opened in New York. So, I cleaned out my desk, walked literally across the street, and went to work on another show.

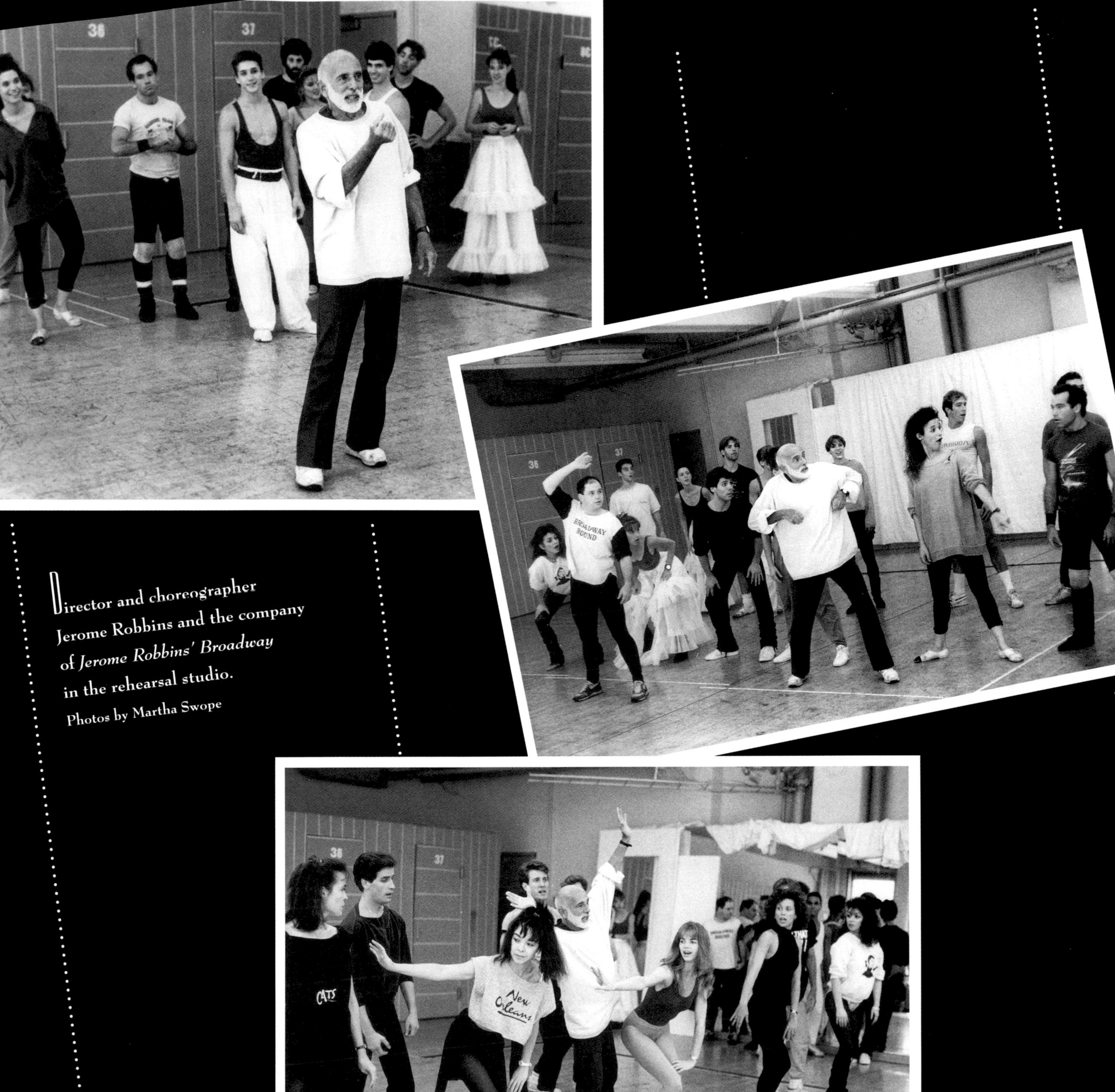

Director and choreographer Jerome Robbins and the company of *Jerome Robbins' Broadway* in the rehearsal studio.

Photos by Martha Swope

The musical number "On a Sunday by the Sea" from *High Button Shoes* in rehearsal and onstage in *Jerome Robbins' Broadway* at the Imperial Theatre.

Photos by Martha Swope

VICTOR GARBER

I was riding on the Second Avenue bus. I can't tell you what the weather was like that day. I can't even tell you what year it was. I have never been good at time. I can tell you I was on my way to Stephen Sondheim's house. The man who had composed the music and written the lyrics for *Anyone Can Whistle,* a show that had beguiled me completely as a young singer in Toronto. My friend Peter and I would stay up all night doing our own extremely unique rendition of "There's a Parade in Town." On this particular day, I was humming "Anyone Can Whistle," a more appropriate selection for bus riding. I was struck with the realization that I was in New York City, actively pursuing the dream that had begun so long ago in London, Ontario, and that I was about to meet the man who had unwittingly helped guide me toward that dream. His music and lyrics had resonated so deeply within me I just knew I had to be there. Wherever "there" was. New York.

I approached his front door with considerably less assurance than I had boarded the bus. I was let in by a very gentle man with a warm, calm face as Stephen Sondheim came bounding down the stairs, his arms outstretched, skewed smile, talking faster than the speed of sound. I was definitely out of my body now. As I floated up the stairs after him, I made some inane comment about the weather (fortunately I hadn't forgotten it yet), and then we were in his office-study-temple. I have since been in that room on several occasions, and I'm pleased to tell you I am never blasé. I simply behave better.

I had passed the preliminary audition for the role of Anthony Hope in the new Sondheim musical *Sweeney Todd.* Now I was to learn a song from the show and come back to sing it for the composer, director, producers, assistant director, stage manager, press agent, ushers, and cleaning staff. No problem. I was to go to Mr. Sondheim's house to learn the song. This seemed logical if slightly fantastical. Now here I was, tape recorder poised, as he sat down at the piano, apologizing for his voice, his intonation, the key, which would of course

be changed several times. He struck the first few chords of "Johanna" and proceeded to sing one of the most beautiful songs I have ever heard. I remember feeling totally present in my body, suddenly, in that room, in that moment. A feeling I have aspired to many times since. I was there, and I knew it. That was the gift.

Victor Garber

Victor Garber with director Jack O'Brien in rehearsal *(top)*, and onstage at the Cort Theatre with Brian Bedford and Zeljko Ivanek in *Two Shakespearean Actors*.

Black-and-white photo by Marcia Lippman
Color photo by Brigitte Lacombe

In rehearsal and onstage at the Booth Theatre with Spiro Malas and the company of *The Most Happy Fella*.

Black-and-white photos by Ken Howard
Color photo by Jay Thompson

AUGUST WILSON

Robert Judd was a big man with a wide smile that was not always ready. He was a black man who had learned to live in a world of truncated possibilities by refusing to recognize the impossible. He was an actor. He got into acting the old-fashioned way. He said, "I can do that." Then he went off and did it. With style and grace. I met him at the Eugene O'Neill Theatre Center's National Playwrights Conference the summer of 1982 when he was cast as Toledo in my play *Ma Rainey's Black Bottom* and where he often held court under a tree in the sunken garden telling stories.

Robert Judd was a great storyteller. I've seen few people do it better. He understood words were just a necessary part of it. Attitude and style, the ordinary dressed in fine clothes and made extraordinary, were the other parts. Robert Judd worked many years as a clothes presser. The creases he put in a pair of pants stayed there. But that was not always so. He spent many years wrestling with his machine until he decided to talk to it, much as one talks to a balky mule, and won it over and became *Robert Judd, Presser Extraordinaire.*

Pressing clothes is a hard, hot, sweaty job and he was a hardworking man who liked an occasional bourbon whether on the job or not. He told me a story about a half pint of bourbon that he gently set down on the top of his presser and told his boss, "That stays there or I go home." The bottle stayed, as did Judd. A black man in America making his own rules.

Like any actor I guess, Robert Judd always wanted to be on Broadway. *Ma Rainey* gave him his opportunity. I watched him wrestle with the character of Toledo much like he wrestled with his pressing machine. He pushed and pulled, shoved, bent, and twisted, until Toledo became in Robert Judd's hands very much like a piano. When he struck a chord, it gave him back just what he wanted to hear. But it wasn't always so. During rehearsals, and even during performance, when Judd would forget his line, he would cough. The cough was his way of buying time for him to remember his next line. So frequent were these occasions Charles Dutton suggested he get a bottle of cough syrup and a spoon and work them into his character. Robert Judd rejected the idea out of hand and went on with his work, coughing and sputtering through the lines he couldn't remember. He brought a camera to rehearsals and documented the whole process.

It was a different Robert Judd during the rehearsals for the New York production. The stories were fewer and he withdrew into himself. We put it down to his being, like most of us, scared. I visited him in his dressing room opening night October 11, 1984. He told me, "We gonna run the possum up the tree tonight. You look when the show's over and see if he ain't up there." It was a splendid performance, and yes, the possum was up the tree surrounded by a pack of baying hounds.

During the run of the show Robert Judd was usually the first of the cast to leave. He would, without stopping, give me a wave and head on down

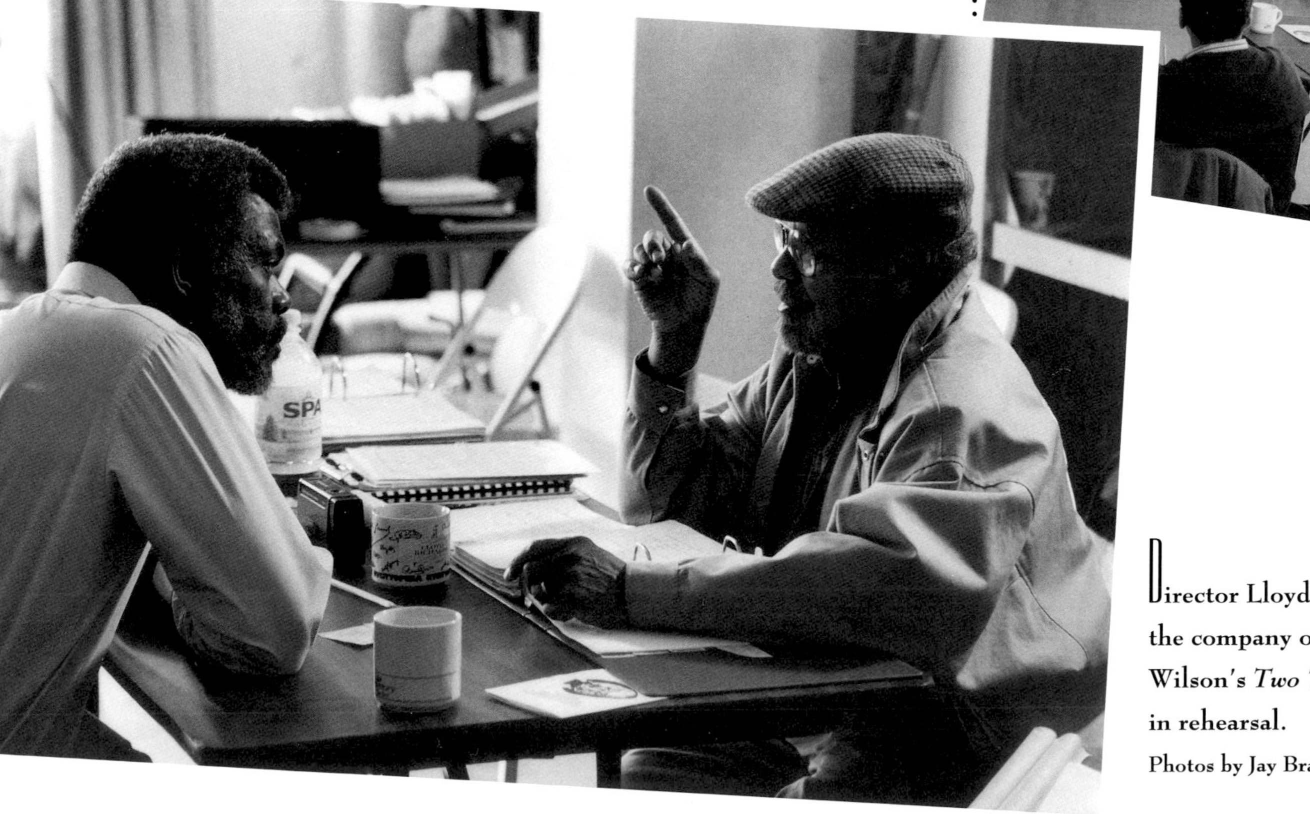

Director Lloyd Richards and the company of August Wilson's *Two Trains Running* in rehearsal.
Photos by Jay Brady

Forty-eighth Street to the subway and go on home. Once after the show I shared a drink and much conversation with him and his brother. If I was in town, I saw the show and visited Charles Dutton in his dressing room often. I would stop by Judd's dressing room, but he never appeared to want to talk much and I gave him his space. "Man," Charles Dutton told me one night, "Judd still scared. He be in his dressing room throwing up almost every night."

Ma Rainey closed in June 1985 after an eight-month run on Broadway. Shortly thereafter Robert Judd died from stomach cancer. He never told anyone. He allowed us to tease him about not knowing his lines and to misread fits of coughing. He was a big man in more ways than one. When I heard he was dying, I called him up. He didn't want to talk. He didn't want anyone's sympathy. He asked me how my wife and daughter were, he wished me good luck with my plays, and hung up the phone. Typical Robert Judd. A black man in America making his own rules. He talked to Charles Dutton about dying and told him, "That's just the way it goes. If I had messed around and became a rich man, I would be really pissed."

A few days after my phone call he died. I had written the role of Bono in *Fences* for him when I thought he would be able to play it. After he died I continued to write roles for him in each of my plays. Seth in *Joe Turner's Come and Gone,* and Doaker in *The Piano Lesson.* Even though I knew he couldn't play them, he served as the inspiration and helped me get them on the page. For anyone who missed *Ma Rainey's Black Bottom,* they missed seeing Robert Judd on Broadway: a black man reclaiming his moral personality, making his own rules in which the deprivation of opportunity did not exclude the highest of possibilities.

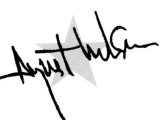

LLOYD RICHARDS

One of my most unexpected experiences and yet one that taught me a great deal was the occasion of my first Broadway play as an actor. I had been trudging the streets of New York City with the pack of unemployed actors for many years, learning to absorb the rejections of the agents and producers and to survive. I would walk the streets of Broadway and look at the theatres, at the marquees, as I hustled hopefully from one rejection to the next. The thing that seemed to keep me going was the fact that one day my presence in those canyons would be acknowledged and my name, too, would go up on the marquees in the lights and in the papers.

The day arrived. I was cast in a Broadway show. I had a wonderful agent who got me a decent salary and, of all things, good billing. I was informed that my name would go up on a billboard at the corner of Forty-seventh and Broadway. I was elated. On the appointed day I got off the subway fully one stop ahead of my destination so that I could walk down Broadway and encounter the sign that would include my name. I walked those blocks in high anticipation. There was the sign, the name of the play, the author, the producers, and a list of actors in the middle of which was the name "Floyd" Richards. My jaw dropped. I must confess to tears. I called my agent, who called the producers, who called whoever was to be called, and I was assured that that evening someone would be up there and change the *F* to an *L*.

They did as they'd promised. They changed the *F* to an *L*, but somehow the paint was not exactly the same as had originally been used. The square of yellow beneath the *L* was different from the rest of the billboard. I had not learned the lesson but had been reminded that no matter how valuable we consider these manifestations of value, true value lies elsewhere. For me it now rests firmly in the work, and in that extraordinary moment when it all comes together and there is magic. That moment is the memory and the reward.

ROSCOE LEE BROWNE

One evening, in 1956, over dinner, I announced to three friends, "Tomorrow, I shall become an actor." Of course, I meant that "tomorrow" I would abruptly leave a splendid position at Schenley Imports Corporation and begin to pursue a career in theatre. My friends were outraged that I would leave fabulous pay and guaranteed security for the uncertain, unprotected life of an actor.

One of my dinner guests, Josephine Premice, left, saying, "I'll be right back." The other two, Leontyne Price and Susan Fonda, cajoled, warned, and begged me to leave off this capricious decision. When Josephine returned, she had three trade papers, which she and the others said would show the difficulties for one with no training as an actor and no particular assets. The first paper was *Variety,* and because it was full of acronyms that were Greek to me, I put it aside. The second was, it seemed, tabloid . . . and the third was *Show Business*. There, on page twenty-five, I read that the next day was the last day for actors to audition for the inaugural season of the New York Shakespeare Festival in Central Park. Having acted in only a couple of college productions and three amateur outings, I did not presume to think I was on the level of actors for whom the theatre was already their lives; but armed with bright determination and some knowledge of the literature, I went.

After my audition, Joe Papp introduced himself and said, "You are new to me. How long have you been an actor?" I replied simply, "Twelve hours, but I have no intention of bearing torches." He laughed and said, "No. You're good. You have much to learn, but you'll have words. There are characters you are already ready to play. Shakespeare is a whole world, you see, and you're in it." So I was cast in the role of the Soothsayer in *Julius Caesar.* I was supremely happy, surely the happiest new professional actor in the land.

There were then in the park marauding herds of young men, teenagers, most in emblazoned jackets and all looking for a little action. We could be just their mark. Yet rehearsals took place without incident. Soon we were ready for

Larry Fishburne and Roscoe Lee Browne onstage at the Walter Kerr Theatre in *Two Trains Running*.
Photo by Schwartz/Thompson

our first audience, with a glorious summer sky, with a breeze enough to be dramatic as it gave our robes a lilting flow. Here, at center stage, were Brutus and Cassius carrying on, with Casca telling them what was the great shout, and there, off right, coming from the games, were Caesar with Antony by his good ear, attendant lords and ladies and shouting citizens. The director, Stuart Vaughan, knew during rehearsals that my first line, a single, conjured word, "Caesar!" would not be heard over the loud and constant cries of "Hail, Caesar!" So, it occurred to him to have one actor, on the step just below Caesar, raise his long arm only once—a signal for all shouts to halt for a split second. The din would still be in the air, but my first "Caesar!"—thrust in that split second—would be heard.

Up on the rocks by Belvedere Castle were some of the young fellows who had been daily attendant to the play throughout rehearsals and knew the play as well as we. And it went this way: the lords and rabble were all hailing, shouting to a fare-thee-well, and then the long-arm signal was raised and I cried out "Caesar!"—but on the precise instant, my cry was drowned out by a long, trailing, *"Fu-u-u-ck Caesar!"* The audience gasped, then roared with laughter, it seemed, forever. Staats Cotsworth, as Caesar—patrician, never nonplussed—merely sought out my startled eyes, waited for me to speak again, realized at long last that I would not, gave me a look that scorned all novices, certainly this one, and then charged the air with the unfortunate next line: "What voice is that I hear more shrill . . . ?" Of course, the audience, having heard only the more shrill voices from the Belvedere, roared again.

Only the horror of Caesar's death got the play back for us, with no thanks to the absent and absentminded Soothsayer, who was last seen dodging borne torches.

Roscoe Lee Browne

..... OPENING NIGHT .....

1. theatre term meant to hint at phenomenon that occurs when the audience appears for the first time, in the theatre, at night, constructed by use of gerund *opening,* beginning a course or activity, and *night,* n., the time from dusk to dawn when no sunlight is visible.
2. an evening or night taken as an occasion or point of time.

Photo by William Gibson

HOWARD KISSEL

For many years an integral part of the mythology of Broadway was the drama of opening night—the arrival of a glamorous audience, the tension backstage, the even greater tension between the time the critics dashed up the aisle and the moment the early editions of the papers rolled off the presses, and finally the jubilation of success.

This element of Broadway ritual has long been in decline. The audience no longer glitters. It consists largely of the myriad backers now necessary to bring a show to Broadway. There isn't much glamour left. Noël and Marlene no longer glide into their aisle seats as the houselights dim. The aisle seats are seldom even occupied by critics, most of whom have seen the show during the final previews.

These days closing performances are likely to be more exciting than openings. To begin with, the audience does not consist of people nervous about their investments. It is full of people who know how much a last performance means to the performers. Being in a long-running show takes on the protective aura of dwelling in the Garden of Eden; the final performance has a special kind of energy, a desperate desire to make the most of things before the Expulsion.

Openings are like blind dates, with the excitement of anticipation and too often, the disappointment of one's expectations. Attending the closing is like taking leave of a beloved friend. It has a particularly deep emotional charge in an age—in the theatre and elsewhere—when we say farewell to so many friends prematurely.

Perhaps the last show whose opening and closing were *both* high-powered events was David Merrick's *42nd Street.* The opening, August 25, 1980, was probably the last of the old-fashioned Broadway opening nights. Merrick was the only producer powerful enough to force all the critics to attend the opening. The theatre still had vestiges of its aristocracy left, and among the opening nighters were Ethel Merman, Garson Kanin, Ruth Gordon, Joshua and Nedda

Logan, and Carol Channing. What made the evening unforgettable was Merrick's appearance onstage during the curtain calls to announce that the show's director-choreographer, Gower Champion, had died that morning, which created pandemonium on both sides of the footlights.

The show ran for eight and a half years. Its closing, at a Sunday matinee in January of 1989, seemed to represent the end of a certain kind of musical, the unpretentious American show that had no higher aim than to entertain, a form in which Merrick had specialized. When Jamie Ross, as *42nd Street*'s tough producer, uttered the line about "the two most glorious words in the English language, *musical comedy,*" it drew laughs and hearty, sustained applause. Even the term has a nostalgic ring: musical *comedy*? The producer of *42nd Street* himself, sitting in the very last row on the aisle, was seen to weep.

The most simultaneously joyful and sad closing in my "collection" was that of *A Chorus Line,* in April of 1990. My wife and I had seen the show four times, a paltry figure to be sure. For my sister, the closing performance was her twentieth. The nineteenth had occurred earlier the same week, when she attended it on her birthday, as she had the previous umpteen years; she had also gone to see it anytime she needed her spirits raised. Even she was a piker compared to an Englishman in the balcony, who had made the *Guinness Book of World Records* by seeing it 356 times.

At this performance you had the feeling everyone in the audience knew the show by heart. There was a wild burst of applause as soon as the lights came up on the auditioners, and another a few minutes later when the first group of dancers is thanked and sent into the wings, then heartfelt ovations at every particularly pointed line, almost every song cue, especially the one leading into "What I Did for Love."

For all the high spirits, there was an unbearable poignance to the evening. The man who should have been there to celebrate this triumph had died three years before at the age of forty-four.

Not all closing nights convey a sense of loss. If the final performance "ignites," it is a kind of miracle. Nothing, after all, is more evanescent than a live performance, but a truly incandescent theatre memory is indelible. It can erase time.

That is certainly true of a memory that goes back thirty years, to a blustery night in March of 1961. Even if you didn't know it was the closing night of *Gypsy,* you would have been certain something special was going on because the overture, an explosive piece of music to begin with, was exceptionally so that night. The trumpeter went berserk during his solo, and the audience responded with a tentative ovation before the piece was over, which it repeated unrestrainedly when the music stopped.

I, then a hopelessly stagestruck college freshman, clapped so hard my watch fell into the aisle. As I scrambled to retrieve it before the star of the show made her determined way down that very aisle, I saw her making chitchat with the fat boy who sold orange juice at the back of the theatre. Moments later she strode down the aisle with a clarion, "Sing out, Louise," that demonstrated—lest there be any doubt—that her own trumpet was also in very good shape.

When she reached the stage, the audience, warmed up by its exertions during the overture, gave Ethel Merman two minutes of sustained hearty applause. (This, I might note, was in the days before it was customary to season an ovation with those odious hooting noises that I assume have come from the world of rock.) There was no mistaking the intensity and the warmth of the tribute that was being paid.

Merman, by all accounts a pretty tough customer, at first maintained her composure. But as the applause continued, her face broke into a grateful, possibly even tearful smile. The applause sealed an already strong bond, and Merman performed that night with the same fervor the trumpeter had.

What I particularly remember was the way she sang "Everything's Coming Up Roses." As she looked at the perplexed, frightened Louise and declared, "Mama is gonna see to it," her voice became an implacable growl, marshaling resources in her lower register that had probably not seen active duty in some time. I doubt that even the opening-night audience saw a more thrilling performance than we did.

On all these evenings what seems to be constant is the active, nay, the aggressive, participation of the audience. We live in a society that does not encourage overt displays of emotion. One of the exceptions is a leave-taking, when we can be as blubbery as we wish. Closing nights allow us to declare our love for performers, our love for the theatre, with a lack of restraint that might seem gauche or excessive during the normal run. On these occasions parting is unusually sweet sorrow.

Howard Kissel

Photo *(top)* by William Gibson
Photo *(bottom)* by John Huba

Jonathan Pryce, Hinton Battle, Willy Falk, and Barry K. Bernal onstage and outside the Broadway Theatre on the opening night of *Miss Saigon*.

Black-and-white photos *(top left,* and *bottom)* by William Gibson

Black-and-white photos *(top right,* and *opposite)* by E. Ira McCrudden

Color photo by Michael Le Poer Trench

ET
NEWS

BETTY COMDEN AND ADOLPH GREEN

The year was 1944. *On the Town* was the first show for Leonard Bernstein, Jerome Robbins, and the two of us as writers of the book and lyrics, and as actors in leading roles. The show, however, did not become a reality until George Abbott suddenly appeared on the scene as our director. Mr. Abbott was then in his fifties, and already a legendary figure in the theatre, and at our first meeting we were stunned that this rugged, handsome American monument would consider working with us. Lenny and Jerry had already made their marks on the theatre scene with their ballet *Fancy Free,* but we were still pursuing our sordid existence working in nightclubs when we could get the jobs and were completely unknown to him. We soon found out that he considered everyone he worked with a professional equal. In no time at all we were unselfconsciously calling him George, and we embarked on an exciting creative journey.

We had only ten days out of town in Boston because George had an immediate commitment coming up in Hollywood. In our happy ignorance we thought ten days was an ample amount of time, indeed, and before we knew it we had opened in New York and were a smash. That opening night was a storybook occasion. Some of the greatest names in the theatre came streaming up onstage to congratulate us, but we were in a daze and felt depressed. The actor in us had taken precedence over the writer, and all we could think of was a surefire laugh we had missed. A line that had always rocked the house had been greeted in stony silence. Amid all the cheers and hugging and joyous crying, we were huddled together trying to figure out what we had done wrong. Finally we stopped brooding about the laugh, but even after several great reviews, we remained emotionally disconnected and couldn't begin to feel anything.

The next day we had a matinee, and not having the sense to use the stage door, we entered through the lobby, or tried to. There was an endless snake line of eager ticket buyers all through the lobby and down the block, and disbelieving, we had to push our way through them. We did our eight shows that week, still somewhat numb and detached. Then toward the end of the week we found a letter in our backstage mailbox from Mr. Abbott. In it were warm words of praise, plus some advice. He told us that what was happening to us comes along rarely in any lifetime, and that we must be aware of it and not let the moment pass; to live it fully, to savor it to the hilt and not let superficial daily annoyances spoil it. Enjoy it! said George. This was just what we needed to hear. We laughed out loud and for the first time realized that a great thing was taking place in our lives. We had a hit on Broadway.

Betty Comden
Adolph Green

Writers Betty Comden and Adolph Green and composer Cy Coleman *(middle)* backstage at the Palace Theatre on the opening night of *The Will Rogers Follies.*
Photos by William Gibson

Dick Latessa, Keith Carradine, Jerry Mitchell, Dee Hoty, and Cady Huffman *(opposite)* prior to the opening-night performance of *The Will Rogers Follies.* Director Tommy Tune *(center)* and the company of *The Will Rogers Follies* in "the circle" backstage at "half-hour" before the opening-night curtain.

Black-and-white photos by William Gibson

Color photo by Martha Swope

HELEN HAYES

The year was 1909. I was appearing in my first Broadway show, *Old Dutch,* a musical by Victor Herbert, playing at the Herald Square Theatre at Thirty-fifth and Broadway. At night, after the show, Lew Fields, the producer and star, commissioned his brother Sidney Fields to walk Mother and me up Broadway to Forty-second Street, where he put us on the crosstown streetcar to Lexington Avenue and home, which was Mrs. Nathanson's rooming house.

Those eight blocks between Herald Square and Forty-second Street were a glorious playground for an eight-year-old. We had wild snowball fights, chasing back and forth from one side of Broadway to the other. There weren't too many hansom cabs and carriages to dodge at that hour; everybody was happily at supper in Shanley's or Rector's or the Knickerbocker Grill after the theatre. I dreamed about getting inside one of those magic places one day when I was grown-up, and sure enough I did.

The Empire Theatre at Fortieth Street was where the Barrymores, Maude Adams, Billie Burke, and William Gillette held forth regularly. Years later I saw my first play in that theatre, Maude Adams in *Peter Pan.*

On my first opening, the lobby of the Herald Square Theatre was lined with flowers sent to the cast members. In those days a Broadway opening was very grand. Ladies wore their jewels and décolleté gowns, gentlemen wore black tie. I would like to see it like that again today, but there is little hope for that. The Herald Square Theatre is gone. Several years ago, I went to an important Broadway opening with the producer of a successful London play. We were bedecked for the occasion. In front of us sat two young couples in leather jackets and jeans, the ladies with hair I yearned to take a brush to.

No, we can never get back to those days of elegance, and the high respect for the fairy-tale people who inhabited the theatre. However, I have my memories. Lucky me.

Helen Hayes

LUCIE ARNAZ

February 11, 1979, was my opening night and my Broadway debut in Neil Simon and Marvin Hamlisch's *They're Playing Our Song.*

That night will always be a beautiful, backlit memory for me. The show went better than anyone would have dared predict, and it seemed that everyone who was ever in show business was in the audience.

My official escort for the evening was Michael Bennett, my mentor, my first official Broadway director in the national company of *Seesaw,* and the midwife to my birth in the theatre. Michael's smile after the performance let me know that, whatever the reviews, whatever the fate of the show, I should be proud because of the work I had done.

Michael "choreographed" my entrance to the traditional opening-night party at Sardi's. When the doorman opened the double door in front of that famous chocolate awning, Michael took hold of my arm for a moment and said, "Walk slowly, dahling! This only happens every couple of hundred years."

This was great, sage advice for a rookie with her first big hit. I had no idea, then, how very true it would turn out to be. Being on Broadway was like the college years I never had. It was a campus where on Wednesday or Saturday afternoons on your way to class, all of the "dorms" would be buzzing, and as you'd pass your classmates, you'd share the jitters and joys of life at "Broadway U."

Of course, it's different now. Faces are new. But when you've been in one of those ancient temples, with your name out in front, you know you've got a right to the street. And to me, there's nothing more thrilling than walking into a crowded Sardi's, Joe Allen's, or Sam's and seeing the same smile that says, "Come on in. We have your table. You're alumni, now. You will always belong."

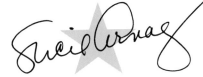

GLORIA ROSENTHAL

The Gypsy Robe passes backstage from *Miss Saigon (top)* to *The Secret Garden (middle)* to *Nick & Nora (bottom).*
Photo *(opposite, middle)* by Marc Bryan-Brown
Photos *(opposite, top* and *bottom)* by William Gibson

Opening night on Broadway. People delivering cards; gifts; telegrams; the ubiquitous flowers and bouquets of balloons; and if it's a musical—a *Broadway* musical—the Gypsy Robe. The adorned, the exquisite, the legendary Gypsy Robe arrives at half hour on opening night in the hands of its previous recipient, a chorus member from the last musical to open on Broadway.

The Robe, which begins its exciting journey as an extremely plain muslin dressing gown, will have been decorated with a significant piece of memorabilia from that last show, and by the time it has passed through about fifteen shows, it will be so loaded down with mementos and elaborately decorated sleeves that the original color is totally obscured. Even the shape is somewhat altered by the addition of, for example, a hood with rabbit ears from *Wind in the Willows;* an oversize collar from *Mame;* a long, flowing train carrying a *Pirates of Penzance* frigate.

The ritual of the Gypsy Robe began in 1950 when Bill Bradley, a dancer in *Call Me Madam,* talked another chorus member into letting him have (in his words) "her tacky dressing gown." He sent it to a friend in *Call Me Madam* as an opening-night present with a note calling the dressing gown the "legendary Gypsy Robe." The friend added a rose from Ethel Merman's gown and sent it to the next Broadway musical on opening night.

Bill, who left Broadway to become choreographer for the Ringling Brothers and Barnum & Bailey Circus, had no idea what he had started that day. He didn't know that the words he'd said in jest were prophetic: the Robe had, indeed, become legendary, and written rules concerning the Robe's transfer from one show to another were soon in effect.

Though many decorations are drawn and painted, such as the beautifully sketched likeness of Joel Grey for *Cabaret* and a magnificent helicopter scene from *Miss Saigon,* most additions are imaginatively created three-dimensional items: a full-size straw hat from *Dancin';* a big, fluffy cloud with "beads" of

The Rules of the Gypsy Robe

The Gypsy Robe blesses every Broadway musical! Please keep the tradition and stick to the rules. Let's not lose what is ours alone.

1. The Gypsy Robe goes only to Broadway musicals with a chorus.
2. Robe goes to chorus member *only* with most number of Broadway shows.
3. It must be delivered by half hour on opening night to member selected.
4. New member must put Robe on and circle the stage three times, while cast members reach out and touch Robe for good luck; new member visits each dressing room while wearing Robe.
5. New member adds memento from show to Robe, with opening-night date, and cast members all sign it; each Robe should represent about fifteen to twenty shows so mementos must occupy a reasonable space.
6. New member must determine when next Broadway musical is opening (contact Terry Marone of AEA); find cast member who is "*the* gypsy" in that show and be responsible for delivering the Robe on opening night, making sure the above rules are followed.

Barry Bostwick, Joanna Gleason, and company touch the Gypsy Robe for luck on opening night of *Nick & Nora*. Photo by William Gibson

rain (*Singin' in the Rain*); fans, feathers, an umbrella, a stuffed cat, dancing shoes, a strategically placed pillow (from *Baby*); a real rope from—of course! —*The Will Rogers Follies;* and in the case of *A Chorus Line,* a full-size, stuffed T-shirt picturing the entire line's eight-by-ten glossies.

When a Robe is so loaded down that it can hardly be lifted, much less worn, it is retired and another started. Some retired Robes are in custody of Actors' Equity, others at the Library of the Performing Arts at Lincoln Center.

The ritual begins when the stage manager makes the eagerly waited-for announcement: "Everyone onstage for the Gypsy Robe." Cast members, some already in costume and makeup, come down, crowd around the stage, and wait to hear who will be honored on this night. Since the selection is based on number of shows, and cast members are not normally familiar with each other's credits, the recipient's name is always a surprise, and the honored gypsy is thrilled to be so designated.

In some cases, the rules are ignored in favor of a featured performer or a star who is still considered a "gypsy at heart." Chita Rivera, Gwen Verdon, and Sandy Duncan received the Robe after they were out of the chorus.

The following note was written by Chita Rivera when the Robe went from Fred Mann in *Merlin* to David Gold in *On Your Toes*:

Dear David, The life and honor of being a gypsy has been with me for (cough here) years and it is the thing that gets you thru. Continue to "Pick 'em up and put 'em down" for as long as you want to. Long live us all—I think I beat you by a few years. Congratulations, Chita.

Chita's note sums up that very special gypsy feeling that, like the Robe, goes on and on, a vital part of every Broadway musical with a chorus.

Gloria Rosenthal

ALFRED UHRY

From 1980 to 1982, I was connected with the revival of *Little Johnny Jones,* the 1904 George M. Cohan musical that introduced "Give My Regards to Broadway" and "Yankee Doodle Dandy." My credit read "adapted by" in tiny little print. What I really did was completely rewrite the book and go through the Cohan archives to supplement the score with appropriate songs. Some of the original songs were no longer in existence. Others had titles and no music, or we came up with music, fully orchestrated, without words, titles, or any indication where it fit into the show. Some songs were simply unplayable to modern audiences and offensive to modern ears, such as "The March of the Frisco Chinks" and "Welcome to the Land of Wang."

I pruned, I hacked away, I invented, and I had a wonderful time trying to recreate plots that held together the MGM musical films of my childhood. Not the great ones like *Meet Me in St. Louis* and *Singin' in the Rain.* I mean movies like *Dangerous When Wet* or *Summer Stock* or *Good News* (my favorite!). In my memory they were genial and dopey and just weighty enough to hold the songs together.

Of course the presence of James Cagney and the more musical *Yankee Doodle Dandy* loomed large. He was still very much alive then and the rumor kept circulating that he was going to show up at a performance. I was relieved that he never did because, in truth, he had a lock on that lead role. It was impossible to see the show and not think of him. Maybe that's why we went through four leads during our two-year travail. Most of the cast, however, remained with the show for the whole run (Maureen Brennan, Jane Galloway, Anna McNeeley, Jack Bittner, Ernie Sabella, and Peter Van Nordan). This was no "take the subway to work and arrive at half hour" job. It involved summer stock, cable television, a nine-month, cross-country tour, and finally Broadway—about five hundred performances in all. The show was in a constant state of flux. Songs came and went and came again. Scenes were rewritten and cut. All of these talented people genuinely wanted the show to work.

And finally it did. Audiences adored it. We started off with rave reviews, but somehow, as we came close to New York, the notices grew more ominous.

We were supposed to play four weeks of previews in New York, but it was shortened to two. Opening night was moved forward as well—to a Sunday. We all knew what that meant. If you open during the week, you at least play out your eight performances, but Sunday is the end of the week. Unless you get good notices, you're over and out in one shot.

Opening night at the Alvin. We all hoped for the best despite the obvious signs and portents. The entire company assembled early for the tradition of the Gypsy Robe. This was my third Broadway musical, but I had never heard of the Gypsy Robe before. At half hour, a tall, elegantly slim dancer named Richard Dodd paraded around the stage of the Alvin in a long muslin coat on which were scrawled the logos and signatures of other shows. Richard was chosen because he had the most Broadway credits, including the original production of *My Fair Lady*. In the glare of the work light onstage, Richard passed among us. We all touched the coat for luck. On the other side of the curtain we could hear the audience filing in. We had been working on this show for two years. Now it was all on the line. We all hugged each other. My job was done, but the actors had that all-important performance ahead of them. I remember thinking, "My God, these people are brave!" We ended up being excoriated by Frank Rich of the *Times* and closed the night we opened. But . . . I was proud to be a part of the company and this business.

CHRISTOPHER DURANG

s a child growing up in New Jersey in the midfifties, I was lucky enough to be taken by my parents to several vintage musical comedies on Broadway.

The first one I saw was *Fiorello!* and my favorite song was the belter "I Love a Cop."

My Fair Lady was almost my first one: my mother wrote for tickets that would have included me, but some local bluenose told her the story wasn't suitable for a child (age eight) because Eliza Doolittle lived with Henry Higgins in the same house without being married to him. Horrors, indeed! Later, after my mother saw the show and loved it, she apologized and said it would have been perfectly suitable. And of course, I loved the record.

I went to Harvard College and didn't come to New York much during those four years, with two memorable exceptions.

The first was for a nightmarish production of Brecht-Weill's *Rise and Fall of the City Mahagonny,* starring Barbara Harris and Estelle Parsons. I adored Barbara Harris from her Broadway records and from the movie *A Thousand Clowns,* and her voice sounded good in the show (especially in the "As You Make Your Bed" song), but otherwise the show was a horrifying failure. Indeed, act two began with a map projection showing a hurricane coming toward the city of Mahagonny and then missing it: when the hurricane bypassed the city, many in the audience booed, so much did they want the show to be over. Poor good actors. And it is a very hard show. (Later I was in a really good production directed by Alvin Epstein at Yale Repertory Theatre; and years later Sigourney Weaver and I parodied lots of this idiosyncratic, strange show in our off-Broadway cabaret act *Das* Lusitania *Songspiel.*)

The other show I came from college to see was a milestone—*Company,* music and lyrics by Stephen Sondheim, book by George Furth, directed by Hal Prince.

The book was witty and current about the intricacies of relationships, both married and single.

And although I grew up loving the Rodgers and Hammerstein musicals where songs grew directly out of the book—Lady Thiang says, "You must go to him, Mrs. Anna," suddenly the music swells, and some contralto voice soars into "He will not always be, what you would have him be . . ." In *Company,* the songs didn't grow predictably out of a scene; usually they commented on the scene.

For instance, Robert and two of his married friends would bicker and not quite get on in a scene, then another character not even in the scene would come on and sing, "It's the little things you do together," wryly cataloguing and complaining about the problems of living together.

Or that brilliant comic showstopper, "You Could Drive a Person Crazy," where three of the women Robert was dating (and frustrating) came out and did a hilarious trio complaining about him, even though in realistic story they didn't actually know one another.

Or Elaine Stritch's great "The Ladies Who Lunch," a blast of bitterness about a wasted life, which admittedly came out of the scene she was in, but it was really her mood that led to the song, not some traditional story development where you felt the buildup coming.

Anyway, I adored *Company.*

And probably the next show I liked as much was *Follies* by Sondheim and Prince again, with a book by James Goldman. I saw that one twice and felt lucky to have witnessed this fabulous show, which used spectacle to contrast with and to intensify the ache that lay at the core of the characters' disappointed lives.

There were so many indelible moments: Ethel Shutta at eighty years old (or something) just about shaking the entire theatre with her "Broadway Baby"; the vicious diatribe "Could I Leave You?" with the charismatic Alexis

Smith; and the truly exhilarating "Who's That Woman?" number, with Mary McCarty, Smith, and Dorothy Collins redoing an old Follies number, while their younger selves appeared, dancing with them in mirror reflection and inadvertently mocking them with youth and optimism. (This last number was choreographed by the late and deeply lamented Michael Bennett.)

Several years later I was in professional theatre myself. I've had two plays on Broadway, though, alas, I haven't had the same thrill as an author on Broadway that I did as an audience member.

My play *A History of the American Film* was briefly at the ANTA Theatre (now the Virginia) in 1978, but it didn't catch on; and in retrospect, even a few months after it closed, I think all of us realized that among other things we were in a theatre too large for the intimacy of what we were doing. (And we made other mistakes as well, though the cast was lovely—Swoosie Kurtz, April Shawhan, Gary Bayer, Brent Spiner, Joan Pape, among others.)

And in 1982 my comedy *Beyond Therapy* was at the Brooks Atkinson in what I thought was a charming and successful production, and I'm very sorry if you missed the wonderful Dianne Wiest as Prudence and the hilarious Kate McGregor-Stewart as a warm but crazy lady therapist (two standouts in a uniformly delightful cast—John Lithgow, Peter Michael Goetz, Jack Gilpin, David Pierce). The newspaper reviews were mixed, the magazine reviewers were enthusiastic, but without any nice words from *The New York Times,* ticket sales didn't build and the producers felt they had to close it.

So it's hard for me to look at Broadway with the same kind of innocent enthusiasm I had when I was just a fan. I'm kind of aware of the randomness (in my opinion) about what gets kind reviews versus what gets harsh ones. I remember Dianne Wiest gave us all opening-night presents from Tiffany's, something she said she'd never done because she'd always feared her previous shows would close, but which she did this time because she thought "this was the one that was going to do it." When she won the Oscar several years later for Woody Allen's *Hannah and Her Sisters,* I wondered where the people had been to celebrate and to report on her talent in 1982 when she was in our theatrical midst. Oh, well.

(I've had better luck off-Broadway—lest you think I'm only a mass of disappointment—especially with my play *Sister Mary Ignatius Explains It All for You,* which ran for two years.)

And as an audience member I'm sorry to say that I feel kind of disappointed at what one sees on Broadway "these days." (To quote Kander and Ebb's *Chicago*—a show I greatly enjoyed—"Nobody's got no class.") Maybe this kind of feeling happens with age, but gosh, I'm only forty-two, hardly an éminence grise yet.

But still, live theatre is unpredictable. And I did feel that surge of excitement watching most of *Grand Hotel* (especially the great Tommy Tune's staging and especially Tony-winner Michael Jeter with his fabulous dance of joy). And I felt it from the revival of John Guare's *The House of Blue Leaves,* with indelible work from Swoosie Kurtz, and from the latest Guare play *Six Degrees of Separation,* with indelible work from Stockard Channing. (And both these productions were directed by my frequent collaborator and friend, the supertalented director Jerry Zaks.) And from Wendy Wasserstein's *The Heidi Chronicles* with the deeply moving Joan Allen. And from Pauline Collins's exhilarating tour de force in *Shirley Valentine.* And Tyne Daly in *Gypsy.*

So, all told, I guess it ain't dead yet.

Christopher Durang

PLAYERS

1. a person who occupies himself for diversion or amuses himself. 2. a person who undertakes to play against all others in various games. 3. a gambler; a trifler. 4. one who makes a profession of acting in stage plays.

Photo by Jim Brill

LILLIAS WHITE

A typical day on Broadway, if you happen to be blessed and lucky enough to be working, is usually one in which you perform certain rituals that strengthen, fortify, and prepare you for your nightly excursion onstage. However, when you are enjoying a multiplicity of thespian appointments, your typical day turns into a marathon in which you bolt from one theatre to the next and back again. Such was the case during October 1991 when I was playing Asaka in *Once on This Island* and rehearsing the role of Grizabella in *Cats,* as well as appearing as Lillian Edwards on PBS-TV's "Sesame Street."

One gray Wednesday, there was a scheduling problem at "Sesame Street" and it became necessary for me to film a segment between the matinee and evening performances of *Once on This Island.* Further adding to the drama of the day was a technical rehearsal of the "tire ride to heaven" Grizabella takes every performance at *Cats.*

So, on this Wednesday, my Broadway day began at six-thirty A.M., getting my children up and out for school, followed at eleven A.M. by my workout with "body snatcher" Shirley Black Brown. From there I ran to the Booth Theatre on West Forty-fifth Street to make my half-hour call. Then two P.M.—show time on "the Island." From the Booth I taxied up to the "Sesame Street" studio simultaneously conferring with my publicist. We filmed the "Sesame Street" segment, during which I had a total memory lapse of the song I was supposed to be singing. So we had to stop tape in order for the crew to make cue cards. The words from *Cats,* mixed with the words from "Sesame Street," compounded by the words and music from *Once on This Island* created a chaotic cacophony of sounds and images in my poor little head.

But I got through the taping and literally ran to the Winter Garden Theatre on Broadway for my tire ride. I rode to heaven with butterflies in my stomach due to the lack of food that I didn't have time to eat. After my descent back to earth, I dashed back to the Booth Theatre in time to inhale a cup of miso soup, do three or four pliés, a handful of sit-ups, vocalize with my infamous "Yee! Whoo! Hey!" and jump into my Tony-nominated costume. Taking a deep breath, I entered the warm, tropical, nonstop world of the French Antilles.

By the end of the evening, I was both blessing and cursing the predicament I was in. I had been teased and cajoled by the cast and crew of *Island* about the money I'd made that day, but I'd have to say that I was not totally displeased with my situation. The opportunity to be able to work in this medium from day to night is one for which I am truly grateful. I thank God for royal jelly, Dong Quai, vitamin B_{12}, and, most of all, His indefatigable energy within me.

Lillias White

Lillias White in her dressing room *(opposite)* at the Booth Theatre during *Once on This Island*.
Photo by Paulo Netto

Keith Carradine *(top)* with a picture of Will Rogers backstage at the Palace.
Photo by Jean Pagliuso
Alan Alda in his dressing room at the Neil Simon Theatre before a performance of *Jake's Women*.
Photo by William Gibson

HARVEY FIERSTEIN

There is nothing, absolutely nothing, that compares with opening on Broadway with a hit. The audiences are wonderful, the press is eager to meet and write about you, the establishment of theatre producers and owners treat you like an instant old friend, and then there are the celebrities. All the people you've watched from afar, the very people who inspired you to one day be up there onstage, there in *your* dressing room. It's amazing. Such a thing happened to me when *Torch Song Trilogy* opened at the Helen Hayes Theatre. Actually the parade of stars began when we were still off-off-Broadway, but it continued almost nonstop for the next three years. Neil Simon and Anne Bancroft and Ann Miller and Anne Meara. Stockard Channing and Carol Channing and Carol Lawrence and Arthur Laurents. Chita Rivera and Rita Moreno and Leonard Nimoy and Bea Arthur and Arthur Miller. Mike Nichols and Milton Berle and Mel Brooks and Mary Tyler Moore. They came and they came, in a never-ending stream that made any show I could put onstage pale in comparison.

My rabbit, Arnold, who lived in my dressing room, fell immediately and hopelessly in love with Barbra Streisand's full-length fur coat.

Legendary camera-shy Ryan O'Neal insisted that he and Farrah Fawcett be photographed kissing my cheeks.

Cloris Leachman, without comment on the show, asked my dresser if he could steam out her gown for a party she was about to attend. She used my dressing room, my deodorant, my lipstick, but never even said hello to me.

Then Mayor Koch had his bodyguards search my room before he'd enter. I told them, "If you'd seen the show, you'd know there's nothing hidden in my closet."

Joan Plowright stayed for a drink, Henry Winkler stayed forever in my heart, and Dustin Hoffman left at intermission (an ailing baby at home).

Cher and Richard Chamberlain and Maureen Stapleton and Geraldine Page and Brenda Vaccaro and Shirley MacLaine and Rip Taylor. Sondheim

and Styne and Comden and Green and Coleman and Herman . . . They all dropped by and made any dream of a gay boy from Bensonhurst, Brooklyn, seem possible.

But the best, my most never-fading memory is of Ethel Merman. She popped back after the show, with her niece, silencing the most callous of stagehands.

"What did you think of the show, Miss Merman?" I croaked.

She glared at me as only Merman could and bellowed back, "I thought it was a piece of shit, but the rest of the audience laughed and cried, so what the fuck do I know?"

Harvey Fierstein

Harvey Fierstein backstage at the Actors' Playhouse during the run of the revival of *The Haunted Host*.
Photo by Susan Shacter

B. D. WONG

Torch Song Trilogy was the first play I ever saw on Broadway. An overwhelming experience on many levels: what was then known as the Little Theatre loomed large around me; The Play seemed epic; its message felt like it was making history as it unfolded; its presentation, just under four hours, was emotionally draining . . . and of course, there was you know who, who simply commandeered all of the above. Big ol' star.

I particularly remembered, in the third act, David, the street kid Harvey adopts, played then by Fisher Stevens (who is also a friend of mine these days —Fisher Fisher Fisher Stevens Stevens Stevens). To him, Harvey was familiar, loving, maternal. I thought, this Fisher Stevens has a *great part*. . . .

From then on, for months, I longed to play David in *Torch Song*. I was barely twenty and quite suited for it and was pretty naive about being an actor of color on Broadway, etc. Still, it seemed like quite a long shot.

One late night, I realized it was Thursday so I bought the new *Backstage*, which lists all of the upcoming auditions, and there I found what I'd been waiting for: "OPEN CALL DAVIDS TS TRILOGY." But I was immediately filled with ironic self-doubt. What a pipe dream I had, I thought. How could I expect that they would see how I was very different but just so *right?* I began searching for the strength to go to the call. (Good thing I got the paper; the audition was the next morning.) I was afraid that, because of my race, I would be laughed at or told to go home or something. I was pretty tough, but stuff like that happens and it's always awful.

I just wanted to feel it was okay for me to go, so that I could act like I belonged there. I just wanted *permission*.

It was eleven-fifteen P.M. I lived on West Thirty-ninth Street. I put on the "David" outfit I had picked out weeks ago (striped shirt; worn denim overalls; a zippered, faded, hooded sweatshirt; beat-up sneakers) and walked to the Little Theatre on West Forty-fourth Street.

I watched the effervescent audience emerge, scatter, and thin, and eventually I was all alone on the sidewalk in weather that was too cold for my clothing. At about midnight Mr. Fierstein (and Mr. Stevens) emerged, and I approached cautiously, trying to sound as unrehearsed and normal as possible. I felt a little like Eve waiting for Margo Channing: "I hear there's an open call . . . would it be dumb . . . um . . . should I go?"

Harvey smiled, and his response was magical:

"Sure, why not?"

Permission granted.

I ran home, folded my costume reverently, and slept. The next morning, strolling through the stage door of the Royale Theatre, I was personally escorted by the spirit of Harvey Fierstein, and it was my secret. "The playwright says I can be here," I said telepathically as I stepped forward in the lineup and stated my name, head high, shoulders square. Guess what, I was asked to read four times!

They were four of my favorite auditions of my life. . . .

'Cause I was Elwood P. Dowd and I had a big, giant, invisible rabbit named Harvey at my side, the whole time.

Harvey was pretty shocked when he found out that kid was me. He says he remembered his encounter with the Asian boy when they cast a Hispanic actor as David in the movie, almost as if I had planted some sort of seed. But even though I never got to play David, sometimes, nowadays, Harvey is familiar and loving and maternal to *me,* just like Arnold is to David in the play. And that, as you may imagine, is a wonderful, wonderful feeling.

Harvey Harvey Harvey Fierstein Fierstein Fierstein.

Chita Rivera *(top)* in her dressing room at The Supper Club.
Photo by Ken Howard

Judd Hirsch backstage at the Royale Theatre before a performance of *Conversations with My Father.*
Photo by William Gibson

HINTON BATTLE

At the age of fifteen, I came to New York City to study and eventually join the New York City Ballet, under the direction of George Balanchine. However, living on $200 a month in New York and not being allowed to supplement my income made for lots of Greek salads and tuna-fish platters.

My sister, being the Broadway gypsy, knew all the new shows to happen. *The Wiz,* a new hip show going to Broadway, was holding an audition. I took a leave of absence from the School of American Ballet and joined *The Wiz* chorus.

Well, during our pre-Broadway tryout in Philadelphia, our original scarecrow became ill during the first act. Charles Blackwell (our stage manager) came to me during intermission and said, "I know you're not the understudy and I know you have not been rehearsed, but do you think you could go on for the second act as the scarecrow?" I said, "Are you kidding?" Mr. Blackwell, all of six feet six, turned to me and said, "Do I look like I'm kidding?"

So with the makeup being put on me, the lines being read to me, stage directions being told to me, wig put on my head, and a thrown-together costume, I was put onstage.

When it was time for me to speak, I got pulled, jerked, and tugged, and when I didn't speak, I just fell down a lot, but I did something right that night because the next day I got a call asking if I wanted to keep the role—and what do you think I said?

So at the age of fifteen, I debuted on Broadway in a show that beat all the odds, and I even received my first Broadway reviews. I think it was Rex Reed who said that I "looked like Diana Ross in drag." But hey, six shows and three Tonys later . . . I'm still lovin' it!

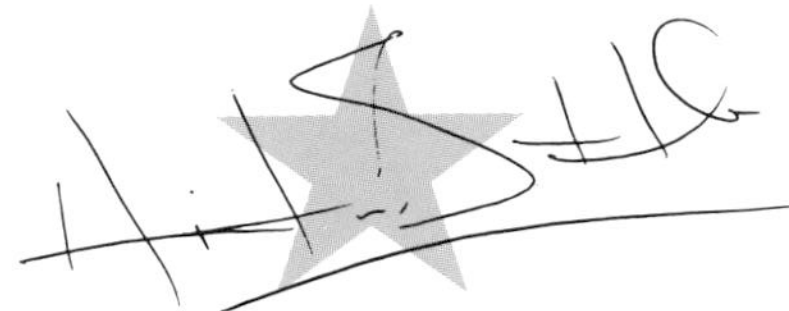

LYNN REDGRAVE

Nineteen sixty-six. It's winter. It's New York. The play, Peter Shaffer's *Black Comedy,* and last year's Manhattan power-out is still being talked about. The gimmick of the play is the reversal of light and dark. So the opening scene has the characters walking about the room with complete confidence, talking as though they can see, while in fact the whole place is blacked out.

It's an SRO, Saturday-night crowd at the Ethel Barrymore Theatre, and you can bet that no one has read the program note that would tip them off to the light-is-dark, dark-is-light gimmick. While the houselights are still up, a Sousa march blares out of the onstage speakers, then groans to a halt accompanied by a sudden blackout as called for in the stage directions.

The curtain rises. Michael Crawford and I are onstage, our dialogue all but drowned out by audience groans, whistles, and appeals to the Almighty. Michael: "There! How do you think the room looks?" Me: "Fabulous! I wish you could always have it like this." *Man in the audience:* "It may look great to you, but we can't see a fucking thing!" Michael and I raise our voices and continue as matches, and flashlights, are pulled from audience pockets and purses. Ushers race down the aisles snuffing them out. "Sir, madame, please, it's all part of the show. Please, miss, we have to keep the theatre dark."

We reach the moment when the onstage plot blackout is supposed to occur, and as planned, the lights bump up to full power. The audience applauds and cheers, "Yeah! About time! Damn right."

Don't they get it yet? Michael and I stumble and trip about the stage. Can't they tell that we are behaving as if it's dark and we can't see? Twenty minutes and no laughs later, Michael does his spectacular fall down the staircase and I creep down spider fashion, my bottom in the air.

Woman in the audience (loud whisper): "You know what, Martha, I think that girl is pretending it's dark."

Lynn Redgrave

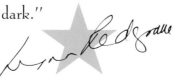

The cast of *Pageant* in their dressing rooms and onstage at the Blue Angel.
Black-and-white photos by Arturo E. Porazzi
Color photo *(opposite)* by Scott Humbert

MICHAEL CRAWFORD

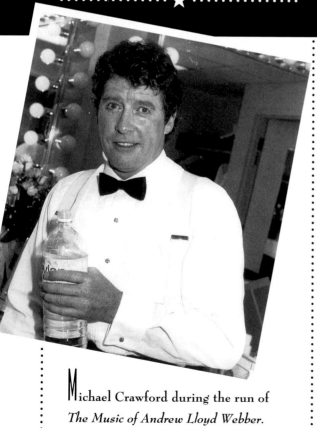

Michael Crawford during the run of *The Music of Andrew Lloyd Webber.*
Photo by Yacek Samotus

I came out of the Majestic Theatre's stage door one night in 1988, long after the crowds had gone, heading through the long alley on my way to Forty-fifth Street and the cab ride home. Suddenly a woman appeared from round the corner, striding toward me, full sail, followed by four young people at the trot. She spoke to them in tones that reeked with resolution: "It's *got* to be here somewhere." (That voice. Where had I heard it before?) She paid no attention to me and strode past. Then she abruptly changed her mind, turned and started back, quickly gaining on me.

"Young man," she called—her voice resounded along the walls of the alley—"where's the stage door to the Golden [Theatre]?"

I turned and looked into Katharine Hepburn's marvelous face. "Uhhh," I stammered, mentally grappling for a brilliant phrase to stun her with the force of my personality, "it's right there." I pointed the way. (That's *terrific,* Crawford: this is a chance meeting she'll never forget!)

"Right," she said. "Thank you." She brushed past me, and she quickly disappeared down the alley with her guests in tow. Only in New York, I thought. Where else would you meet Katharine Hepburn in a dark alley!

A week later she came to see *The Phantom of the Opera* and visited my dressing room afterward. It was clear that she'd been crying. "You!" she drawled in that crisp metallic voice of hers. "I have *never* seen *anything* like *that* in my *life!* And I'm going to bring people back ah-gain and *ah-gain* and *AH-GAIN.*"

"Thank you," I said, "and I give good directions, too."

She raised a perplexed eyebrow, smiled a polite—if puzzled—smile, and left. But she is a very generous woman, and she forgave my bit of brash humor. She kept her word as well and returned on many occasions with members of her family. She was reportedly seen in the orchestra, crying happily every time.

JANE ALEXANDER

It was 1968. We'd been marching for civil rights for years, but black had never been more beautiful. The black power movement was at its height. Stokely Carmichael was sending out the message and it was being heard: *Black is beautiful.* Thousands were letting their hair grow out, and Afros the size of basketballs were everywhere.

No one was more beautiful than a honey-colored boxer named Cassius Clay who changed his name when he became a Muslim: he was now known as Muhammad Ali. A rose by any other name still spelled world heavyweight champion. The boxing commission had taken his belt away when Ali, a conscientious objector on religious grounds, refused to register for the military draft, which was fueling the Vietnam War. He was angry, he was frustrated, and he let the world know it.

The Great White Hope, by Howard Sackler, opened on October 3 at the Alvin Theatre. James Earl Jones played the first black heavyweight champ, based on the life of Jack Johnson, who won the belt in 1908. I played Jack's white mistress.

Directed by Ed Sherin, it was a taut, sprawling epic that had audiences leaping to their feet at the curtain. The play won the Pulitzer that year, and all the other awards you could name. The play had such deep reverberation for all of us at the time with its examination of racism: Jack has his belt taken away on a trumped-up charge of violating the Mann Act, which was taking a white woman—me—across state lines for nefarious purposes. He escapes to Europe and I follow; we're buffeted from pillar to post all over the Continent as he seeks some measure of comfort. Nothing works.

Back home, the country is searching for a "Great White Hope" to challenge him, regain the title, and strip Jack of all power.

In Eastern Europe, we drift into despair, and at the end of the second act, alone at midnight in a Hungarian railroad station when he's just told another lackey from the boxing world that he will *not* return and face charges,

Glenn Close *(above)* at her dressing table during *Death and the Maiden* at the Brooks Atkinson Theatre. Jane Alexander in her dressing room at the Roundabout Theatre's production of *The Visit.*
Photos by Stewart Shining

James Earl lifts his great fists, looks down the length of the deserted tracks into the darkness of the audience, and with a controlled ferocity says: "You tell 'em: If they want me, they'll have to come and get me." Then he beats his chest slowly three times and chants, "Here ah is! Here ah is! Here ah is!" It was a devastating and powerful moment for those of us onstage and in the house.

Muhammad Ali came to see *The Great White Hope* several times. He was so excited by the play and James Earl's performance that the first time he saw it he busted into Jimmy's dressing room afterward and burst into the bathroom, where the star was taking it easy for a few minutes after a demanding three hours onstage. Later, Ali wandered the theatre congratulating everyone, and in his enthusiasm gathering them under his wing like baby birds. All, that is, except me. He would not acknowledge me. He proclaimed loudly, "This is my story. Yes, this is my story. All except that white chick. Yes, this is my story."

The exclusion was palpable. And it hurt. I had been surrounded by black people for months. The black women in the company were gorgeous, and I worshiped James Earl Jones. My skin seemed pasty and unfinished by comparison. I'd even gone so far as to shop for an Afro wig, which looked ridiculous on top of my skinny, pink face. To be snubbed by the greatest of them all was more than I could bear. He came again to the theatre, and again. He made his rounds of the dressing rooms after the show, and I took to following him surreptitiously, hoping for a glance, but he gave me nothing.

One night, we two were the last ones left in the theatre. All sixty-three actors, except me, had gone. The audience had gone, the stagehands had gone, only the doorman sitting by the stage door remained. The curtain was raised and the one standing stage light placed by the last electrician was all that lit the darkened auditorium. Muhammad Ali emerged from the shadows of stage right, crossed to the center of the stage, and stopped. Quiet as a mouse, I scurried thirty feet behind him and hid in the wings watching. He never saw me. I don't think he knew I was there. He raised his huge fists, gazed out at row upon row of darkened, empty seats, then brought his arms down thunderously upon his massive chest chanting over and over again: "Here ah is. Here ah is. Here ah is." Then he disappeared into the night.

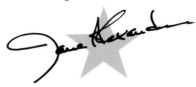

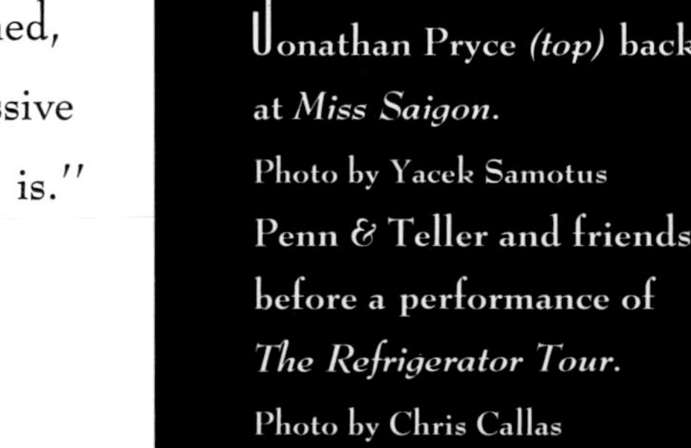

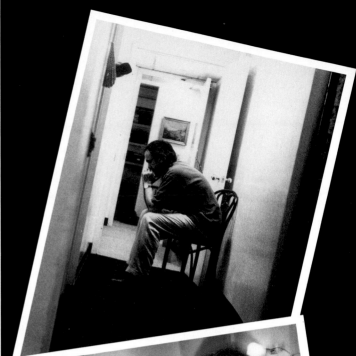

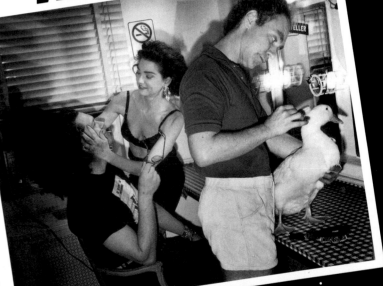

Jonathan Pryce *(top)* backstage at *Miss Saigon.*
Photo by Yacek Samotus
Penn & Teller and friends before a performance of *The Refrigerator Tour.*
Photo by Chris Callas

DANA IVEY

George C. Scott gave me my first real job on Broadway in *Present Laughter* at the Circle in the Square. He both directed and starred in it. It was also the beginning of friendships that have lasted with Kate Burton and Michael Ritchie, Nathan Lane, and Jim Piddock.

My unemployment insurance had ended and I was going to get a job stuffing envelopes when a playwright friend, Percy Granger, spoke to Ted Mann and got me an audition for the play, something my agent hadn't been able to do. Percy called me on a Monday morning at ten-thirty and said I had the audition at noon! I hadn't read the play, but knew it was Coward, and I'd done lots of "style" plays, so I thought, "I can do this." I hastily put myself together and raced down to the theatre. The subway stalled, and I got out at the next station I could, grabbed a cab, and got out at Fiftieth and Ninth, not realizing it was two long blocks away. I had a few minutes to look at the scene before going in to read, and after I'd read the scene they asked me to read one I'd never seen before. I said, "This will be a really cold reading," but did okay with it. When I left, I thought I should buy the script and read the play because I might get a callback. Instead, that afternoon they called to offer me the job, and we started rehearsals the next day!

Months later, when I left the show, George C. Scott stopped the applause during my last curtain call when we were all onstage, and he gave a little speech that was a tribute to me. I was overwhelmed by his generosity in acknowledging me like that.

Dana Ivey

John Mahoney and Dana Ivey onstage before the opening performance of the Roundabout Theatre's revival of *The Subject Was Roses*.
Photo by Yacek Samotus

JOHN GIELGUD

Nineteen twenty-eight and I am in New York for the first time—hastily summoned from London to play a small part as a replacement in a grand Gilbert Miller production. I am met at the docks and driven straight to the theatre, where a dress rehearsal is proceeding. We go on the following night, but the play is a complete failure and closes after very few performances. The management fails to fulfill my guarantee, so I have only enough money to stay on for a week or two but have a thrilling time exploring the city and seeing as many plays as possible. Helen Hayes in *Coquette,* Judith Anderson in *Behold the Bridegroom, Show Boat* with Helen Morgan and Edna May Oliver. Harlem and the Cotton Club, Mabel Mercer at Tony's, exciting speakeasies with fears of bathtub gin (it is Prohibition)—enthralling experiences I have never forgotten.

Then *Hamlet* in 1936 with McClintic directing and Lillian Gish and Judith Anderson, and in competition with Leslie Howard. Our production carried off the honors. Taxi drivers would ask which *Hamlet* I was, and Beatrice Lillie put a "Battle of Hamlets" sketch into her revue.

Since those two unforgettable visits, I have acted on Broadway so many times. *The Importance of Being Earnest, The Lady's Not for Burning, Home, No Man's Land, Much Ado About Nothing, Ivanov, Medea,* and *Tiny Alice.*

I found an enchanting apartment on Central Park West overlooking the reservoir and across to Fifth Avenue, which I sublet when I was not there. I still miss it very much.

New York will always be a second home to me. I fondly wish I could return to it someday, though it has changed so enormously over the many years. The hospitality and vitality of the city are ever stimulating and revitalizing and have meant so much to me over my long career.

UTA HAGEN

At the Shubert Theatre in the spring of 1938 I made my Broadway debut as Nina in the magnificent production of *The Seagull* starring the Lunts. For me this event became the yardstick of excellence against which to measure each stage of the development of my career. In the fall of 1943, once again at the Shubert, I opened in the landmark production of *Othello* starring Paul Robeson. The momentous occasion elicited a standing ovation—a rarity in those days. It heralded the longest run ever for a Shakespearean play on Broadway or anywhere else in the world. This experience shaped and influenced the actions of my life up to this very day, serving to open my eyes to the virulence of racism—even in New York.

At the time, Paul Robeson was a national hero, renowned as a singer, actor, and a leader in the progressive movement in America. Yet, if he wanted to have a bite and a drink after the performance, he was not allowed in any of the restaurants frequented by white performers. We had a choice of private parties, clubs in Harlem, or Barney Josephson's Cafe Society. On a hunt for a taxi, Paul walked at a distance because he didn't want to "embarrass" me. I insisted on taking his arm and gradually learned to ignore the hostile stares and occasional epithets that greeted me. (Once, in an elevator, an elegantly dressed woman actually spat in my face.)

The following season, the Theatre Guild sent us on a national tour, which was even more enlightening. After convincing Actors' Equity, all the performers signed contracts that guaranteed for the first time that we played only in theatres in which the audience would not be segregated. I was amazed at the number of playhouses in the *north* which up to that time had practiced segregation, and we all felt like pioneers as we broke one precedent after another. St. Louis was the farthest south where we were successful in our endeavor. The high tension emanating from the auditorium was often terrifying, and it was fascinating to discover that it was not generated by the action onstage—by a black man kissing, slapping, and strangling a white woman—but rather by the presence of black people sitting among whites in expensive orchestra seats and loges. Indianapolis, the northern headquarters for the KKK, and Detroit, right after the worst of race riots, were particularly adventurous.

Jose Ferrer, to whom I was then married, and I decided at the outset of the tour that we would always go to the same hotel in which Paul could get a reservation, which meant that the rest of the cast were sometimes in the best hotel while we were housed in a fleabag. Restaurants were taboo and we had to rely on room service. In Indianapolis not a single hotel could be found for a black guest so the Guild offered to cancel the booking. Paul felt it was far more important that the townspeople should see the play, and we were housed by his friends. In Sacramento we were actually relegated to a brothel. At our arrival only one of the rooms was ready and we and all the suitcases waited there until the other one was cleaned up. When at last the bellhop came to fetch us, he looked at us in confusion and mumbled, "How do you want me to segregate the luggage?" Paul gazed heavenward and groaned, "Oh, God—now they're doing it to the luggage!"

Although this production of *Othello* was deemed to be a "historic" one, to me it is as though it had taken place yesterday—until I realize the enormous progress that has been made in human rights in the interim. Since this progress has of late begun to erode, I need to remind myself that all artists must continue to take a stand, to make themselves responsible for being in the forefront of social change and betterment.

Lea Salonga *(top)* in her dressing room at *Miss Saigon.*
Photo by Yacek Samotus
Raul Julia in his at *Man of La Mancha.*
Photo by Chris Fesler

The company of *Mule Bone* backstage and onstage at the Ethel Barrymore Theatre.
Black-and-white photos by John Huba
Color photo by Brigitte Lacombe

JONATHAN HADARY

Jonathan Hadary making up as Herbie for *Gypsy*.
Photo by Stewart Shining

As I entered the room, Eva Le Gallienne stood up. It was an ordinary rehearsal studio somewhere midtown a decade ago, and I was auditioning for the Broadway revival of her adaptation of *Alice in Wonderland,* which she herself was directing as well as acting in. As I came through the door, she rose from her chair behind a long table, four or five people seated on either side of her, and extended her hand to me. She was eighty-three.

I had seen her onstage only once, on Broadway in *The Royal Family,* and had been thrilled to discover for myself that she was indeed a great actress. I'd known of her since high school and had some sense of both the duration and breadth of her career. Now, clasping my hand, her eyes gleaming, she tilted her head, regarding me with interest and what seemed like hope. I was honored to meet her and told her so. She was gracious, regal, but at the same time downright friendly, her handshake firm. Our hellos concluded, she offered me the chair in the middle of the room and we both sat down.

It went well. I was pretty good. She leaned forward on her elbows watching me as I read the scene. She chuckled appropriately a few times and gaily laughed outright once. When I was done, she complimented me in a nicely specific way, we chatted a bit, she thanked me, and I got up to leave. She again rose from her chair and held out her hand to me. I gave her mine, we said good-bye, and I left.

I didn't get the job. I didn't even get a callback. But twice Eva Le Gallienne had stood up for me, twice. Maybe she just had better manners than I'm accustomed to, but I think not. I think she stood up for everyone who auditioned. She stood up for me because I was an actor and so was she, because we were both actors.

EILEEN ATKINS

One night when Laurence Olivier was playing Othello, he was particularly brilliant and word spread among the cast that something extraordinary was happening onstage that night and the performance was very special, and they gathered in the wings to watch.

As the curtain fell to tumultuous applause, the cast lined the path to his dressing room applauding him. He stumped through them with his head down, went into his dressing room, and slammed the door. Derek Jacobi, who was in the company, knocked on the door, went in, and said, "What's the matter with you? We were applauding you because you were so incredible tonight. The performance just soared into another dimension."

"I know," said Olivier gloomily. "But I don't know *what* I *did!*"

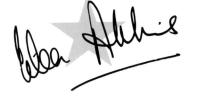

Eileen Atkins

Eileen Atkins at her dressing table before a performance as Virginia Woolf in *A Room of One's Own.*
Photo by Robin Platzer

KATE NELLIGAN

I met Ira in December of 1987. I was looking for a dresser for the Broadway run of *Serious Money,* and Ira came to the rehearsal room at 890 Broadway to interview for the job. He was in his late thirties, tall and slim, with shoulder-length hair of a color not generally found in nature. He wore hot pink socks and a hot pink scarf. He had done the show off-Broadway and knew the terrifyingly quick changes, and so I hired him.

Two weeks later he appeared for work at the Royale Theatre on West Forty-fifth Street carrying his bicycle, wearing a hot pink crash helmet and a very big smile. His first words to me were: "How are you feeling, sweetie? Can I get you anything?" To my surprise, I liked him calling me sweetie. I liked it a lot. Backstage during our first attempt at a thirty-second complete quick change, I ran right over him and hissed, "Get out of my way." Ira smiled from his prone position on the floor and murmured, "Sure, sweetie." We never looked back.

Serious Money closed almost instantaneously, and Ira and I went on to do *Spoils of War,* first off-Broadway and on tour and then at the Music Box Theatre, up the street on Forty-fifth Street from the Royale. Ira had stayed with me and *Spoils of War* for months out of town when I could not afford to pay him what he would have earned working on a Broadway show. For an opening-night gift, he presented me with a twelve-inch rubber alligator dressed in an exact replica of my party outfit from the play complete with earrings, red wig, and high heels—all made by hand by Ira.

During the previews I had run out of the laughter I needed to enter a scene. Ira appeared backstage walking on his knees dressed as a little girl (he called her Audrey) at her first communion—veil and all. He then started playing my part. In a high-pitched lisp he intoned lines like, "Am I or am I not wearing a bra?" I entered laughing that night and every night thereafter. The closing notice for *Spoils of War* went up just before Christmas after a three-week run. I dragged myself into the dressing room that night and found

Marcia Lewis *(top),* and with Ruth Jaroslow onstage *(middle),* and backstage *(bottom)* at the Gershwin Theatre in the revival of *Fiddler on the Roof.*

Black-and-white photos *(opposite)* by William Gibson/Martha Swope Assoc.

Color photo *(opposite)* by Carol Rosegg/Martha Swope Assoc.

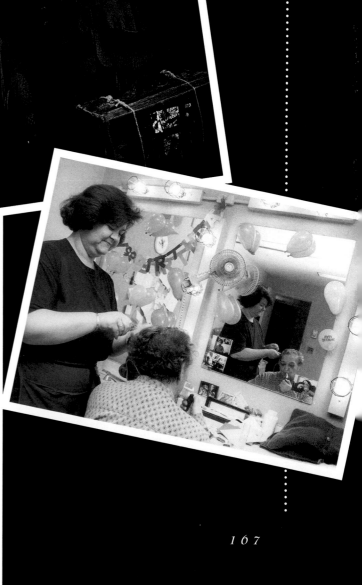

the place festooned with Christmas lights. Ira stood smiling in the middle of the room. "Happy Hanukkah, sweetie!"

After the play closed, Ira and I traveled to Toronto together to do a television miniseries and recover financially from the year spent nursing *Spoils of War* to Broadway. When we had been there a week, Ira began to hiccup. He hiccuped for many days without a break. He couldn't eat or sleep. He flew to New York and was diagnosed as having toxoplasmosis—an infection of the brain. His first battle with full-blown AIDS had begun. Three weeks later I saw him. He had lost a lot of weight and could not walk more than a few paces. His thinking and his speech were scrambled. I couldn't believe he would ever recover, but of course, he did. He fought back with steely courage, kindly humor, and no self-pity. He has devoted his life to the art of living with AIDS. He has taken it upon himself to find and use every available means of help (financial, emotional, and spiritual) to stay alive and heal.

It has been three years since the first bout with toxo. Ira and I are still good friends. We look forward to the time when we will be back together working on a show. In the meantime he does for me what he always has—he shows me how to live gracefully *no matter what.*

I called Ira to invite him to the New York premiere of the film *Prince of Tides*. He was thrilled and asked what he should wear. I said, "Well, Ira, the invitation says, 'Dress festive.' "

Ira said, "Sounds like Muppet fur to me, sweetie."

Colleen Dewhurst backstage at the Lincoln Center Library during a reading of Larry Kramer's *The Desti*

CAROLE SHELLEY

With the loss of Colleen Dewhurst, my thoughts turn back to 1979. A year of immense highs and terrible, terrible lows. Opening off-Broadway in *The Elephant Man* to an incredible reaction and a sold-out four-week run. We are extended. My mother Charlie's illness begins to escalate. Three days before we reopen on Broadway, Charlie has a heart attack and goes into a coma. Five days later she slips quietly away with my loving permission. We open at the Booth Theatre, and she isn't there. Six months of applause, awards, and battling egos, but still an extraordinary and spiritually gratifying time.

At the end of my contract I am offered a movie in Canada. A wonderful script (starring Colleen Dewhurst) and for me a very different challenge. I accept and look forward to letting go and moving on. The night after I closed, George Grizzard took me to a reading of a new play at the New York Shakespeare Festival, with Miss Dewhurst and Jason Robards as Carlotta and O'Neill. Nerves, excitement, and George's hand in mine are moving me to where she stands, like the prow of a ship. He introduces us, and a quick shadow passes over the sun.

"Great to meet you, and I'm so sorry," says that voice like no other.

"Sorry? About what?" I babble.

She looks at George and back at me. "You don't know, do you?"

"Know what?" I reply with Pinter-like earnestness.

"Oh, God." It's drawn out like a terrible sigh. "Oh, God, baby . . . the movie . . . it was canceled last Tuesday."

I know I didn't cry. I was in shock. Colleen pulled me to her and held me tight and rocked me. The Mother Earth image that was always hers, and that she had shared with so many audiences, was mine alone for that moment. In that year, when I needed to be held, her incredible love and compassion were life-giving to a drowning child.

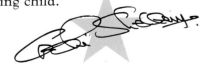

JULIE HARRIS

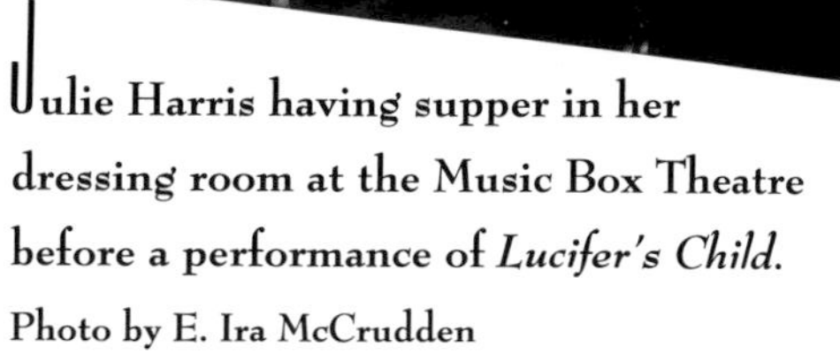

Julie Harris having supper in her dressing room at the Music Box Theatre before a performance of *Lucifer's Child*.
Photo by E. Ira McCrudden

It began for me sitting in the balcony of the Cass Theatre in downtown Detroit, Michigan, watching Miss Ethel Waters in *Cabin in the Sky* and then in *Mamba's Daughters*—and I said to myself, aged thirteen or fourteen, "She is the best, the very best!"

Some years go by and I've been given the part of F. Jasmine Addams, otherwise known as Frankie Addams, in Carson McCullers's play *The Member of the Wedding,* and Ethel Waters will star in the play as Berenice Sadie Brown and Brandon de Wilde has been chosen to play John Henry West, Frankie's cousin, who lives next door to the Addams family—the place, a small town in Georgia.

We meet for the first time, Ethel, Brandon, and I, at our producer Robert Whitehead's apartment. I think it was early November 1949. New York City, and I feel as if I've died and gone to heaven. From that first meeting the three of us feel "we belong together." Brandon, the brightest, sweetest little boy, had never acted, though—never! And he said his lines like a little bird; all the notes were there but no melody.

Toward the end of the second week of rehearsal we were in a tiny theatre downtown having a run-through of the play. I was saying something to Brandon—Frankie to John Henry—and suddenly Brandon answered *as* John Henry. Ethel and I looked at each other. Ethel winked at me as if to say, "You see, I knew my baby would do it."

I looked out into the auditorium at Fritz de Wilde, Brandon's father, who was our stage manager, and the tears were running down Fritz's cheeks. Brandon had made the transition from small boy to actor; he'd found that keyhole and gone through.

So, on we went to Philadelphia, the Walnut Street Theatre, to try out the play. On our opening night there, "Places" was called and we all assembled for the first scene on Lester Polakov's set under the grape arbor: William Hansen, Frankie's pop; Margaret Barker, Aunt Pet, John Henry's mama;

Jimmy Holden, who played Frankie's brother Jarvis, and his bride-to-be, Janice, played by Janet de Gore; and Harry Bolden, who played T.T., Berenice's friend; and our Berenice Sadie Brown, Miss Ethel Waters. The curtain is down, about to go up, when Brandon begins to cry. Fritz came from the wings to calm him.

"Why is he crying?"

Brandon tearfully asks, "What is all that noise on the other side of the curtain?"

"The audience," Fritz said.

And Brandon wails, "I didn't know there'd be all these people watching us."

Ethel scoops him up in her arms and says, "Sugar, it will be all right."

The tears are dried, back to our opening positions again, and the curtain goes up. Our boy is fine and sweet and sassy and *is* John Henry West. And Ethel is sweet, funny, heartbreaking, and powerful as Niagara Falls.

We leave Philadelphia and go back to New York City to the beautiful Empire Theatre on Broadway.

January 5, 1950, another opening, no advance sale, no money in the box office; if the play doesn't make it now, no second chance. Tonight or never.

The curtain rises. There we all are. I feel as if I'm in a dream, but I'm right next to a giant performance, part of a magical experience, a rare piece of writing and a sweet, angelic boy. The curtain goes up and I hear a sound, a sound I'd never heard before and never have quite like that again; a heavenly roar, of joy, of approval, of love.

Julie Harris

La Chanze *(top)* backstage at *Once on This Island* at the Booth Theatre.

Photo by Jean Pagliuso

Paul Hipp on the set of *Buddy* at the Shubert.

Photo by Josef Astor

Backstage, onstage, and in the parking lot with the company of *Nunsense* at the Douglas Fairbanks Theatre on West Forty-second Street.
Black-and-white photos by John Huba
Color photo by
Carol Rosegg/Martha Swope Assoc.

ELIZABETH IRELAND McCANN

I have been a Broadway producer forever. There is a wall of posters in my office—voices pop out of them all the time.

Maggie Smith starring in *Night and Day*. At half hour, when Maggie was having a touch of stage fright, I backed out of her dressing room saying, "Maggie, just relax, and have a good performance." Her reply: "Liz, darling, why must you always get things backwards."

Jessica Tandy in *The Glass Menagerie*. One day I asked to review the production photos and some other matters with her. Her response: "Liz, darling, I'm an actress. It's what I concentrate on. If I didn't think you all knew your jobs, I wouldn't be doing this play."

Vanessa Redgrave, in *Orpheus Descending:* "Liz, darling, I can't go on for the matinee until the stage manager gets an asbestos tester for the wardrobe department."

Frank Langella in *Dracula:* "Perhaps you might explain why everything happens to me in this production."

Glenda Jackson in *Rose:* "Lizzy, I know she's a great actress, but don't you think Jessica Tandy is a bit old to play my mother?"

Glenda Jackson later: "God, she could play my daughter."

Ian McKellen in *Amadeus:* "I just don't believe Americans will know that Mozart wrote *Don Giovanni*. Can't we change the line to read 'his *Don Giovanni*'?"

Maureen O'Sullivan in *Morning's at Seven:* "I've always warned Mia about short musicians, but I just know she is going to get mixed up with Woody Allen."

The head usher at the Booth Theatre during *The Elephant Man:* "They have nudity in the second act, but it's really very tasteful because they also read the Bible."

Boston, *Mass Appeal,* Eric Roberts: "Please release me from my contract. I'm really too unhappy."

Richard Gere in *Habeas Corpus:* "I have a chance to do *Streetcar,* someplace in Pennsylvania, so I'm giving my notice."

Roger Rees in *London Assurance:* "It's too bad we didn't run, Liz, but I would like to come back to America sometime."

Roger Rees in *Nicholas Nickleby:* "Well, I made it."

Maggie Smith in *Night and Day,* standing center stage and viewing the ANTA, now the Virginia, for the first time: "Darling, it's not a theatre that cuddles me."

Alan Rickman in *Les Liaisons Dangereuses:* "After ten weeks in this play, I fail to understand why I can't find an apartment in the Village, with a fireplace and a garden, for less than five hundred dollars a month."

Mike Nichols, the director of *The Gin Game,* at the Golden Theatre: "The lobby is too noisy."

Peter Hall, the director of *Orpheus Descending,* at the Neil Simon Theatre: "The air-conditioning is too noisy."

John Dexter, the director of *The Glass Menagerie,* at the O'Neill Theatre: "The heating plant is too noisy."

Frank Dunlop, director of *Habeas Corpus,* during technicals at the Martin Beck Theatre: "How do you expect me to direct comedy in a haunted theatre?"

Dennis Rosa, director of *Dracula,* during technicals at the Martin Beck Theatre: "There's something very spooky about this place."

Lynn Redgrave in *My Fat Friend:* "Liz, I want you to meet my daughter, Kelly Clark. She's just three years old."

On a winter afternoon in 1991: "Hello. Do you remember me? I'm Kelly Clark. I've just gotten my Equity card and you're the only producer I know."

Stockard Channing *(top)* and Courtney B. Vance in their dressing rooms at Lincoln Center's Vivian Beaumont Theatre during the run of *Six Degrees of Separation.*
Photos by Stewart Shining

KELLY BISHOP

Kelly Bishop and friend during the run of *Six Degrees of Separation.*
Photo by Yacek Samotus

I stood on the stage of the Shubert Theatre looking out at an ocean of dancers from all over the world. It was August 6, 1987, and the first meeting of this select group, who would participate in what is lovingly remembered as "the celebration." Michael Bennett had summoned us for a command performance to mark *A Chorus Line*'s becoming the longest-running show in Broadway history. I remember the swell of pride I felt from having helped create such a project. During the course of that day we greeted old friends, renewed acquaintances, and made new friends as we relearned the parts of the show that would be performed by "the original company." Only four days were allotted to put together this extraordinary performance (I remember love and generosity and excitement and cooperation), but Michael Bennett's genius made it happen.

Then came "The Day," which I recall in flashes: the thunderous reaction of the audience as they realized that behind the eight-by-ten glossies we held stood the original company; they greeted each of us as we stepped forward and introduced ourselves. It was like tossing beach balls of love back and forth across the footlights, the ultimate bonding of performers and audience. The show grew in depth and richness through the finale. We "originals" who started it were joined by wave after wave of subsequent companies until it was, more than ever before, "one singular sensation."

As we sang the final "One," the houselights came up to reveal the full house, orchestra to balcony, surrounded by top-hatted, sequined performers dancing and singing in the aisles. The view from the stage was astounding. At the end, 332 of us were crammed onto the stage, and I could have died happy at that moment.

When I think of that experience, I know why I'm in "the business" and I'm grateful.

Kelly Bishop

MICHAEL RUPERT

I was walking down Broadway on my way to a matinee of *Sweet Charity* and I saw Bob Fosse walking up Broadway toward me, and he looked very depressed, very down. We stopped, and for about half an hour we stood at the corner of Forty-ninth and Broadway looking at Times Square, seeing all these skyscrapers, these tall, ugly buildings. And Bob said, "Look at what they've done. This isn't Broadway; this looks like Third Avenue now. I'm writing this picture about Walter Winchell, and where am I going to shoot it? I'm going to have to build Times Square in Astoria, Queens."

This was just after *Big Deal* had closed, and I remember Bob had told me at one point he felt no one understood him anymore—that people no longer wanted to see the kind of stuff that he did. Then along came *Sweet Charity,* this revival of a twenty-year-old show of his, and the critics, everybody, loved it. So here's Bob, who has always been a hero of mine, feeling that everything is changing and that the New York he knew and loved was disappearing right in front of him. After about thirty minutes of standing there talking, we parted, and I turned and watched him walk up Broadway for a while.

Michael Rupert

Michael Rupert in his dressing room during the run of *City of Angels.*
Photo by Susan Shacter

IAN McKELLEN

Sir Ian McKellen during rehearsal at the Brooklyn Academy of Music for London's Royal National Theatre presentation of *Richard III*.
Photo by Carol Rosegg/Martha Swope Assoc.

In 1961, just out of Cambridge University and waiting for my first professional acting job, I found myself in an amateur production with recent graduates from the Royal Academy of Dramatic Art. Also in the cast was Curt Dawson. Curt was from Texas, although the RADA had almost erased any aural evidence. To look at, though, he was perfectly all-American. Tall, healthy, golden hair, big, big smile: ex-army pants and sneakers.

One evening in London, he introduced me to three great Americans—Ethel Merman, Stephen Sondheim, and Sara Lee. He had presented me with an apple pie from a packet, and, having won my heart, then serenaded me with an original cast recording of *Gypsy*. "Everything's Coming Up Roses" was Curt's favorite refrain. He made Broadway, which produced such glories, seem like the center of the theatre world. London's West End, by contrast, was still in the lull between Ivor Novello and Andrew Lloyd Webber, dependent on American musical imports, just as British cinema has always relied on Hollywood.

Yet, like so many Americans who study drama in England, Curt longed to settle in Shakespeare's country, where the classics are alive and well and waiting to be performed. After he went home to work and I had started acting in regional repertory companies, our letters exchanged envy of each other's theatre culture.

In 1967, I walked into Times Square for the first time and saw a man urinating against the statue of George M. Cohan. Some critic. Those days, Broadway was a dirty, gutsy thoroughfare: no posh hotels then, although the original Lindy's still served blissful cheesecake. Eighth Avenue was out-of-bounds, except to gypsies rushing across to the newly opened Joe Allen restaurant, where Joel Grey ate and they played *Cabaret* songs nonstop.

If you're interested in what else played on Broadway at that time, check out *The Season,* where William Goldman analyzes them all, hits and misses.

He gives little space to the Russian play *The Promise,* which was why I was there. Indeed no one in New York cared much for us (Eileen Atkins, Ian McShane, and me), despite the worldwide success of the play. On opening night at Henry Miller's Theatre, our audience was picketed by local Equity members chanting that only American actors should be allowed on Broadway. Their wish was soon granted; twenty-three performances later, we closed. *The New York Times*'s critic, then an Englishman, had not been overgenerous to his countrymen. I felt like George M.'s statue.

Before I flew home, I met up again with Curt. He had done a few bit parts on Broadway and a few better parts off-Broadway. He had done the classics out of town, but he made his money in the soaps. He still romanced about working in London. I warned him that there might be pickets there, too.

In 1981, I was back on Broadway in a hit. Others will have recorded how thrilling that sort of thing can be. Yet through the eighties there were so many changes. Henry Miller's was a porno-movie house. They (who?) had destroyed three intimate theatres to make way for one monstrous auditorium and a hotel in Times Square. *Cats* was purring and the British musical invasion was under way.

In 1984, Curt died, the first friend I knew with AIDS. I wanted him to be in this book.

Ian McKellen

Kevin Spacey and pal *(top)* in his dressing room following a performance of *Lost In Yonkers.*
Alec Baldwin backstage during the revival of *A Streetcar Named Desire.*
Photos by Stewart Shining

FRANCES STERNHAGEN

In 1975, while appearing in the hit production of *Equus,* I would walk to the Plymouth Theatre and back to Grand Central Station every night to board my train home. As I walked briskly along Forty-fifth Street at eleven P.M., dressed down for safety and comfort with my backpack and boots, I would pass a topless bar. In the doorway, a rugged hustler in a watch cap, dirty jacket, Coke-bottle-bottom glasses on his nose was hawking, "CheckitoutCheckitout. Beautifulgirls, gorgeousgirls. CheckitoutCheckitout . . . ," and my nerves would tighten ever so little, and my stride would grow brisker as I contineud to Grand Central.

On New Year's Eve, as soon as the show came down, I hurried out to get through the rollicking crowds in Times Square and on to my train. I pushed through, allowed by the police to continue east on Forty-fifth Street, and pursued my trek toward Sixth Avenue. I heard the familiar chant, "Checkitoutcheckitout . . ..," and my nerves tightened as usual. Then, as I passed the Troll at the Bridge, I heard, "Checkitoutcheckitout. There'smygoodgirlgoinghometobed. HappyNewYearsweetheart. Checkitoutcheckitout . . ." I waved and called, "Same to you!," and my step lightened all the way to the train. *We* weren't tourists, like all those people in Times Square, we were *on Broadway*—both of us: it was *our street!*

Frances Sternhagen

ELLEN BURSTYN

During the run of *Same Time, Next Year* on Broadway in 1975, I was onstage with Charles Grodin one Wednesday matinee when I became aware of a stir in the audience. People were whispering to each other. Something was going on that I didn't know about.

I could see that the audience was still focused on the stage, and whatever it was, it was happening behind me. I was downstage and Charlie was up from me. As we continued our dialogue, I casually turned to look up at him and then I saw it. A cat! A strange gray-and-yellow cat was crossing nonchalantly across the stage. She had just about reached center stage, and as I turned, I saw her become aware she was not alone.

She stopped and turned her head toward the darkness beyond the fourth wall and seemed startled to discover that the darkness was alive. It had presence, as though there were a thousand pairs of eyes out there, which of course there were. That realization stopped her dead in her tracks. She arched her back, raised her hackles, and hissed into the frightening presence of the dark monster and turned and fled into the wings. I remember thinking, "I know just how she feels."

I've often told that story to the actors at the Actors Studio because I think it shows us what the job of the actor is: to make contact with that kitty inside each of us that wants to turn and run when we feel those thousand pairs of eyes on us. And to find the way to quiet the kitty and just go on doing what we have to do.

Ellen Burstyn

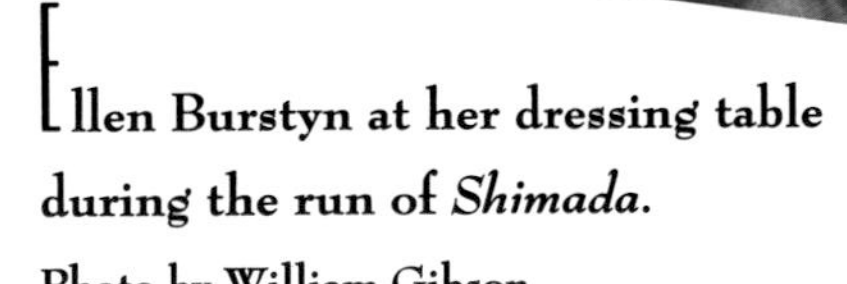

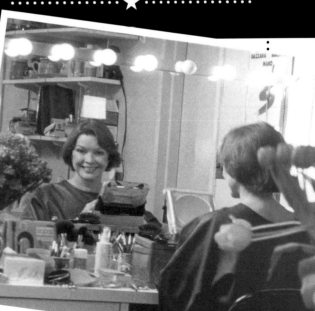

Ellen Burstyn at her dressing table during the run of *Shimada*.

Photo by William Gibson

MANDY PATINKIN

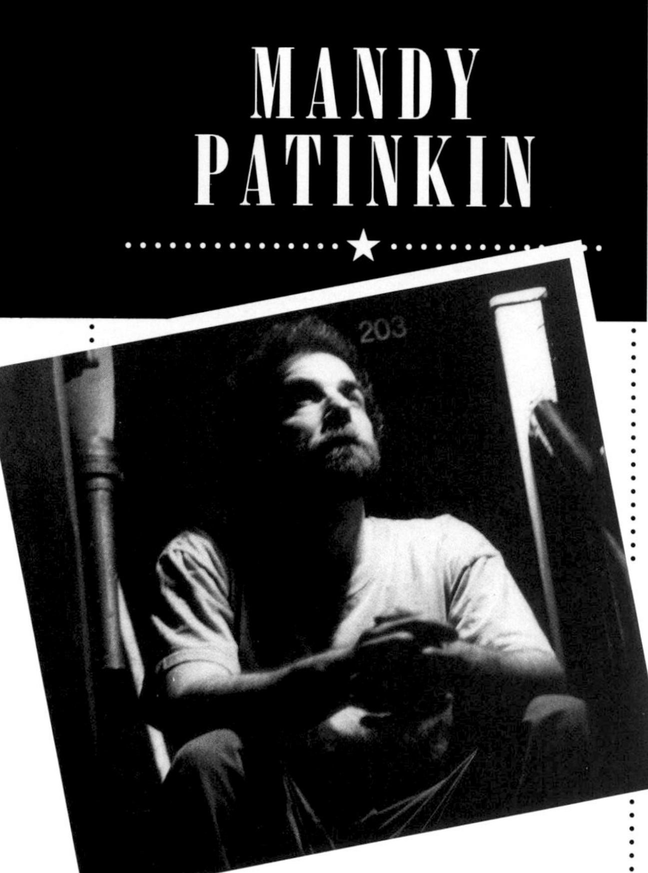

Mandy Patinkin backstage during *The Secret Garden*.
Photo by Yacek Samotus

I don't like to read reviews because I don't believe in the process of them, basically allowing any one single individual or group of individuals to change the opinion of other individuals. The reason I read this pile of . . . reviews for *The Secret Garden* was because I walked into the theatre the day the reviews came out after spending a great day with my kids and having a wonderful time. But when I got to the theatre that night, whew! It was awful. They were having a meeting and everyone was putting his hand on my shoulder. I thought, "What is this?" So in the middle of the first act I just couldn't take it anymore. I called my wife and said, "All right, read it to me." So she read it to me. And some of the other ones. And I said, "Well, that's pretty much as bad as I thought they were saying." Then what happens is that as hard as you try to fight it, you get the flu a little bit—even if they are wrong. You feel awful. Because the theatre is different from a book, movie, or painting. There the work is done and you put it on a shelf and go on to other things. But the theatre happens right there, right that second.

My goal is to really believe in what *I* think about my work. What *I* feel. I say this like a mantra to myself because I feel you have to fight hard in this world.

When we started playing *The Secret Garden,* people came in droves and loved it! The way they reacted brought things out in us and it was wonderful. Just thrilling. The reviewers came and the night they were there all the people still loved it. The reviews were written that day and there were negative reviews, mixed reviews, and positive ones, too. The next day, after three weeks of previews, the same human beings . . . a different crowd but human beings . . . came into the theatre and they were critical. Their hands tied. And it is cold! And they are not giving. And they are making it hard. And they are making you fight. And you can't do it alone. Because the theatre is not just me and the other actors up there.

Then a few weeks pass. And then come the Tony Awards. And then the Tony Awards are over. You won three Tony Awards. I defy anyone to say which three Tonys we won, except for Daisy Eagan, because she broke everyone's heart. But the ads are in the newspaper the next day: "Winner of Three Tony Awards!" And what happens? The houses are full! And the reaction is, "This Is Phenomenal! This Show Is Great!" The same thing happened to *Evita*. *Evita* got killed in three cities—Los Angeles, San Francisco, and New York City. Across the board. Killed! And then it won Best Musical awards. And was a huge success.

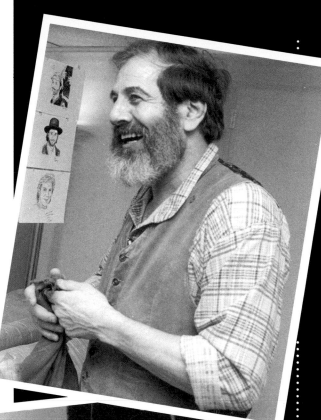

And that's how it works. And it works that way every year.

Topol *(top)* before a performance as Tevye in *Fiddler on the Roof*.
Photo by William Gibson
Michael York in his dressing room at the Belasco Theatre after a performance in *The Crucible*.
Photo by Yacek Samotus

JAMES EARL JONES

The Journey from Arkabutia, Mississippi, to Manistee, Michigan, to Broadway can be long and convoluted. I set out to be a doctor, not an actor, enrolling in the pre-med program at the University of Michigan. My father, Robert Earl Jones, is an actor, and he and my mother split up before I was born. My mother's parents raised me in Mississippi and then in Michigan, and they had no use for troubadour actors. As a small child I began to stutter, essentially losing the power of speech. If I had harbored any early fantasies of acting, they would have been mightily discouraged.

One day when I was a teenager, I was sitting on the porch in Michigan with my Uncle Randy, who was close to me in age, more a brother than an uncle. Randy had an innate talent for building things and making things work. He always knew he wanted to be an engineer, and he spoke of his future plans with conviction. He not only knew what he wanted to do when he grew up, but he knew his parents—my grandparents—approved of his plans. I admired that. I knew I couldn't top him.

"Yep, I'm going to be a mechanical engineer," Randy told me that day on the porch. "What about you? What are you going to be?"

Now I had to try to top Randy, or at least match him. "Well," I said, "I am going to be an actor on the stage."

All of a sudden I felt a blow. My grandfather had been standing behind the screen door listening. He was still suffering from that image of an actor being irresponsible. He did not want to hear that kind of talk from his grandson. He flew out from behind that door and gave me a whop to the head.

For a long time, that put a stop to my dreaming out loud about becoming an actor. Yet a question always remained in my mind, and in my grandfather's. Did that whop to the head knock *out* the idea of acting—or knock it *in?* About twelve years later, I got my first job on Broadway playing a small role in *Sunrise at Campobello.*

James Earl Jones

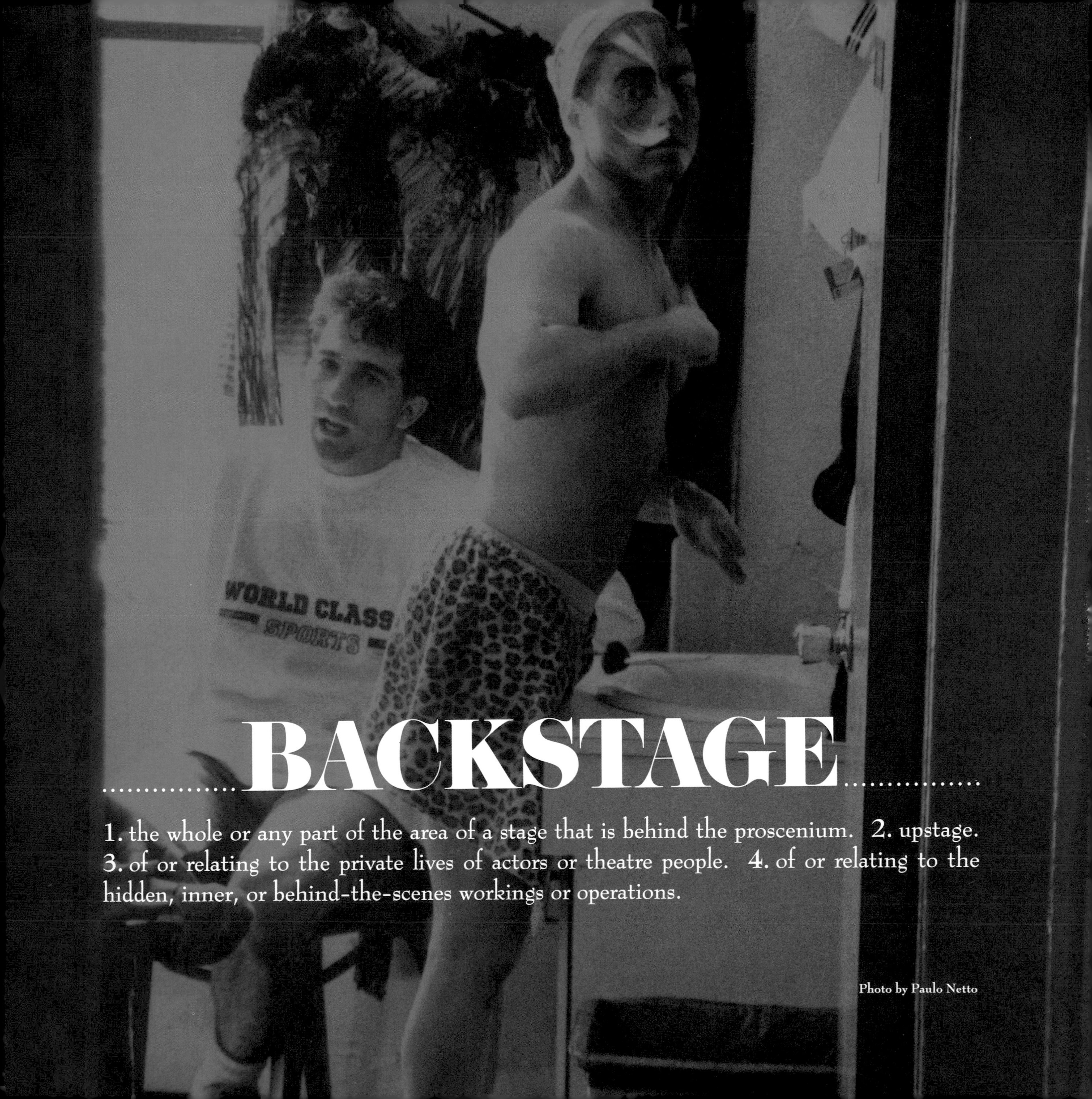

BACKSTAGE

1. the whole or any part of the area of a stage that is behind the proscenium. 2. upstage. 3. of or relating to the private lives of actors or theatre people. 4. of or relating to the hidden, inner, or behind-the-scenes workings or operations.

Photo by Paulo Netto

JUDY KAYE

It's March 6, 1978. *On the Twentieth Century* has been open since February 19 and it looks like we're a hit. And though at first I resisted even taking this job, so far away from a cozy bungalow in Los Angeles, I'm very glad that I accepted. Being part of a new Broadway musical, even as a lowly understudy, has turned out to be very exciting, indeed. Just being in the same room with Hal Prince, Cy Coleman, Betty Comden, and Adolph Green has been thrilling to say the least. And the talent on the stage! Madeline Kahn, John Cullum, Imogene Coca—and this fabulous new guy, Kevin Kline—incredible! And while playing the maid is not the most fulfilling role I've ever done, it does have its moments: eight solid laughs on a good night. And of course, waiting in the wings for Madeline to miss a performance feels ghoulish, at best. Still, maybe I'll get to play Lily Garland in stock somewhere.

I've been in my sublet apartment all day watching a Carole Lombard movie, picking up pointers on Hollywood starlets of the thirties. It's about one in the afternoon. Time enough to run an errand, go to the gym, have a leisurely dinner, and get to the St. James Theatre well in time to don my rather fabulous Flossie Klotz–designed maid's *shmatte* and hit the stage.

I've had a good stretch and gotten the old heart pumping and decide to take a little steam. (I do a little vocalizing in the steam room.) I should call my service, but there's a long line of naked, betoweled women waiting to use the phone. And besides, it's late and there've been no calls all day. So, I just hop back into my jeans and plaid shirt, boots, and green parka and go to that little Belgian restaurant between the gym and the theatre.

Dinner is terrific! Sole meunière, salad with Dijon vinaigrette, rice, and what the hell, a glass of white wine. I know I shouldn't, but jeez—I don't go on for over an hour. And it's really just one little scene. What could it hurt?

I check my watch. It's seven-ten. Plenty of time to stroll to the St. James. Well, here's the stage door. I unzip my army-surplus parka and open the door. *Surprise! You're on!* My God, there's the whole cast draped around the foyer telling me news too impossible to be true. And I'm five minutes slow. All I can say is, "No shit . . ."

Madeline's dresser rushes me up to her dressing room. She helps me off with my lumberjack outfit and starts trying Madeline's costumes on me. There are no understudy clothes yet, and the dresses are rather intricate: a breakaway middy dress, a wool traveling dress with matching fox-trimmed cape, and of course, the peignoir. It all fits fine, if a little short. After all Madeline is perhaps six inches shorter than me. The wigs are tight, but okay. Somehow I'm getting my brunette mane under the platinum tresses. I have no fake eyelashes—Agnes the maid doesn't wear them. I borrow a pair from Imogene.

Well-wishers keep knocking at the door. Imogene climbs the stairs to wish me good luck. Kevin asks if there's anything I want to go over. I'd love to *go over* a number of things, but there's only time to assemble myself and *go.*

I wish I could tell you that I remember every millisecond of what happened. But, as in all otherworldly experiences, you go into a zone of semireality. I know I *did* the show. I'm sure I made some mistakes. But it went well, for at the curtain call when I finally came to, I was greeted by a standing ovation from the audience and gorgeous yellow roses from the cast. I had lived through the understudy's dream, and what a dream it was. True reality reintroduced itself two days later when I put my maid's uniform back on. But I have spectacular memories of that magical night, and the bow I kept from the roses.

Judy Kaye

tainment
9404

Backstage and onstage at the Shubert Theatre with Harry Groener and the company of *Crazy for You.*

Photos by Joan Marcus

PATTI LUPONE

Funny, the things you remember. I shall never forget . . .

Being booed.

My "first time" was in *Next Time I'll Sing to You* at the Billy Rose, in 1973.

It happened again at the Harkness in 1975, when Mary-Lou Rosato, Mary-Joan Negro, and I were hissed and hooted at our *Three Sisters* curtain call.

(One of the offending theatres was razed; the other renamed.)

Being nude.

Then there was the night my strategically placed hair shifted during the "Nuthin' Up" scene in *The Robber Bridegroom,* and I inadvertently flashed the audience. (Again the Harkness.)

Having windows!

Dressing room space was limited during the 1978 run of *The Water Engine* at the Plymouth, so instead of sharing stage-level quarters I chose to climb six flights of stairs to a chorus dressing room in order to be alone. One of the advantages—aside from blessed privacy—was that I was actually able to open my windows. And we all know what a rarity that is in a Broadway theatre.

I remember throwing those windows open every night at seven and hearing the carriage trade six floors below: cab horns honking, the strains of a violin (whatever happened to that guy anyway?), and the clopping of horses' hooves.

(Never again on Broadway have I had dressing room windows that opened.)

Getting threats.

There've been opening-night bomb threats in every single Broadway production I've ever been in.

And then there were those death threats during *Evita* in 1979.

(Broadway afforded me my first brush with the FBI. And I'm here to tell you, some of those boys are pretty cute!)

Singing without amplification.

Possibly the most profound and exciting memory I have is of standing center stage at the Broadway during tech dress for *Evita*. It was the first time we got onstage, before the orchestra came in. Just a piano. I remember hearing my voice reverberate throughout that darkened theatre. . . .

Ghost hunting at the Belasco.

I remember being given a tour of David Belasco's suite above the stage of the theatre that bore his name during the rehearsals for *Accidental Death of an Anarchist* in 1984, and being told that his ghost had put in an appearance on every single opening night in that house since his death.

Well, we waited every night of our one-week run for his ghost to appear, but Belasco was a no-show.

(The legend was later revised to the effect that his spectral presence never missed an opening until *Oh, Calcutta!* came along. After that one opened, Mr. Belasco was never heard from again.)

Getting married at the Beaumont.

Then, on December 12, 1988, fifteen months into the run of *Anything Goes,* I made what was surely my most memorable Broadway entrance—as a real-life bride.

My leading man was Matthew Joel Johnston, and thankfully neither of us went up in our lines as we were united in matrimony.

Backstage and onstage at the Nederlander Theatre with the company of *Our Country's Good*.
Black-and-white photos by T. Trompeter
Color photo by Martha Swope

BETTY BUCKLEY

Merlyn Davis lives in my heart. He first befriended me in the musical *1776*. I was twenty-one years old, straight from Texas, cast as Martha Jefferson my first day in New York City. He was a property man and to hear him tell it he thought I was "really young, really naive, very new in New York and in need of friends."

Merlyn taught me the layer method of dressing in cold weather. We opened in New Haven in the middle of a blizzard. At my first performance the weight of my 1700s panniers created an unexpected momentum. I tripped through the door, lurched down the steps into the Philadelphia street. I stumbled on for my talk with Benjamin Franklin and John Adams, wondering if my one-scene part would be cut from the show. Our producer, Stuart Ostrow, assured me that despite my grace my part would stay. Onna White gave me floating lessons. Patty Zipprodt redesigned my dress, and thereafter, Merlyn opened and held the door.

1776 was the surprise hit of the season, and Merlyn and I hung out in the basement of the Forty-sixth Street Theatre. He gave validity to my dreams of being a Broadway star. He believed in my talent. One night after I had blown an audition for the London company of *Promises, Promises,* he encouraged me to go with my inner voice. It was prompting me to talk to the New York *Promises* stage manager, Charlie Blackwell, about his working on the role with me so that I might secure a callback. So I did and I got the part.

A few years later my favorite show on Broadway was *Pippin*. I ran into Merlyn on the street—Jill Clayburgh was cast in the role of Catherine and was leaving the show six months into the run.

"They're auditioning for her replacement—the callbacks are next week—you've got to get in," he said.

"My agent says they won't see me."

"I'll talk to the casting guy," Merlyn said.

A couple of days later I received a letter from Michael Shurtleff, "the casting guy."

Elation! I auditioned—got the part for a really long stay on Broadway all through magic by Merlyn—and fired my agent.

Years passed. I did a film and a TV series in Hollywood, but always longed for Broadway. My TV show was eventually canceled, and after six months of auditions, a battery of tests to convince a reluctant Trevor Nunn that I could deliver his vision of Grizabella, Merlyn and I were working together again.

The job assignment was simple: *Stop the show!* The key to my past show business success had been the art of surprise relative to nonexpectation. It was not the easiest thing to meet the standards set by Elaine Paige in London, who originated Grizabella, and Barbra Streisand's hit recording of "Memory."

There was tremendous pressure, private memorable meetings with Trevor and Andrew Webber, and over and over they told me, "Just sing the song!" And I did, trying hard to sing every note the way Andrew wrote it, fulfill every mental picture Trevor described and every piece of the perfect, delicate choreography Gillian Lynne had given me. But all through previews I had yet to stop the show.

It was critics' night, the night before opening night.

In my whole life, I have not felt either before or since such panic. My dresser, Marci Olivi, did everything she could to calm me as she got me in costume. I went on for the opening number and came off for the Grizabella costume change a bit more settled, a little more devil-may-care. Marci walked me to my next entrance position in the wings, stage right. As we were standing in the dark, the sound man, Dale, raced over and said to Marci, "Her mike's broken!" She flew into action—stripped me down, three layers of costume, changed the body mike, and had me back together in seconds. Dresser extraordinaire! Dale went to his monitor board and returned with the news: "That mike's broken, too!" And in the dark the process was repeated.

Merlyn had come close to me as I stood spread-eagled and about to faint with fear and said on the first change, "Spread'em, lady! Eighty-sixth Precinct!" I tried to laugh. On the second change he came very near, looked into

Dear Miss Buckley, Merlyn Davis says you're in town and available. We have repeatedly tried to find you for the role of Catherine in Pippin *and were told by your agent that you were out of the business. Please contact us directly at . . . to schedule your audition.*

Backstage and onstage at the Winter Garden Theatre with the company of *Cats*.

Black-and-white photos by Paulo Netto

Color photo by Martha Swope

Thanks for the Memory
Betty Buckley
Your Prop Department
"Cats"

Charlie Rosen George Green
Dan Foley Merlyn Davis
Winter Garden Theatre
June 4, 1983

my panic-stricken face, and softly said, "Look in my eyes! It'll be okay. Breathe, breathe, just keep breathing." I was back in costume after the second mike change and Merlyn took me to my entrance position. My legs would barely move. He led me. And just as the intro to "Memory" played for my cue, Dale dashed back over in the dark and said, "That mike's broken, too!"

I moved forward as Grizabella and entered the Jellicle junkyard. From the wings, Merlyn yelled, "You don't need a mike! Remember when you were eleven and filled the whole house—sing like you did when you were eleven!" And so I did. One critic said I had a strident voice. Merlyn and I had a laugh over that one—I, being the girl singer in *Cats,* a $5.5-million musical wherein all cats but me were miked.

There was another Merlyn gift in the week before the Tony Awards. He and the rest of his prop department presented me with a beautiful black Egyptian cat trophy on a base with an engraved gold plaque.

I saw Merlyn on the street a couple of times after my stay in *Cats.* There were no new casting reports. I couldn't wait to see him along with all the rest of the original team at our ninth-anniversary gala in October 1991. I saw his wife, the beautiful dancer Sally Neal, and stalwart son, Neal Davis, at the party. The grief in their faces told me before their shocking words that Merlyn had died, of lung cancer at the age of fifty-one on January 24, 1990.

Merlyn did props and scenery and worked twenty-four Broadway shows. I was privileged to be in three of those shows. He was one of my teachers. He gave me the antidotes for cold, fear, and a sometimes fickle business. His warmth, humor, and freely offered faith live on in my heart. Thanks for the memory, Merlyn Davis—Your Girl Singer.

Betty Lynn Buckley

BILL IRWIN

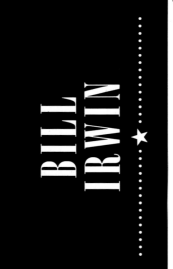

Understudies have to sit ghostlike in the rehearsal room until a show moves into a theatre, then they sit and wait and watch through the tedium of tech rehearsals. There is rarely any place for them, they are just supposed to be ready.

In the fall of 1984 a cast of six of us began uneasy previews of *Accidental Death of an Anarchist* at the Belasco on Forty-fourth Street. There were things lacking in our production, but one thing was clear: Jonathan Pryce in the lead role was charged with a brilliant, comic energy.

In the second week of previews Jonathan got the flu and his voice weakened a little. One night at the end of the first act the stage manager told us that Jonathan would not be finishing the show, that Seth Allen, the understudy, would be doing act two. I don't think we went up to the dressing rooms during the intermission. We stayed onstage listening to the house on the other side of the act curtain. At some point Seth came toward us, swimming in the judge's robe and gray wig Jonathan had been wearing a few minutes before. A stage manager was on either side of him, and though I doubt that they were actually pushing him, it did look like it for a moment as he stumbled slightly in the wings. Alex Cohen stepped before the curtain to give a terse little speech of explanation. The house sounded different after that. We all gave each other a look—pursed lips, raised eyebrows—and the curtain went up.

Seth knew every word. His tenor voice and thin face were so unlike Jonathan's, his presence was completely different, but he spoke every word and the audience stayed with the play. At the next day's matinee he knew both acts. Everyone knew Seth wasn't Jonathan, Seth certainly knew, but he held the fort and got the production through a weekend so that Jonathan returned with a strong voice and his manic energy recharged. Seth rejoined the other understudies on folding chairs in a hallway, we faced our opening and soon after, our closing, and then everyone went on to the next thing in life.

Two and a half years later Seth Allen died of AIDS. I last saw him on Eighth Street, handing out leaflets for something. I'm sure I congratulated him profusely back on that fall weekend, but I'll always feel that I didn't congratulate him enough.

Backstage and onstage at the Plymouth Theatre with Dearbhla Molloy *(left)*, Donal Donnelly *(middle)*, and Catherine Byrne *(right)* and the company of The Abbey Theatre's production of Brian Friel's *Dancing at Lughnasa (opposite)*.
Black-and-white photos by Ken Howard
Color photo by Tom Lawlor

Views of the orchestra pit at *Fiddler on the Roof* (*top, left*/photo by William Gibson) *and Black & Blue* (*bottom, left*/photo by John Huba); conductor Paul Gemignani in the pit of the Shubert Theatre during dress rehearsal of *Crazy for You* (*right*/photo by Joan Marcus).

PAUL GEMIGNANI

Late in the run of *Jerome Robbins' Broadway,* we were well into a Saturday matinee—relaxed and sure that the show would proceed as it had many times before. We knew where the laughs were and which of the numbers would receive little or much applause.

We had finished "The King and I" and were about half through "Gotta Have a Gimmick" when onto the stage strolled an eighty-five-pound canine! He stood about three and one-half feet high and reeked of stage presence. He entered, crossed down right, and looked at the three strippers (Suzanne Fletcher, Faith Prince, and Karen Mason) as if to say, "They get paid for this?" He looked at me in the pit—did a perfectly timed take to the audience—and made a slow exit stage right with the same relaxed professionalism that he'd entered with!

I don't think any of us have been the same since!

Pit singers and percussionist under the stage at *Buddy.*

Photos by Paulo Netto

ROBERT BILLIG

From the time I was around twelve years old, I was fascinated with the idea of conducting an orchestra. I was a piano student at the New England Conservatory of Music Preparatory Division. This entitled me to use the music library of the New England Conservatory. One day I asked my father to stop at the library on his way home from work and get me the orchestral score to Tchaikovsky's *Nutcracker Suite*. Delighted, I sat with the open score in front of our hi-fi system, listening to the music, following along with the instruments on the score. There it was, right there on the page. That was it! I was enthralled. Somehow I knew, then and there, I would be a conductor someday.

A few years later, I bought my first original Broadway cast recording. It was *Bye Bye, Birdie*. Once again, I sat in front of our new *stereo* system, and what a new thrill I got—to hear the string section of the orchestra coming out of the left speaker. That's where the string section actually sits—to the left of the conductor. And I could hear Chita Rivera and Dick Van Dyke singing on opposite sides of the stage. It was *great!* From that point on I was hooked on musical theatre. My dream was to conduct *on Broadway*.

About eight years later, after high school and college, I began my professional career in an off-Broadway musical and went on to do summer stock, bus and truck tours, national tours, and finally, Broadway. The one thing that nobody ever mentions is the danger of conducting in a pit. It's amazing, what can fall off a stage and nearly land in your lap.

When I was conducting *Singin' in the Rain,* Don Correia, who played the Gene Kelly role, was very enthusiastic, dancing and splashing in the puddles on the set for the title song. It was a wonderful number, but I got soaked nearly every performance. In fact, some of the musicians started wearing those umbrella hats to protect them from the splashing onstage.

A few years later, while conducting *Les Misérables,* I had a few other interesting experiences. In the hospital scene, after Fantine dies, Javert comes to recapture Jean Valjean. In the ensuing confrontation, Valjean picks up a nearby chair, smashes it on the floor, and uses one side of it as a weapon against Javert. On many occasions, a leg of that chair would fly downstage, once whizzing just past my right ear. I began to think that I should find a hard hat to match my tuxedo.

Another time at *Les Miz,* during "Master of the House," all the characters had been drinking through the scene, and an actor got up from a table center stage and accidentally (I hope) knocked it offstage. I looked up just in time to catch it with my left hand, push it back onstage, and not miss a beat with my right (conducting) hand. Pretty good, if I do say so myself.

With that, management placed nets over the orchestra to catch any other loose props or actors from falling on the musicians in the pit. Since then, in separate touring companies of *Les Miz,* actors have fallen off the stage and landed on the net. All managed to keep their composure and pull themselves back up onto the stage and continue the scene. Revolutions, particularly French ones, are never easy.

Unfortunately, however, the net does *not* protect the conductor, who must be able to see the actors onstage and likewise be seen by them. In *Miss Saigon,* we will occasionally have a fallen beer can or cigarettes land on the now standard net.

Yet, in spite of all the aforementioned hazards, there's no place I would rather be than standing in front of a wonderful group of musicians and a talented cast, and bringing these great musical theatre pieces to life.

Conductors Paul Schwartz and Robert Billig in the orchestra pits of *Phantom of the Opera* at the Majestic Theatre and *Miss Saigon* at the Broadway.

Photo *(top)* by Paulo Netto

Photo *(bottom)* by Allen Frame

Backstage and onstage at the Imperial Theatre with the company of *Les Misérables*.

Black-and-white photos by Paulo Netto

Color photo *(opposite)* by Joan Marcus

WILLIAM M. HOFFMAN

I always like to stand near the back of the house when a show of mine is on, anonymous, so at the intermission and the end I can overhear what audiences really think of my work. I've learned a lot that way. (I've rarely learned anything of value from critics, except which way the winds of critical fashion are blowing.)

For example, years ago when Playwrights Horizons had its home at the Clark Center on Fifty-first and Eighth, I was spying, as usual, during an experimental dance-theatre piece of mine. In the middle of what I considered my best scene, a couple got up and left. Just as they closed the door, I overheard the woman whisper, "What a pretentious pile of shit!"

I was outraged. What stupid people, I thought. Didn't they understand that I was making a statement about the transitoriness and futility of *their* lives—about all human life, as a matter of fact? Hadn't they read Campbell's *Hero with a Thousand Faces* or Blofeld's *Taoism?*

But when I think back, the woman was right. Of what significance was the girl twirling and twirling, holding a gold chalice? Why was the stage suddenly transformed into a gigantic chessboard? How could the couple have possibly comprehended why the man was hoisted up in the air by one foot?

But ten years later, one warm June night early in the run of *As Is* at the Lyceum, as I leaned over the rosewood-covered back wall, discreetly parting the velvet curtains, I wasn't hostile to, just fascinated by, the conversation of a middle-aged suburban couple in the last row. It was the moment after Rich reveals to his ex-lover Saul that he is HIV-positive.

MAN
I told you they were fairies. Let's get the hell out of here.
WOMAN
I'm not going nowhere. We spent fifty bucks for these seats. I don't care if they're cannibals.

They were quiet a few minutes until Saul discovers a Kaposi's lesion on Rich's back:

WOMAN

He's going to die.

MAN

I'll meet you in the lobby.

WOMAN

Don't you dare! Joe! . . .

Their neighbors shushed them as the husband got up and left. The play went on. I was so absorbed in the performance—the two Jonathans, Hogan and Hadary, were really cooking that night—that I forgot about the pair in the audience until the very end of the play, which takes place in Rich's hospital room. Saul was about to climb into Rich's bed to make love when I realized that Joe was standing to my left, not five feet away.

Oblivious to the tears streaming down his face, his eyes were glued to the stage. But just as soon as the hospital curtain was drawn around the bed and the applause started, he looked around with an embarrassed expression, wiped his face with his sleeve, and dashed out the door. When I looked down at his wife, she was slumped back in her seat, devastated.

A few minutes later in the lobby, as I talked to my agent, I overheard Joe talking to his wife.

MAN (*Bitterly*)

That's the last time I'll let you drag me to one of these. What's wrong with musicals?

Backstage and onstage at
the Martin Beck Theatre
with the company of *Grand Hotel*.
Black-and-white photos by Marcia Lippman
Color photo by Martha Swope

TINA HOWE

In life, as in art, the transcendent moments always come unannounced. There you are tending your stew when Opportunity suddenly comes crashing through the roof and *Blam!*—you're covered with gold dust. My night of gold dust occurred during the 1986 run of *Coastal Disturbances* at The Second Stage.

Rosemary Murphy suddenly took ill one afternoon and called the theatre to say she couldn't go on that night. Because there were no understudies, it meant the entire performance was in jeopardy, which translated to some $2,000 at the box office—$2,000 that The Second Stage couldn't afford to lose. What to do?

At five-fifteen my telephone rang. It was Carole Rothman, director of the play and co–artistic director of the theatre. She explained the dilemma and then said, "Tina, *you're* going on for Rosemary tonight!"

"Me?" I gasped. "But I can't act. And I don't know the lines. The audience will storm the box office for their money back!"

"No, no," she said. "It will be a novelty, everyone will love it."

To be honest, I *had* entertained fantasies about taking to the stage. It's quite the rage for playwrights these days—witness the acting careers of Wally Shawn, Chris Durang, and Sam Shepard. I might even have voiced this longing to Carole, but when the call came, my answer was loud and clear. "No way! It's bad enough when the *actors* mess up my work, there's no way *I'm* going out there. Forget it! Don't waste your breath!"

"You won't mess up, you can carry the script with you," Carole purred. "It'll be fun, the rest of the company will support you, and if you don't do it, the theatre will lose two thousand dollars!"

I stepped onto the stage sometime around eight-twenty that night, and it was one of the most extraordinary experiences I've ever had in my life.

When you're sitting in the audience at one of your plays, you're always judging the actors, noting this one should calm down and that one should take his time—pick, pick, pick. But if you're suddenly put onstage with them, they're not acting anymore, it's *real!* They come rushing at you with real tears streaming down their eyes and real pain contorting their faces. I was afraid they were going to burst into flames. I kept wanting to shake them and say, "Hey, calm down, it's just me, Tina. It's only a *play,* for God's sake. Take it easy, it's no big deal!" After about ten minutes of this, I couldn't look in their eyes anymore. It was too harrowing. Because of sitting in the house all these years, I'd thought acting was just "acting."

The other revelation had to do with Jockey shorts. I had no idea actors walked around backstage in just their underwear—and such skimpy, colorful underwear! Reds, midnight blues, blacks—it was stunning! I was afraid to look for fear my eyes would leave a stain. I didn't know the etiquette. Maybe you were *supposed* to look, that was the whole point. Lucky for me I had quite a bit of time to sort it out since Rosemary wasn't in every scene.

So there I was—undone onstage, and agog off. So, *this* is the actor's life, I mused. Not bad, not bad at all. Then came the curtain call. The company had chipped in to buy me flowers, a bouquet was presented. I had fantasies that the audience was on its feet as I clutched it to my bosom. For a moment I thought I spied a famous movie director in the audience. Was he winking at me?

No doubt about it, Wally, Chris, and Sam definitely have a good thing going!

Tina Howe

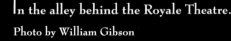

In the alley behind the Royale Theatre.
Photo by William Gibson

Backstage and onstage at the Majestic Theatre with the company of *The Phantom of the Opera.*
Photos by Paulo Netto

Under the stage of Broadway's Majestic Theatre, and onstage in the catacombs of *Phantom's* Paris Opera House.

Black-and-white photos by Paulo Netto
Color photo by Clive Barda

GWEN VERDON

When I decided to become a performer, everyone warned me what a tough business show business was, and what terrible dangers were found on the path to a career in the theatre. But I had no idea how dangerous it was until I was already starring in a Broadway show!

The show was *Sweet Charity* and it opened at the Palace Theatre in January 1966. Shortly after opening night I received letters from someone who threatened to shoot me. The producers didn't think those letters were funny. They took them very seriously; so seriously, in fact, they hired what seemed to me like a platoon of Pinkerton men, all masquerading as civilians. They were everywhere, guns at the ready, anxious to protect me. They protruded from the wings, they hung out of the boxes. Wherever I was, they were. No head of state was ever treated with such care. And the entire operation was kept completely under wraps. No one wanted to leak this story. It might frighten away the potential customers.

The first day after the arrival of my personal army was in every other way the same as those that had preceded it. I got into my costume, put on my makeup, and did a few vocal and dance exercises until the "Five minutes" call. Then I walked onstage to my place behind the curtain. I assumed the position that was the *Sweet Charity* logo: me standing, my back to the audience, looking over my left shoulder, one foot cocked saucily upward, and my right hand clamped on my right hip, which I present provocatively toward the audience. I am all alone on that great stage as the overture ends and the curtain parts.

And suddenly the realization hits me! I look at my conductor, Fred Werner; our eyes meet and we both break up! I know he is thinking the same thing: *I am going to get shot in the ass!*

I didn't and ten days later the troops are removed and life goes back to what passes for normal on the Broadway stage.

Gwen Verdon

BEHIND THE SCENES

1. out of public view. 2. in secret. 3. that not usually revealed. 4. in a position to see the hidden workings. Among those found behind the scenes: scenery, screen, flat, wing, border, teaser, teaser curtain, cloth, hanging, drop, drop scene, backdrop, fire curtain, set, stage setting, stagehand, grip, gaffer, scenes painter, stage manager, props, costumes, makeup, greasepaint.

Photo by William Gibson

LIZ SMITH

I came to New York from Texas in the fall of 1949. All through the fifties, I was so dazzled by Broadway and the theatre that I don't think I ever saw a movie. So there are great gaps in my cultural lacunae for this period. But I was busy making up for a much worse cultural desert; I had grown up in Fort Worth and the plays I had seen had been at my high school. There were three exceptions—*Tovarich* with Eugenie Leontovich . . . *Tobacco Road* starring Henry Hull . . . and the Lunts in *Amphitryon 38*. Those legit plays on tour constituted my entire personal knowledge of professional theatre. The rest was all in my scrapbooks—pictures of Katharine Cornell, Tallulah Bankhead, Helen Hayes, the Barrymores, etc. And talk, talk, talk in my high school drama classes about "the theatre."

I will never forget that I had to bring a note from my mother to be excused from Pascal High so I could see the matinee of *Tobacco Road*. My mother was oblivious of the play's reputation for profanity and sexual vulgarity. (Had she realized, she'd no doubt have considered it an object lesson to warn her children about the dangers of falling into the ways of poor white trash.) Anyway, we heard a joke back then about the demure religious grandma who went to see this play. At the intermission, she was seen bending over in the aisle and heard to say: "Oh, shit, I've dropped my goddamned program!"

Armed in idealism and ignorance, I landed in New York and, on my very first night, was driven through a glittering Times Square with the Camel cigarette sign blowing smoke rings. I thought I had landed in Wonderland.

I immediately started going to the theatre with all the vengeance of any out-of-towner. There were so many plays then and some of them one could attend for only $1.25. I remember seeing Carol Channing and her bright blue eyes onstage as Lorelei Lee in *Gentlemen Prefer Blondes*. I was miles from the stage, sitting in the very last row of the Ziegfeld Theatre balcony. I comforted myself that this was the view Flo Ziegfeld himself liked best as he viewed the stage from the peephole in his office. I did a lot of standing room as well.

Luckily, I began to hang out with some lovely folks who were theatre wise. One was Tom Wenning, then the theatre critic of *Newsweek.* (His wife, Joan, and I had gone to the University of Texas together.) Through the Wennings, I met the *Newsweek* writer Walter Osborne, a handsome blond devil who was the grandson of the writer Herman Melville. Walter liked taking a wet-behind-the-ears hick around town. He loved how impressionable I was. He would quote great gobs of Shakespeare, right along with Maurice Evans, when we went to see *Richard II.* I was entranced; I began to accumulate lore.

I was working for the last of the movie magazines, *Modern Screen,* typing nights for Blue Cross, and spending weekends proofreading at *Newsweek.* In between I went to Saturday matinees. On Sundays, a gang of us would read *Newsweek* out loud to one another on Forty-second Street, then go with our boss, Robert Austerlitz, to eat in *The New York Times* cafeteria. We had no affiliation with the *Times* and no right to use their facilities, but those were the good old days. Nobody barred our entrance to buildings, there were no guards, and if one "behaved" one could crash anywhere. What we talked about for pleasure was—"the theatre."

Austerlitz, who always wore a black knit tie, "in mourning for the world," often took me to Bleeck's, pronounced Blake's. This was a newspaper and theatre hangout where Lucius Beebe and James Thurber had made "the match game" famous. It was a haunt for the old Metropolitan Opera crowd, more authentic than the Algonquin Roundtable. Here, again, we inevitably talked —theatre. And I gathered theatre lore. It was a mark against me, a definite lapse, when it would be revealed that I had never seen Laurette Taylor onstage. Saying that she was "before my time" didn't help.

I met more theatre people. The Broadway director Burt Shevelove. Jay Presson, who had understudied Elaine Stritch in *Pal Joey.* Stritch herself, who, having a date with Marlon Brando, made me talk to him on the telephone. (I gulped and almost died.) Actor-turned-agent Michael Garrison, who

Photographer Martha Swope *(top)* shooting Rosemary Harris, and on the set of *Lost in Yonkers.*

Black-and-white photo by William Gibson

Color photo by Martha Swope

told me how he had lost his job in *Death of a Salesman* because "I looked too much like Lee J. Cobb." The comedienne Kaye Ballard. The man I adored and had assisted at CBS Radio—Mike Wallace, who translated himself into a stage actor in *Reclining Figure*. Through Mike, I met the agent Gloria Safier, Arlene Francis, and Martin Gabel. Mr. Gabel often lectured me that the theatre was a temple, saying I should dress better to go to worship. I dutifully began to wear pearls and little white gloves like Grace Kelly.

I collected more lore. What Tallulah had said from her apartment door to a departing reporter she didn't like. As the woman stepped into a crowded elevator, Tallulah said, "Dahling, you're my favorite lesbian!" I met Dorothy Parker and failed to make enough of an impression to be insulted by her. I worked in summer stock for the tempestuous Gus Schirmer, Jr., and discovered at Westport that it was important to put a long-stemmed rose in the toilet backstage as the performance began, to remind the actors never to flush during the show.

My lore became massive, fascinating, incredible. The years rolled by. One day I turned around and the theatre had mostly disappeared. What had been the core of my early life in Manhattan had become a sometime thing. We who want to continue worshiping at the temple of the theatre now only get occasional glimpses of the glory.

I deal in television these days, working with Young Turks who do not know Mary Martin from Ethel Merman. And I ask myself often—what am I to do with my vast and valuable theatre lore? Who wants to hear how Miss Fontanne used to stand offstage before her entrance in *The Great Sebastians,* holding her arms up over her head so that when she was first seen by the audience, her hands were snowy white?

Who cares now about the divine story of every comedienne in town auditioning for the London company of *Touch and Go*. As the brilliant Mary Wickes (you've seen her as a maid in many a movie; and as Carrie Fisher's

Daisy Eagan, Mandy Patinkin, and company at a press rehearsal for *The Secret Garden*.
Photos by William Gibson/Martha Swope Assoc.

grandmother in *Postcards from the Edge*) went down the line to say good-bye to her peers after they'd all read in front of one another, she said, "So long, Nancy. . . . So long, Bibi. . . . So long, Alice. . . . Bon voyage, Kaye." (Kaye Ballard went to London.)

Does it matter that I was there the night Shirley MacLaine went on in *The Pajama Game* for the ailing Carol Haney . . . that I was once at a matinee sitting near Marlon Brando. He was so besieged by fans at the intermission that he sat with a jacket draped over his head until the lights went down . . . that I saw Jose Ferrer break his stride in *The Shrike,* stopping to face the audience and say, "Please be quiet. We can hear you up here. *This* is the theatre, not television!" . . . that I was there the night Bette Davis opened in *The Night of the Iguana;* she went out of character and took a bow for her entrance ovation . . . that one of the great theatre stories is of John Barrymore's going backstage to tender praise to fellow actors. He invariably dropped to his knees, clasped his hands, and said in tones of mock reverence: "Oh, let me go down on you! Let me go down on you!"

Having seen the opening nights of *West Side Story, Candide, Bells Are Ringing, Kiss Me, Kate, Wonderful Town, Mr. Wonderful, House of Flowers, Kismet, Gypsy, She Loves Me, Top Banana, Guys and Dolls, No Strings, Company*—oh, I could go on and on—it's hard these days to wait for the theatre to strike its magic. Such magic is now so rare.

Now it's all British entrepreneurs, high ticket prices, puny themes, ordinary music, and the power of Frank Rich. My lore has no place to be heard because it comes from what seems to be a dying art. And I have no place I want to go at night.

Liz Smith

STEPHEN SONDHEIM

Stephen Sondheim *(seated, with crutches)* and company at the recording session *(above,* and *opposite)* for the cast album of *Assassins.*
Black-and-white photos by Nick Sangiamo
Color photo by Martha Swope

I suspect that the most accursed opening night in the history of the musical theatre took place in New Haven on September 1, 1947; the first public performance of *Allegro,* Rodgers and Hammerstein's third show. I was seventeen. Oscar, who by that time had become a second father to me, wanted me to learn about the professional theatre and hired me at $25 a week to be his assistant and a general gofer on the show.

Expectations at the Shubert Theatre that night were high. R&H had created a revolution with *Oklahoma!* and *Carousel,* both of which were enormously successful, and this new venture was even more experimental: nothing less than the story of a man's life told with a Greek chorus (a true "chorus") and for the first time on the commercial stage, a fluid scenic concept (Oscar's idea), which did away with forestage/full-stage scene-change tradition by substituting a curved curtain that "wiped" scenes from side to side in a cinematic style, along a curved track set into the stage floor.

Fifteen minutes into act one, during a tap-dance ballet choreographed by Agnes de Mille, Ray Harrison (the lead dancer) caught the tap of his shoe in the track, ripped a ligament in his leg, and was carried off into the wings screaming in pain.

Thirty minutes later, the ballad "A Fellow Needs a Girl" was being sung by William Ching to Annamary Dickey when the flat behind him slowly started to fall forward. As he noted it out of the corner of his eye, his left hand shot out and he held it back with increasing effort while trying to finish the song tenderly. The audience politely controlled its amusement.

Halfway through act two, Lisa Kirk, making her professional debut on the stage, got to the release of "The Gentleman Is a Dope," caught her heel in the troublesome track, and pitched forward into the string section of the orchestra. Luckily, there was no pit at the Shubert, so she fell more forward than down. Some of the violinists caught her, hoisted her back up onstage, and she finished the song—to a standing ovation, of course.

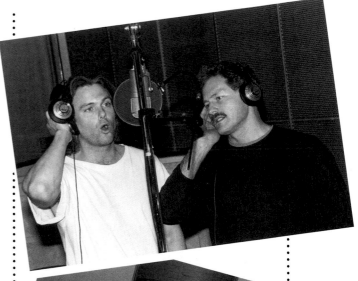

At the climax of the show, during a quiet, uplifting song called "Come Home," the smell of smoke started to pervade the theatre. One by one, or more accurately, two by two, the audience began to leave in a barely controlled panic. The panic spread until about sixty patrons were making their way up the aisles, when the mass exodus was stopped by a voice from the standing-room section (it was Joshua Logan's) yelling, "It's just a rubbish fire in the alley!"—which indeed it was, the evening being a hot one and the alley doors being open. Some of the audience returned.

It would make a neat ending to this story to add that *Allegro* became a smash hit in spite of these four disasters, but life, unlike Rodgers and Hammerstein musicals, seldom follows such a happy course. The show, though it ran the better part of the season, was their first flop.

Stephen Sondheim

FRANK RICH

The Astor Hotel was still standing on the night I took my first solitary walk around Broadway. I know because I was staying there, in a room looking across Shubert Alley to the Booth Theatre. The night was December 28, 1963, a Saturday, and I was fourteen years old.

I had been at the Astor for a week with my family. Presumably we did other things besides go to the theatre, but what I mostly remember is the plays we saw in a nonstop marathon of Christmas-week matinees and evenings: *110 in the Shade,* with real rain, at the Broadhurst; *The Ballad of the Sad Cafe,* with a strapping, two-fisted Colleen Dewhurst—I'd never seen anything like her—and the dwarf Michael Dunn—I'd never seen anything like him—at the Martin Beck; *Chips with Everything,* an angry English drama that lent credence to all my blossoming teenage hostilities, at the Plymouth; Noël Coward's *The Girl Who Came to Supper,* with twirling Oliver Smith sets that looked like *My Fair Lady,* at the Broadway; *Jennie,* a flop in which Mary Martin played to a half-filled matinee of yawning patrons, at the site of her past triumph in *South Pacific,* the Majestic; *She Loves Me,* with Barbara Cook, Jack Cassidy, Daniel Massey, and the whiff of romantic between-the-wars Budapest, at the O'Neill; and tonight, the last night of vacation, *The Private Ear and the Public Eye,* a double bill by Peter Shaffer at the Morosco. I was so keyed up that in between shows I could do little but constantly reshuffle my Playbills and ticket stubs into stacks of variable significance.

Late on our final afternoon, my parents, heeding my persistent claims that I was entitled to special privileges befitting the eldest child, let me go out for dinner alone. They gave me a ten-dollar bill and made a reservation at Frankie & Johnny's, a steak house with a speakeasy's second-story ambience down the block. I tucked the crisp bill in my pants pocket and headed toward the restaurant, but not before stopping at the newsstand at another hotel, the Manhattan, to spend a quarter of my own, hard-earned money on the latest *Variety.* I guess the newsstand dealer was puzzled that a kid would ask for

Variety. "Do you know Eddie Hodges?" he asked. I nodded no, but was flattered to be associated in any way with the child star of *The Music Man* whose delivery of "Gary, Indiana" I had mimicked countless times to the accompaniment of the original cast album in the privacy of my bedroom in Washington, D.C.

At dinner I devoured *Variety,* a sirloin steak, and a glass of milk. After leaving the meticulously computed tip on the table, I walked up the block to meet my family at the Morosco. But I was puzzled by what I had read in my newspaper. *Variety* said that seemingly half the plays on Broadway were closing that night, fleeing town just as my family and the rest of the tourists would be, as if Christmas on Broadway were a charade put on exclusively for our benefit. When the curtain fell on *The Private Ear and the Public Eye,* I asked my parents: What happens when a play closes? And they said: Why don't you find out?

What followed was an adventure that no parents would allow a fourteen-year-old to undertake in today's Times Square. For a good hour after the shows let out, I traipsed from theatre to theatre by myself, scooping up discarded Playbills and watching the striking of scenery and its removal into waiting trucks. On Forty-seventh Street, I found two departures: *The Irregular Verb To Love* starring Claudette Colbert and Cyril Ritchard, at the Ethel Barrymore, and *Man and Boy,* written by Terence Rattigan and starring Charles Boyer, at the Brooks Atkinson. On Forty-fifth, there were three: an Irish revue titled *Double Dublin* at the Little; a Dore Schary comedy called *Love and Kisses* at the Music Box (starring Larry Parks, famous to me as a martyr to the witch-hunts of the House Un-American Activities Committee); and at the Royale, Jean Anouilh's *The Rehearsal.* I remember so well the airy, Gallic set of *The Rehearsal,* but even as I tried to picture such elegant actors as Coral Browne and Keith Michell inhabiting it in the style advertised by the production photographs at the front of the house, stagehands were dismantling the

Behind the scenes and onstage with the company of *And the World Goes 'Round,* the Kander and Ebb musical.
Black-and-white photo by William Gibson
Color photo by Joan Marcus

doors and revealing the stage's rear brick wall. Yet the exposure of the seams of the play's illusion seemed every bit as theatrical to me as the creation of such an illusion. The plays came and went, I saw, but the theatre stayed.

Only at one closing could I not see the sets being struck: the backstage of *Jennie* was obscured by a long walkway that led to the Majestic's stage door. By now, midnight, the neighborhood was lonely, but one young man was standing at the street exit of the Majestic's cul-de-sac. In retrospect, I realize that he was a fanatic: he clutched a stack of Playbills even larger than my own. His eyes were large and unfocused, as if he did not reside completely in this world.

Sensing a somewhat kindred spirit—or perhaps protecting his own, carefully staked-out turf—he struck up a conversation, explaining that he loved *Jennie* and was waiting to get the star's autograph. I didn't have the heart to say that I didn't like *Jennie* and didn't think Mary Martin was going to turn up at this hour, now that the theatre's marquee had dimmed.

Incongruously the marquee across the street, at the St. James, still burned bright, heralding John Osborne's *Luther* to no one on the deserted street but us. The young man pointed at it and knowingly informed me that the producer David Merrick was about to move *Luther* to another theatre so that he could bring his new production, a musical, to the St. James the next month.

As it happened, I had seen that musical, *Hello, Dolly!,* in its tryout in my hometown the week before coming to New York. It seemed incredible and thrilling that even the gargantuan image of Martin Luther towering above us would soon be struck to make way for its usurper's logo. Venturing what may have been my first, gingerly expressed critical opinion to a total stranger, I advised the young man to buy a ticket to see *Hello, Dolly!* in advance. "It's going to be a hit," I promised.

I have no idea if he believed me or not. He was still waiting for Mary Martin as I turned to walk back to the Astor.

Of course, the Astor is gone now, and so is the Morosco, and so is Mary Martin. It would be years before I learned that some closings on Broadway, as in the rest of life, are for keeps. On the night of December 28, 1963, the country was still mourning its dead president, and Broadway seemed a refuge from mortality, a place where the show always went on, where a closing would always be followed by an opening, where a *Luther* would always give way to a *Hello, Dolly!* As the chill wind of an incipient new year propelled me up Forty-fourth Street, I felt terribly grown-up, when in truth I was more of a child of the theatre than I had yet begun to understand.

Frank Rich

Behind the scenes and onstage at Steve McGraw's with the company of *Forever Plaid*.

Black-and-white photo by Seth Gurvitz

Color photo by Carol Rosegg/Martha Swope Assoc.

TERRENCE McNALLY

Broadway! (I still think it deserves an exclamation point.)

I'm old enough to remember—and want to talk about—the old days. The receding hairline I saw coming, but this attack of nostalgia I was completely unprepared for. I thought nostalgia was remembering my parents taking me to see Ethel Merman in *Annie Get Your Gun* when I was five years old and my grandfather taking me to see Gertrude Lawrence in *The King and I* when I was ten. How could anyone not remember seeing those two fabulous ladies in those two fabulous shows for the rest of his life?

Nostalgia was remembering my first opening night on Broadway and walking into the opening-night party at Sardi's and responding with (I thought) becoming modesty to the unexpected standing ovation I was receiving only to discover that the cheers were for Eileen Heckart, the play's star, who had made *her* entrance only a few paces behind me. Most of the first-nighters had no idea who I was.

Nostalgia was being at the opening night of *Who's Afraid of Virginia Woolf?* and knowing you'd seen a great play. It was remembering Colleen Dewhurst and Jason Robards in *A Moon for the Misbegotten* and rejoicing that an American masterpiece had been reclaimed from oblivion. It was anything that had Gwen Verdon in it. It was remembering the Morosco and the Helen Hayes and gritting your teeth every time you walked by the dreadful building that had replaced them. It was sleeping on the sidewalk in front of the Mark Hellinger to get standing room for the next evening's performance of *My Fair Lady*. It was remembering Carl Reiner's *Something Different* with Gabe Dell and Linda Lavin and Bob Dishy, which I still think is the funniest play I ever saw (probably because it's about a playwright who can tell you every single production a play of his has received, including stock and amateur ones in towns and places no one ever heard of, even the people at Samuel French and Dramatists Play Service!). Nostalgia was grumbling about having to rent a tuxedo for an opening night but secretly agreeing everyone really did look terrific for their efforts. Nostalgia was seven or eight newspapers and no televised reviews. Nostalgia was being part of something bigger than yourself or your play. That something was a fraternity. It was a royal family. It was magic.

If that was nostalgia, I could handle it. The past was something we could fondly recollect at leisure and at the same time steer and measure ourselves by in times of doubt. When you remember Tennessee Williams and Eugene O'Neill, you can't get too far lost from where you want to be as a playwright yourself. The same for an actor, a director, a designer, or a producer who remembers an Olivier, a Guthrie, an Aronson, or a Kermit Bloomgarden. People like that are great maps for where any of us in the theatre should want to go.

But the nostalgia I'm feeling today is also one of sadness and loss and anger. AIDS has decimated the New York theatre and Broadway. We have lost people long before their time. People who still had so much to give us are gone. We miss and honor them and we will never stop grieving for them. It's the plays that won't be written, the performances that won't be seen, the heart-stopping musical numbers that won't be choreographed, that have become a part of the new nostalgia. We don't sweetly summon up this nostalgia. It leaps out at us and strikes our hearts when we least expect it. There is not a theatre in Manhattan that is not haunted by these ghosts of What Was Not to Be.

I am mourning not the Broadway that was but the Broadway that AIDS has seen to it will never be. If this is nostalgia, I don't know how we're expected to handle it except to continue to do the best work we can. It's the only fitting memorial for those we love and have lost.

Terence McNally

Playwright Terrence McNally, Nathan Lane, Swoosie Kurtz, Christine Baranski, and Anthony Heald backstage at Manhattan Theatre Club's *Lips Together, Teeth Apart.*

Photo by T. Trompeter

KATHY BATES

I guess my fondest memories of Broadway would have to be from the time I spent performing the role of the suicidal daughter in Marsha Norman's Pulitzer Prize–winning play, *'night, Mother.*

I was sitting backstage one night with Anne Pitoniak before one of our previews, or maybe it was opening night. We could hear the audience moving to their seats. I remember it was Anne's birthday and she was sitting on a step behind the scenery waiting to go on. She had her knees drawn up to her chest like a little kid, and all of the sudden, she looked over at me and she squealed, "Ooooooh, Kathy, we're on Broadway!" I'll never forget that.

We ran the show for eleven months at the John Golden Theatre, and I often brought my little Yorkshire terrier, Pip, to work with me. After a while he got to know the backstage routine. When Steve Beckler, our production stage manager, called, "Five minutes," Pip would walk out of my dressing room door and climb the stairs to the dressing room just above mine where Betty Lee Matelli, our wardrobe supervisor, was. She would give him a snack and he'd curl up on her sofa for a puppy snooze while we did the play. As Betty Lee tells it, each time Jessie Cates committed suicide an hour and a half after the play began and a single gunshot rang out through the theatre and over the backstage intercoms, Pip would wake up, jump down off the sofa, and run around the dressing room all excited because he knew that the gunshot meant I'd be coming for him soon to take him home.

LYNNE THIGPEN

LYNNE THIGPEN. *Although she was conceived in the Andes, the daughter of a defrocked priest and a missionary of the Fundamentalist Abyssinian Church of the Divine Right-On, she quickly and erringly devoted most of her early life to dancing and frolicking on the slopes of the magnificent mountains. It was in 1975 when a touring company of* The Sound of Music *played in a nearby hamlet that Lynne was cast as the lovely Maria.*

When you go to the theatre, you find your seat and open your program to see who's who in the cast. Me, too, but I always disliked writing those program bios each time I did a new show. No matter how much I worked on them, they always ended up sounding like laundry lists. My agents, Michael Thomas and Rozanne Gates, had suffered my complaints each time I had to write a new one. So when one was due for the musical *Tintypes,* Michael revised my last one.

Because I had previously worked with the production staff of the theatre presenting *Tintypes,* I submitted this bio, certain that they would laugh and come back with, "Okay, Lynne, where's your real bio?" They didn't, and my agent's first complete work of fiction was published. I did have a moment of concern that people wouldn't realize that the joke was on *me,* and not on them. Most theatergoers, however, recognized the tongue planted firmly in cheek (nontraditional casting aside, an alto singing the role of Maria is quite out of the question); the show went on and I forgot about the bio.

Then, after one Wednesday matinee, two members of the audience waited backstage to see me. I welcomed them into my dressing room, two very patrician, white-haired ladies who excitedly told me they had spent, over the years, much time in and around the Andes. "What village did you come from, dear?" they asked sweetly. My heart sank as they asked me out for a drink and talk of the mountains.

Since then, laundry lists have looked just fine.

Lynne Thigpen

Mandy Patinkin, Robert Westenberg,
Daisy Eagan, and company of
The Secret Garden
in the recording studio and
onstage at the St. James Theatre.
Black-and-white photos by Joan Marcus
Color photo by Bob Marshak

ALEX WITCHEL

In school, when we had to pick heroes, it seemed that most people—the girls at least—picked Eleanor Roosevelt. I liked her, too, especially the part about being her husband's legs, but there were two I liked even more. Joseph Papp and Annie Sullivan. I figured if Annie Sullivan could get through to Helen Keller, it was no less of an achievement that Joseph Papp could get through to Robert Moses.

And so in the summer of 1978, when I was still in college, I got my chance to work for Joseph Papp as an intern at the Public Theatre. An intern meant working for free, I explained to my openmouthed parents. Which meant they would have to lend me the money to commute from Scarsdale to the East Village, a prospect they found as appealing as Harlem at midnight. Couldn't I find a hero in a better neighborhood?

My goal was to meet Mr. Papp, as he was called by his staff, and I spent most of my time at the makeshift desk across the floor from his office trying to get a glimpse. I sat there day after day dutifully pasting every scrap of newsprint ever written about him into memory books, waiting for the moment he would notice me. I even envied the terrified souls whom he summoned when he was displeased—which was often. They may have been yelled at, but at least he knew who they were. When I occasionally did see him, he would walk through the halls with great concentration, gesturing, talking to one or two or six people trailing behind him with clipboards, trying to keep up.

Though my intern duties finally changed—from pasting to Xeroxing—my relationship with him was the same. I worshiped, he ignored. Then one day, Mr. Papp's receptionist asked me to answer the phones during her lunch break. I don't remember her name, but she had a sweet, long-suffering face, and cut perfectly symmetrical pieces of the Entenmann's cakes she brought to the office, without once ever washing the knife.

She said Mr. Papp was expecting some people from *Runaways,* the Elizabeth Swados musical that he had recently transferred from the Public to

Joseph Papp and friend in his office at the New York Shakespeare Festival.
Photo by Cori Wells Braun

Broadway. It was not Ms. Swados who would come—though she often walked through the stifling offices wearing her thick black tights as if it were January. It was one of the actors, the receptionist confided timidly. One of the teenagers Ms. Swados had found, and he had been missing performances. He wasn't sick, he just didn't feel like showing up.

I was too excited to listen to the details. Finally, after all these weeks, I would meet Mr. Papp. I would tell him what a great man he was. I would tell him I had risked being disowned by my family for the chance to ogle him across the hall. My devotion would impress him. He would thank me.

The receptionist left. Mr. Papp was in his office with the door closed. Should I knock and introduce myself? The actor walked in then, a tall, black teenager with a sullen expression. He was with another man, maybe his father.

I pressed the intercom. The door opened immediately, and without a word, Mr. Papp rushed out, heading straight for the actor. He grabbed him by the lapels of his windbreaker and hurled him against the wall. Then he did it again, and this time the other man interceded, trying to calm him down. Mr. Papp abruptly let go and turned back toward his office. I expected to see fury on his face, rage or hatred. But there was only frustration, almost sorrow. He could not find sufficient words to condemn this actor's sin, this ungrateful child who was given a place in the theatre and did not choose to revere it.

No one spoke. Or even looked in my direction. They all walked into the office and Mr. Papp slammed the door shut. I didn't see him again that summer. So much for my grand introduction. But that moment, with his face so close, so red and fierce with its heat, had overwhelmed me with its unexpected intimacy. That was a face that started fights and finished them, made promises and kept them. That was a face that *believed* in things, in the theatre most of all, and insisted you did, too. That was the face I had waited all summer to see. I see it still.

WENDY WASSERSTEIN

The night my play *The Heidi Chronicles* opened on Broadway, I was waiting for an experience similar to the one described by Moss Hart in his theatrical memoir, *Act One.* Mr. Hart had a lifelong dream of getting to Broadway. On the opening night of *Once in a Lifetime,* his fondest wish as both a New Yorker and a man of the theatre came true.

I anticipated pacing back and forth in the orchestra on my opening night and having my childhood memories of Saturday matinees converge in one ecstatic, overwhelming, sentimental moment. Looking back now, however, as my play comes to the end of its Broadway run this Labor Day weekend, my own version of Moss Hart's theatrical epiphany was not on opening night, but the first time I entered the Plymouth Theatre.

I am from a generation of off-Broadway babies. Unlike Mr. Hart, we mostly don't dare dream of getting our plays to Broadway now. Broadway in the past decades has generally housed three or four new plays a year, one of which is often British.

Our plays, even the most well known, such as A. R. Gurney's *The Dining Room* or Alfred Uhry's *Driving Miss Daisy,* have never been on Broadway. They have long and healthy lives in regional theatres across the country and two-hundred- or three-hundred-seat commercial houses in New York, Chicago, or Los Angeles.

But the day I first walked, as an author, into the Plymouth, I became suddenly envious of Moss Hart and his theatrical era, when at times more than two hundred new American plays were produced on Broadway every year. As I sat in the empty orchestra while Daniel Sullivan, our director, and Thomas Lynch, the set designer, evaluated the sight lines, I thought it was the most beautiful and enormous theatre I had ever seen.

I stared at the delicate gray and white rococo ceiling and wondered what John Barrymore, Laurette Taylor, and even William Gillette, who opened in the theatre in 1917, first thought when they gazed at it. Bernard Jacobs of the Shubert Organization tells me the Plymouth is his shining jewel, the most beautiful theatre in New York—maybe, he says, even in America. I think it is in the world.

During the year and a half that my play has been fortunate enough to be at the Plymouth, I have never missed an opportunity to visit there. I've attended understudy auditions and cast-change rehearsals, and sometimes just come by during a matinee to pace in the back. In fact, what has amazed me as a New Yorker is that the lore of the theatre district is still intact.

For example, for a Broadway playwright there remains the thrill of the stage doorman's knowing your name. I've never missed an opportunity to just say "Hi" to Richard White and Andrew Capps at the Plymouth. Conversely, the Plymouth ushers have never missed an opportunity to tell me their opinions on every cast change, and they're generally right. And I've come to rely on the anecdotes of "Broadway Ernie," Ernie Austin, our props man, who has been an actor, singer, dancer, stage manager, and now has been doing Broadway props for twenty-five years.

My friend the late Edward Kleban, who wrote the lyrics for *A Chorus Line,* told me shortly before he died, "Kiddo, the thing about having a show on Broadway is you'll always have a private rest room in the theatre district." As it turned out, Eddie had the longest-running rest room in musical theatre history.

It breaks my heart that I won't be regularly visiting with Roy Harris, our stage manager, in Lily Tomlin's and Maggie Smith's old dressing room. I've told Roy I think the Shubert Organization should change the theatre's name to "Roy Harris's Plymouth Theatre" with Roy's hand waving in neon above.

But what I will miss the most is simply being inside the Plymouth Theatre. A year ago Labor Day weekend, the original cast gave their final performance of my play in the afternoon, and the new cast was to rehearse for the first time that night. After the actors packed up their dressing rooms and departed, the director and I went out to dinner. Eighth Avenue was abandoned except for the men in white space uniforms. Though we later found out this was due to an asbestos-pipe break, it seemed to us the end of the world. What to do seemed simple: go back inside the Plymouth Theatre.

I have wondered often since that time how many New Yorkers would choose to go to the theatre if it were indeed the end of the world. And I suspect the answer is quite a few. Even in a theatrical climate now beleaguered by censorship, soaring ticket prices, and embattled unions, what makes coming of age and living in this city great is *theatre*.

As I sat for the last time in the empty Plymouth Theatre, staring again at that gorgeous ceiling, I felt a true sadness that all Broadway theatres are not presently occupied with playwrights having the epiphany of Moss Hart. It's all entirely possible. New Yorkers, both in and out of the theatre, have to work together to insure that it survives. Ask any drama student: "Theater is collaboration." It is also our legacy.

Wendy Wasserstein

Linda Hopkins, Carrie Smith, Ruth Brown, and company behind the scenes and onstage during *Black & Blue*.
Black-and-white photos by John Huba
Color photo by Martha Swope

ROCCO LANDESMAN

Rocco Landesman behind his desk at Jujamcyn Productions.
Photo by Allen Frame

In the winter of 1984 I had been a producer, or more properly, an aspiring producer, only a few months. My wife, Heidi, and I had somehow come up with the idea that Roger Miller, the country-music songwriter and performer, could write the score for a Broadway musical, and with a few exceptions, the idea received a response that ranged from polite bemusement and indifference to derision. But we had never produced anything, on Broadway or off-, and we didn't know better. I persuaded Bill Hauptman, an old friend from our days together at the Yale School of Drama, to write an adaptation of *Huckleberry Finn* and after more than a year of cajoling, finally convinced Roger to take a shot. "After all," I told him, "Lincoln did." I cheated at first, assuring him that we could just use a lot of his old stuff. Roger had never seen a musical, and eventually, slowly and tentatively at first, and then with more confidence, he began to produce songs for the show.

I sent a scratchy tape with four songs on it along with Bill's book to Bob Brustein, my old mentor and friend and later colleague at Yale, who was then and is now the artistic director of the American Repertory Theatre in Cambridge. Bob, maybe because he never liked musicals anyway, or because he had known me long enough to know that I wasn't insane, or most likely, because he actually liked the book and songs, agreed to stage the show at ART. But we had only a handful of songs, one of which was, in fact, from Roger's trunk, so Bob was taking an enormous leap of faith. And my own doubts were not deep down or in the back of my mind—they were front and center in my mind and gave me, literally, my first sleepless night since infancy.

In January of 1984 we all—Des McAnuff, who had become the director, Bob, Bill, Roger, the cast, the ART staff, Heidi, and I—gathered around long tables in a room at ART on the first day of rehearsal. The first run-through of any new show is always a time of great anticipation and anxiety. How is it going to sound? How will it play? After what seemed to me like hours, the moment in the book arrived for the first song. Roger picked up his guitar and sang. It was "The Boys' Song." Everyone in the room was watching Roger. Except me. I was watching everyone else in the room. Total silence, then some of the actors took their eyes off Roger and began to look at one another. Some faint smiles started to form. Some fingers kept time on the table. When Roger finished, the room erupted. Broad smiles, whistles, applause. What we had heard was not a "show tune," but a new sound in the musical theatre. It was going to work. Roger could do it. The response to the next song was more tumultuous. And even more so for the one after that. It was my happiest moment in the theatre.

I so vividly remember the passage in *The Season,* William Goldman's delightful book about Broadway, in which he notes that you can almost always handicap the success of a new show on opening night by simply looking at the program and reading the credits of the principals. As at the races, the "track record" is usually decisive. *Big River* was a musical presented by first-time producers with a book by someone who had never written a musical, directed by a director who had never directed on Broadway, and performed by a cast that had only two members who had ever appeared on a Broadway stage. After opening in April of 1985 at the Eugene O'Neill, it ran for more than a thousand performances over two and one-half years and toured all across the country. But in all that time there was never a more thrilling moment—and I would include the night in June when the show won the Tony for Best Musical and six other Tonys—than that winter afternoon in Cambridge, Massachusetts, when Roger Miller sang and played his guitar.

Rocco Landesman

BERNARD B. JACOBS

Bernie Jacobs at his desk in the offices of the Shubert Organization.
Photo by Jay Brady

The first time many people in the business became aware of Michael Bennett was when he choreographed *A Joyful Noise.* I had met Michael before that, way back, during the original production of *West Side Story* at the Winter Garden Theatre. He was a bright young man with enormous self-confidence. He exuded an immense talent and energy.

I caught up with Michael when he did *Promises, Promises* for David Merrick and then again during his work with Hal Prince in *Company* and *Follies.* But most people associate us with *A Chorus Line,* which was in the Shubert Theatre for almost fifteen years.

I saw the first preview of *A Chorus Line* at the New York Shakespeare Festival's Newman Theatre in 1975. I went backstage after the show. Michael saw me and came up to me in a panic. "You shouldn't have come so soon," he said. "I'm not ready for you yet." But he called the next day and asked for my notes on the show. He was very polite and listened as I ran down my list. A week later, I went back to see the show. Afterward he very proudly told me, "I made all the changes you recommended!" But in truth, Michael never made any changes that he didn't want to make. He wasn't listening to anyone but Michael.

By now, *A Chorus Line* was a powerhouse. Michael heard I wanted him to move the show to the Winter Garden. He wasn't happy about that. It was a difficult negotiation. At one point in our discussions, when we were still trying to convince Michael to go into the Winter Garden, I assured him that "nothing will ever dynamite you out of that house." He put his arms around me and said, "You really like my show, don't you?" Yes. "I want the Shubert." And eventually, like most everything else he wanted, he got it.

In 1988, we gave a party for the thirteenth anniversary of *A Chorus Line.* At that time Michael was sick and there were rumors that he had AIDS. But he showed up at the party and seemed to be in very good health, had put on some weight and looked good. Soon after, an article appeared on the front page of the Arts & Leisure section of the Sunday *New York Times* that claimed that Michael had angina.

Sometime after *Ballroom* Michael began to work on *Scandal.* We got together one weekend at his house in East Hampton. Michael and I sat and talked before lunch, during which he told me he was giving up *Scandal.* But before he did so, he would appreciate it if I would read it and perhaps give him some advice. He seemed tired. I took *Scandal* home with me and left him the script for *Chess*. Later I told him I thought *Scandal* was hopeless. He expressed interest in *Chess* and I asked him to go over to London to direct and choreograph it. Subsequently he went to London and cast the show. But he returned to New York, saying he was sick and could not go back to London. He said he wanted to have nothing to do with *Chess*. The angina sickness was a story that Michael had made up because he felt that he should not tell the world that he had AIDS.

Michael retired to East Hampton and subsequently went to Arizona, where he died. Trevor Nunn took over *Chess*. Difficult as it was, the show was a success and ran for two years in London. In New York we tried an entirely different concept and the show failed. Perhaps if Michael had been able to conceive and direct the show in London and New York, the story might have been different.

Another Michael Bennett will not come around again soon. He was a self-taught genius who loved the theatre.

Two things are certain: 1. AIDS is the scourge of this century; and 2. I never dreamed that I would outlive Michael Bennett.

KEN MARSOLAIS

It was February 1975. Jose Quintero and I were having lunch at a small Italian restaurant on Madison Avenue. We had met two years before when I was interviewed by him for a job as a stage manager, actor, understudy, and assistant for a play he was directing called *Gandhi*.

Gandhi was short-lived but my friendship with Jose lasted. When *A Moon for the Misbegotten* came to New York, Jose asked me to assistant-stage-manage and understudy. I accepted because it meant Broadway, and of course, being in the same theatre with Colleen Dewhurst and Jason Robards didn't hurt either. Incidentally, it was during the early run of *Moon* in New York that one evening I casually yelled upstairs to Colleen to join me in a drink. To my surprise, she accepted. We spent the next seventeen years together.

While we were in California in the autumn of 1974 with the final weeks of *Moon* at the Ahmanson, Jose and I began talking about forming our own production company. He would direct and I would produce. We thought we would be a good team.

So we were having lunch. I asked Jose what he wanted to direct. He said he had always wanted to do *The Skin of Our Teeth*. I said, so why don't we, but how do we get the rights? Since he knew Thornton Wilder, I asked Jose if he would mind calling him. By this time we had finished lunch and were on our way out of the restaurant. On the sidewalk Jose asked me if I had any change. I gave him what I had. He immediately stopped and called Thornton, who was at his home on Martha's Vineyard. I thought, my God, here I was, a neophyte producer standing at a pay phone with one of our great directors who is talking to one of our greatest playwrights to option a classic American play. Thornton said yes and I was launched into the world of producing.

Since then I've learned that it doesn't always happen that way, but keep a quarter in your pocket just in case.

Ken Marsolais

ALAN EISENBERG

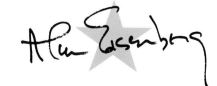

On October 5, 1981, I started a new job as executive secretary of Actors' Equity Association. I was an "outsider" to theatre and was working hard, putting in long hours, in order to get this industry under my belt. I met Michael Bennett early in the game, and we got to know each other pretty well pretty quickly because of negotiations over the terms of a new workshop agreement. I liked him very much.

Dreamgirls opened on December 20, 1981, and I thought it was absolutely wonderful. (It was the best musical of the eighties.) I saw it several times within a couple of weeks of its first performance, and each time it thrilled me.

At this point, I had an idea: since I was at the office late so often, I should work until close to nine P.M., go over to the Imperial, listen to Jennifer Holliday bring the house down every single night with her first-act closing, "I'm Not Going," and then go home. Which I got permission to do, and which I started doing.

Each night the doorman would let me in, I'd walk through that long lobby, then stand at the back of the house. Many times I saw Michael—he would be prowling around, most times watching from the mezzanine—I'd see him walking up and down the stairs. He almost always looked drained, haggard, unshaven, wearing dungarees. We smiled at each other and waved, but didn't talk much—I felt he was working and didn't want to disturb him.

Jennifer would sing her heart out. The audience always started clapping too soon, long before the song was over, but she would ride this ever-increasing crescendo, going higher and higher, more and more, she and the house meeting in some new place—and then it was over, the song ended. There was this roar from the audience.

I felt lucky, special, and privileged. I could see Jennifer's number anytime I wanted. I didn't feel like such an outsider anymore, thanks to Michael.

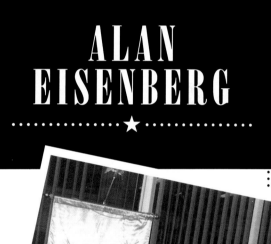

Actors' Equity President Ron Silver, Counselor Frank Converse, and Executive Secretary Alan Eisenberg at a membership meeting.
Photo by Seth Gurvitz

DAVID HENRY HWANG

Behind the scenes and onstage *(above,* and *opposite)* at the Astor Place Theatre with Blue Man Group in *Tubes*.
Black-and-white photos by John Huba
Color photo by Kevin Joseph Roach

I was twenty-one years old and my first play, *FOB,* had been accepted to be workshopped at the prestigious Eugene O'Neill National Playwrights Conference. Months before, while still a college undergraduate, I had received the Mailgram informing me of my selection and had rushed breathlessly across campus to tell anyone who might cross my path. In all my subsequent career to date, this remains the only time that good news has taken me completely by surprise.

Now I was sitting amidst empty audience bleachers breathing in the muggy country air of Waterford, Connecticut, thrilled to be observing a technical rehearsal for *FOB.* The director had not yet arrived. I was somewhat concealed in a corner of the outdoor stage area. I saw a sound operator on a wooden platform, and beside him, a stage manager. I saw the sound operator turn to the stage manager and mutter with a smirk on his face, "What are we going to be using for this one? Chink music?"

The problem with a good deal of racism nowadays, particularly if one travels within a relatively enlightened circle, is that it catches you unawares. The incidents may be small, but they are reminders nonetheless: at the moment you are preparing to revel in your first professional tech, someone else might just be seeing you as something other than another young playwright.

The stage manager's face blanched with horror. She gestured furtively in my direction. The sound operator's eyes met mine for an instant. He, too, was shocked. At me? At himself? I don't know. I looked away quickly, toward the ground. I was sitting far enough away that it was possible I never even heard his remark. The question always arises in such instances, is it worth making an incident? On the one hand, I am humiliated and angry. On the other, it seems almost impossible to calculate an appropriate response. Statements like "I am not a chink!" are self-defeating in their absurdity. "There's no reason to use racist terms like that" sounds insufferably academic. "Fucking asshole!" is useful on the streets of Manhattan, but I am loath to disturb the serenity of this theatre community, though my own peace has been shot to hell. Perhaps I misheard him. People don't really *say* things like that, do they? Not *these* kinds of people! How about, "Did I hear you say 'chink'?!" *That* might be a good place to begin.

By the time all those thoughts have run through my mind, the director has arrived and it seems the moment has passed. I salvage some scraps of dignity by fixing the still-dazed offender with a long, accusing stare, the kind that says, "I heard what you said and I know who you are." I try to look like De Niro in *Taxi Driver.* Then the tech begins.

Weeks later, at the closing-night party for the conference, the sound operator approaches me. We have not spoken since that incident; I have made it a point, however, to stare at him whenever he enters my sight. He is carrying a box of chocolates. I think I detect a slight trembling as he offers me one. I hesitate, wondering if this is the moment to release my simmering anger. But he looks genuinely apologetic as he says, "Would you like one?" I take a dark swirl, smile, and reply, "Thank you very much."

Perhaps I've worked with him since then and not even known it. I assume he's still out there somewhere.

I think of myself as a happy and well-adjusted man. When I look at my work, however, I see powerful currents of anger and bitterness, one indication that the oppressive presence of the invisible sound operators continues to haunt me. That one I encountered in Connecticut—I wonder if he still remembers our exchange of stares and his chocolates as clearly as I.

CHARLES BUSCH

Meghan Robinson was a wonderful young actress who, in another time and healthier theatre, might have been a new Katharine Cornell or Lynn Fontanne. I was fortunate to be able to write five roles for her in my plays.

Meghan was mercurial, tempestuous, madly loyal, and the embodiment of the word *actress.* When she was stricken with AIDS, she handled her illness as if it were a challenging classic role to be shaped and conquered. She was determined to continue her career onstage.

The opening in the summer of 1989 of our show *The Lady in Question* at the Orpheum Theatre coincided with her last burst of good health. She played a beautiful actress being held prisoner by the Nazis, and who must escape through the Nazi baron's castle. The comic high point of the play was when I had to divert the Nazi's attention while she, a cripple, agonizingly dragged herself up an enormous staircase. Her progress up that staircase was a physical tour de force, involving pratfalls and climaxing in a somersault out the upstairs door.

Two days after we opened and she had received her usual rave review from *The New York Times,* she arrived at the theatre ashen and gasping for breath. I could see she was terrified that she was coming down with another case of pneumonia. Ken Elliott, our producer and director, was prepared to cancel the performance. The understudy hadn't been put on the contract yet. Meghan wouldn't hear of it. She was determined to get through the show.

We played our first scene together on the sofa. Meghan's timing was perfect and the audience laughed at her every line. Sitting so close to her, I could see the beads of sweat at the edge of her wig. Immediately following each of her laughs, she'd turn her head upstage and begin wheezing and desperately trying to catch her breath.

During the intermission, Ken begged her to at least cut the somersault. She could barely speak but nodded that she agreed. We got to the big scene and I began my routine of trying to divert the Nazi's attention downstage. From the corner of my eye I could see Meghan begin her agonizing ascent up the stairs. The audience was laughing at what they took to be a slapstick scene when in reality the actress was truly struggling to make it. I began sweating more profusely than Meghan and slowed my delivery to give her more time. I must have gone too slowly because when I looked upstage, she shot me a fierce look that my change in timing was screwing up one of her bits. My back was to her when she reached the top landing. The suspense was too much for me and I had to turn around. Sure enough, with all the strength left in her, she did that goddamn final somersault and exited to a great round of applause.

The cast was emotionally drained from witnessing this act of defiance in the face of great odds. Ken had a cab waiting outside the stage door and took Meghan, still in her stage makeup, straight to the hospital.

Not long ago I met a wonderful veteran movie character actress, Iris Adrian. I asked her all about working with such stars as Joan Crawford and Ginger Rogers. Her very wise answer to all my questions regarding the legendary temperament of those ladies was simply, "Kid, you gotta love an actress." Iris, you are so right. And I most certainly did.

Charles Busch

Julie Halston *(center)* and Charles Busch *(right)* backstage at the Lucille Lortel Theatre during *Red Scare on Sunset*.
Photo by T. L. Boston

CHARLES NELSON REILLY

Dorothy Stickney is most remembered for playing Vinnie in *Life with Father,* a 1939 comedy by Howard Lindsay based on Clarence Day, Jr.'s *New Yorker* reminiscences. It remains the longest-running nonmusical play in Broadway history—3,224 performances. It was first done in Skowhegan, Maine, by the resident stock company. As the opening approached, Howard Lindsay could get no one to play the male lead. He tried Henry Hull, Roland Young, and other "names" of the time, but no one would do the play. He could not give away the lead in what was to become the longest-running show on Broadway, an affectionate portrait of nineteenth-century homelife evoking a past of simple values.

I first heard this story about Dorothy Stickney from Jon Cypher, who played the prince in the original Rodgers and Hammerstein *Cinderella* with Julie Andrews. Miss Stickney and Howard Lindsay played the king and queen. I have told the story over the years on talk shows at Christmas. When I suggested it was right for Kendall Hailey's new play *Race You for the Wings,* I called Miss Stickney, who is very much alive, in New York. She corrected "my" version, and what stands in this excerpt from Kendall's play *is* the accurate story as verified by Miss Stickney.

ACTRESS
You know Dorothy Stickney, the actress, don't you?
FANATIC
Sure. Mother in *Life with Father,* Mother in *Life with Mother,* Edna St. Vincent Millay in *A Lovely Light,* Mollie Molloy—
ACTRESS
All right, I'm convinced, you don't need to list all of her credits.
FANATIC
Married to the playwright Howard Lindsay of the partnership of Lindsay and Crouse.
ACTRESS
Enough! Dorothy Stickney's mother died when Dorothy was a very young girl. And she was buried on Christmas Day. Dorothy promised

her father that day that she'd stay with him for a year and then she was going to New York to be an actress. And so exactly a year later, she left for New York. And arrived on Christmas Day. The only person she knew in the city had been an old family friend who turned out now to have a lot of red wigs, and a lot of different lingerie, and went out at odd hours. But she said Dorothy could stay in her hotel room. So there she was, this young girl, all alone in this hotel room on Christmas night. From her window, she could see the theatres. And she finally got up the courage to go out and mingle with the theatre crowds. She was standing outside the Empire Theatre when the crowd began going in. Blanche Bates was starring in a musical called *The Famous Mrs. Fair.* Dorothy ran to the box office and asked if there were any tickets. The box office man said, "You're a very lucky little girlie; there's one single left." Second balcony. Last row. Against the wall. But she got to see her first show on Christmas night.

Years later, she was performing in *Life with Mother* at that very same Empire Theatre. And it was once again Christmas night. It was long into the run and Dorothy had a terrible case of bronchitis. Her doctor told her not to go on. Howard Lindsay told her not to go on. But she insisted. And the audience that night turned out to be the best the show had ever had. At intermission, the house manager came back to ask her how she was feeling. And she said, "How do you think I'm feeling with an audience like that? Wonderful! But where did they come from? It's Christmas Day. At noon, we had half a house." And he said, "The strangest thing happened, Miss Stickney. At the last minute, we sold a lot of singles."

Charles Nelson Reilly

The box office at the Shubert Theatre.
Photo by Paulo Netto

HENRIETTA DERASMO

I never saw a Broadway show until I became an usher. My first job was at the Roxy, a movie theatre that had reserved seats. We all wore uniforms that looked like sailor suits with hats. I was first hired as an usher at the Lunt-Fontanne Theatre in 1959 during the run of *The Sound of Music.* I came over to the Palace when it reopened as a legit house in 1966 with *Sweet Charity.*

I love the Palace. It has history. We've had a lot of wonderful shows here. Judy Garland in 1968. They were hanging from the chandeliers for that. Bette Midler in 1973. *Man of La Mancha, Applause, George M!, Frankenstein, La Cage aux Folles,* and now *The Will Rogers Follies. Frankenstein* was a great show. I was very surprised when it closed in one night. Usually we can get a pretty good feel for how a show will do. But I sure missed on that one. I thought *The Grand Tour* with Joel Grey was pretty good, too. But it didn't last either. I'll tell you one thing, though; some of those critics fall asleep during the shows they're supposed to be reviewing. We only wake someone up if they're snoring.

My favorite show was *La Cage aux Folles.* I watched that one more than any other, especially the "Pebbles on the Beach" song and "I Am What I Am." They were an especially nice cast. Most don't have anything to do with the ushers, but *La Cage* had a lot of parties and they would always invite us.

Audiences aren't much different from one show to the next. But those that came to *La Cage* were fun. A lot of the audience would come "dressed," if you know what I mean. Some of them you couldn't tell unless they spoke to you when you showed them to their seats. We were never sure who should be going to which bathroom. After a while, I stopped trying to figure it out. One gentleman came to *La Cage* every night. Every night! And every night in a different dress. I always wondered what happened to him after the show closed.

People lose many things at the theatre, including husbands and relatives. I remember one woman whose husband didn't come back after intermission. All she knew was that he went to "a tavern" but wasn't sure which one. Lots of things get left behind. Mostly umbrellas.

One night during *The Will Rogers Follies* a man died sitting with his family in the orchestra. They thought he had just fallen asleep. But he had died. Figured it out at intermission. The porters had to carry him out of the theatre. Lots of people get sick, especially if they've been to dinner, gulped down their meal, and rushed to see the show. According to our house manager, 99 percent of these people had some kind of fish and white wine.

Just last week there was a woman here with lights on her shirt that could be seen from the stage. I had to go to her and ask her to unhook her batteries. She did. Usually people don't give you much trouble. Occasionally we'll have mix-ups about seats, and once in a while it will come to fisticuffs. Once a man came back out into the lobby and started punching the concession seller, saying he had gotten the wrong seat. The only way we could stop the fight was by screaming, "He's not an usher! He's not an usher!"

No one hits one of *my* ushers.

Henrietta Derasmo

Henrietta Derasmo *(opposite page, far left)* and the ushers at the Palace Theatre.

Photos by Frank Franca

JACK GOLDSTEIN

In March of 1982 I joined the hundreds of theatre people who had gathered at the northern end of Shubert Alley to protest the destruction of the Morosco, Helen Hayes, Bijou, Variety, and Gaiety theatres.

The weather was abominable. Steel-gray days with intermittent snows were followed by bitterly cold nights. Yet Broadway's actors and playwrights were mounting around-the-clock play readings from the unsheltered back of a flatbed truck parked, protectively, in front of the Morosco. The performers, all but disguised by their scarfs and hats, huddled on metal chairs arranged in a semicircle around a single microphone. Occasionally, when a Lauren Bacall or an Arthur Miller came forward to read, a stir in the street activated the press crews and a battery of television lights would suddenly hiss on. Most often, however, the cameramen sat motionless on their platforms, hibernating deep in their parkas. We, too, had moments of introspection, and it was during these quiet interludes that I began to develop a special relationship with the Shubert Theatre.

We took comfort in the company of all the theatres that surrounded the Morosco. The heritage they jointly embodied validated everything we did, but the Shubert became a special talisman because, at that moment in theatre history, it was home to *A Chorus Line.* Ultimately the contest over the Morosco was a philosophical one between those who saw Broadway's future in terms of theatre, and those who saw it in terms of real estate development. The powerful interests of the Establishment might be weighing in heavily on the side of the land speculators, but *A Chorus Line,* that quintessential homage to the very people freezing on the back of a flatbed truck, was definitely a vote for theatre. I came to rely on that marquee for encouragement as, day by day, bits of discouraging news about our lawsuits filtered through the crowd.

The demonstrations came to an abrupt end on March 22 with the announcement that the Supreme Court had refused to hear our case. A steam shovel, christened Godzilla by its operator, tore into the side of the Morosco.

The Helen Hayes would come down in June, the month the Landmarks Preservation Commission began hearings on the rest of the Broadway houses. We were strong advocates of Landmarks designation because without it the destruction would continue. More irreplaceable buildings like the Morosco would be lost, and Broadway would become nothing but a museum, a historical curiosity with musical entertainment.

The theatre owners predicted a host of cataclysms if the theatres were designated: Landmarks designation would kill Broadway. Theatre and its millions in related revenue would decamp to New Jersey. Creativity would be stifled by regulations. This last charge was the most divisive of all. It implied that if a theatre interior was to be designated, the Landmarks Commission would prohibit any changes to it, and shows such as *Cats,* with their "environmental" sets, could not be produced. State-of-the-art technical and mechanical systems, either permanent or production related, would also be banned, and therefore Broadway's ability to attract innovative theatre would suffer. To my dismay, the illustration most often cited in support of this specious argument was the light bridge for *A Chorus Line* suspended from the ceiling of my old friend the Shubert.

Fortunately common sense prevailed and most of Broadway's theatres, including the Shubert, were designated Landmarks in 1988. *A Chorus Line* finally closed in April of 1990, and *Crazy for You* has opened. The theatre is being refurbished from top to bottom with the blessing of the Landmarks Commission, and thanks to a group of dedicated theatre people who were willing to brave the elements on the back of a flatbed truck, the Shubert and its fellow theatres will continue to light Broadway for decades to come.

Renovations of the Shubert Theatre *(above,* and *opposite),* home for fifteen years of *A Chorus Line,* prior to the opening of *Crazy for You.*

Photos by T. L. Boston

WOODY SHELP

Woody Shelp at work in his studio at 890 Broadway.

Photo by Marc Bryan-Brown

Photo *(opposite)* by Martha Swope

In April 1975, I was working in Philadelphia, where Bob Fosse's musical *Chicago* was trying out at the Forrest Theatre. After finishing a variety of headache bands, derbies, and boaters for Bob's unique version of 1930s Chicago vaudeville, I came back to New York and went straight to the shop to begin work on what were to be the first nineteen finale top hats for Michael Bennett's *A Chorus Line.*

A Chorus Line's first dress rehearsal was just a week away. I can assure you that one week is not enough time for anyone to make nineteen top hats. But I did the best I could and came to rehearsal at the New York Shakespeare Festival's Newman Theatre with only a few of the hats still incomplete. The women's top hats had been designed to go over wigs. When you make a hat to go over a wig, naturally it is made to be bigger than what the performer would wear without one. As soon as the girls came out onstage for the finale, Michael cut the wigs because he felt it made the dancers lose their identity in what was essentially their curtain call. So that left me with having to refit all the women's hats before the first performance before an audience, just two days away. But at the finale of that now legendary preview, all nineteen members of "the line" tipped nineteen brand-new, sparkling, handmade top hats.

I sensed *A Chorus Line* was a hit when I received an order for eight top hats for the understudies. Soon after the company moved uptown to the Shubert Theatre, in July of 1975, I received another order for an additional set of top hats for the entire company. That day I knew *A Chorus Line* was going to be around for a long time. So I decided to keep track of how many top hats I made. Seventeen years later I have made, by my last count, 706 top hats for the numerous casts on Broadway, three national tours, bus and truck companies, two London productions, and the current international tour. In all that time, I have never tired of making them. I will always love *A Chorus Line.*

AL HIRSCHFELD

Al Hirschfeld at his drawing board, completing a sketch for *Nick & Nora*. Photo by Marcia Lippman

Some years ago I was assigned by the Arts & Leisure section of *The New York Times* to do a drawing of *Away We Go,* a new musical opening in New Haven.

After the out-of-town opening performance, Billy Rose, Mike Todd, and myself met for a prearranged meeting with Lawrence Langner, one of the producers of *Away We Go,* who said, "Look, I arranged this meeting because, frankly, I don't know if this show is good or not. What do you fellas think?" Mike Todd, being Mike Todd, immediately answered, "If it were my show, I'd close it. I wouldn't open in Boston—forget it; take your lumps like a—" Billy Rose interrupted diplomatically by pointing out the impossibility of predicting the staying power of a song on first hearing. "There are a couple of tunes in there that are not all that bad."

It seemed to me after this impromptu conference that *Away We Go* might not open in either Boston or New York. After reporting my doubts to the editor of the Arts & Leisure section, I was reassigned to do a drawing of *The Ziegfeld Follies* opening in Boston starring Milton Berle.

At intermission at the Boston opening of the *Follies* I was collared by a press agent for the Theatre Guild, who pleaded, "Listen, Al, you've gotta stay over and catch our matinee tomarra. They've made some great changes, even the title *Away We Go* to . . . *Oklahoma!* Since I was not very enthusiastic about *Follies,* I decided to stay over and catch the matinee of *Oklahoma!* Returning to New York, I split the space allotted with drawings of both shows.

Weeks go by and there's the normal insanity of opening night in New York. The song that ended the first act, "Oh, What a Beautiful Mornin'," now opens the show, and a young unknown actor, Alfred Drake, comes on-stage, sings the song, and gets a standing ovation in the first two minutes of the show. And I turned to Dolly, my wife, and laughingly said, "Y'know, this thing may turn into a hit."

HIRSCHFELD

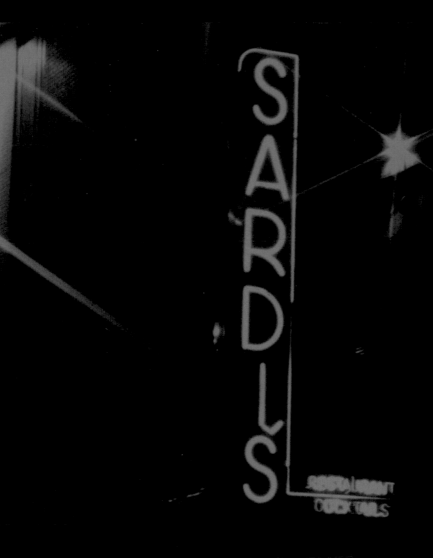

AFTER HOURS

1. engaged in after closing time. 2. operating after a legal or conventional closing time.

Photo by Arturo E. Porazzi

VINCENT SARDI

In the spring of 1991, Sardi's celebrated its seventieth birthday. The two best parties during those years were, first, the night of the Big Blackout in 1965, and second, the day of the kitchen fire.

I was at home on East Ninety-fifth Street when the power blew. Suddenly the lights in my house and on the street began blinking. I called the restaurant. They also were experiencing problems with the lights. I told them if anything should happen to use the emergency candles that had been stored since World War II. I quickly called the garage, which operated with an electric elevator. My car made the last trip down. I drove to the restaurant as lights went out all over town.

When I arrived, candles were lit and there was enough light to illuminate Sardi's with a romantic glow.

People in the dining room took the whole thing as a party. The front doors were left wide open for ventilation, and people wandered in and out from the street. As the street crowds became larger, and in some cases a bit unruly, my car, which was parked in front of the restaurant, became a great asset. It was used as headquarters for patrolmen on duty. They sat in the car with the interior light and air conditioning on. We had no trouble after that.

All the gang from the "Merv Griffin Show" next door arrived and the atmosphere resembled New Year's Eve. Eventually the candles burned out and none were available to buy. I remembered that while visiting Rome in my youth we went to the catacombs. The inhabitants used wicks floating in fat for illumination. We cut strings from new mops to make wicks and floated them in deep dishes of fat. They made excellent emergency lamps. The light was slightly romantic; however, they had an unattractive odor.

Clients who had given up any attempt to reach home asked for shelter. The second-floor dining room was turned into a dorm.

When dawn finally arrived, we ended up with quite a few hangovers, but everyone was well fed and happy.

The second-best party was after the fire in the kitchen. A new employee placed twenty pounds of bacon in the broiler on a plastic tray. This created a flash fire, which swept through the entire first-floor kitchen and part of the second floor. The fire department extinguished the fire safely, but all the wiring was burned out. None of the electrical equipment would work. The main fuse box was inoperable. Once again we were in the dark.

The next day *The New York Times* next door came to the rescue and ran a power line to illuminate the restaurant. The kitchen was inoperable because of the water damage and confusion. But it was lunchtime so I went to the corner of Forty-fifth and Eighth Avenue where a lady sold frankfurters. I asked her how many she had. She said seven hundred plus. I told her I would buy them all if she would set up her wagon and umbrella in the restaurant on the second floor. We gave away frankfurters and ice cream. The bar was open but we charged for drinks. Despite the fire, lunch was served, and before long we were back in business, as we are once again today.

Vincent Sardi

Vincent Sardi and famed friends on the main floor of his restaurant.

Photo by Frank Franca

DON KOEHLER

One of the first things I did when I came to New York was to meet John Effrat. He was doing press for the Actors' Fund, council member of Actors' Equity, stage manager, and the first commissioner of the Broadway Show League. I became his gofer and would deliver the weekly league newsletter to the theatres. This is how I got to know where every stage door on Broadway was in 1958.

I remember my first opening day. There was a race on the field between a horse ridden by a cast member of *Flower Drum Song* and a horse ridden by a cast member of *Destry,* ending in a tie. Paul Newman played for the *Sweet Bird of Youth* team. Bruce Dern played center field in his bare feet and ran down everything hit to him. Sidney Poitier was there from *A Raisin in the Sun* and Michael Tolan from *A Majority of One*. Michael Tolan won MVP that year.

George C. Scott played Shylock in The New York Shakespeare Festival's production of *The Merchant of Venice* in Central Park. It was said that he had a clause in his contract saying that he got out of rehearsal for two hours every Thursday so he could pitch in the Broadway Show League.

My first year as a player/manager was in 1972, for *Two Gentlemen of Verona*. That year, Signa Joy of *Two Gentlemen* became the league's first woman MVP.

In 1973 the Broadway Show League was down to eight teams.

In 1974 I managed and played for my first championship team, "The New York Shakespeare Festival." The league started growing again with teams like "The Turkeys." (You had to be in a flop to be on the team.)

In 1984 I was elected commissioner of the Broadway Show League. At the time, Yul Brynner was starring in *The King and I.* Who else but the King to throw out the first ball. In the years that have followed, many of the stars of Broadway have thrown out a first ball.

Many of the stars still play. When Judd Hirsch was in *I'm Not Rappaport,* he pitched a no-hit game. Jack Lemmon almost gave me heart failure. He was rounding first going to second and ran into the second baseman, who should have gotten out of the way. Jack took a spill but he got up and continued to play. Kathleen Turner turned a few heads in her uniform, and Tyne Daly sat in the stands under a lace parasol.

Many teams have combined for one reason or another, and as a result some interesting teams are created: Tru Lovage (*Tru* and *Lettice & Lovage*); I'm Not Intelligent (*I'm Not Rappaport* and *The Search for Signs of Intelligent Life in the Universe*); Nunsticks (*Nunsense* and *The Fantasticks*); and Song of Plaid and Teller (*Song of Singapore, Forever Plaid,* and *Penn & Teller*).

But the thing the players most fear is the possibility of injuries. Norm Nixon, husband of Debbie Allen and pro basketball star, was shagging flys in the outfield and twisted his knee. Just bending over one day, John Rubinstein did something to his back and was out of his show *Children of a Lesser God* for a considerable time. Thank God John's producer was Manny Azenberg, 1988 MVP and still playing. In the 1989 championship game, Tom Wiggins of Equity and soap opera star of "As the World Turns" broke his leg sliding into second base in the eighth inning. Fortunately the following week he was written into the soap with a broken leg.

The year 1992 is the thirty-seventh consecutive season of the league. *Play ball!*

Don Koehler

Topol, Tyne Daly, Jonathan Pryce, Keith Carradine, Tom Wopat, and friends kick off the 1991 season of the Broadway Show League.

Photo *(top)* by Judie Burstein

Photo *(bottom)* by Seth Gurvitz

CRAIG DAWSON

Places, please. House to half . . . *go!* I am your host. The star of my own Broadway show for some fifteen years now. The unofficial mayor of Forty-fifth Street. I have all the stories, all the accumulated knowledge, and of course, all the "dish."

I was there when *Working* didn't and when *Dreamgirls* did. I saw *A Chorus Line* go into history and wept for the loss of Michael Bennett. Dorothy Loudon's losing the Tony Award and Carole Shelley's winning it, Mary Tyler Moore with a bug in her salad (don't ask), or Tyne Daly's standing ovation are all great stories. One of my most memorable, though, involved the first time Elizabeth Taylor arrived. Always a great fan of Miss Taylor, I never expected to meet her. Who would?

The encounter was simple. Elizabeth was in New York rehearsing for *The Little Foxes.* As we were desperately trying to get everyone out for the theatre at seven-forty P.M. . . . (cue Elizabeth) . . .

My cohost, David Wood, had just sent me to the back of the room with a new party. As I returned to the front desk, David calmly said, "Look who's on table thirteen." I turned around and I'm sure I audibly gasped. In the short time I was away from the door, Elizabeth and her production stage manager Patrick Horgan had entered, David had thrown our friend Danny Kreitzberg off table thirteen, cleared and reset the table, and seated Elizabeth. David never moved so fast.

Well. There she was. Stunning in a simple black dress . . . *there she was.* Well, I could die happy. The funny thing was how the room simply "stopped." No one made any attempt to approach her, as the tourists can sometimes do; no one even spoke. The room had gone silent; I think because we had never seen Elizabeth onstage, as we had Liza or Shirley. There was something unreal about her. As if the movies had come to life. And here she was, and she was very real. My bartender came over and suggested that we play the jukebox, as it was conspicuously quiet. I did, and slowly the room came back to reality. It was very exciting and only the first of several visits we had with Elizabeth, who loved the chili. She was wonderful and remains so today. I can't wait for Katharine Hepburn.

Many celebrities and newcomers alike have passed through, leaving behind them wonderful memories. Even the tourists are usually good for a laugh when they query, "You're great . . . what show are you in?" as you're delivering their desserts. They just don't get it.

I love it all. I know that someone gets it when I am told by Judy Blazer, when she was taking over in *Me and My Girl,* that I am an institution. She said to me, "You are wonderful. You make everyone feel like a star. And you remember us all."

I do remember it all. Call it Charlie's or Sam's. I'm there. Bring on another season, *I got a show to do.*

Craig Dawson

Craig Dawson *(opposite)* and the staff at Sam's.
Photo *(bottom)* by William Gibson
All other photos by Frank Franca

JOE ALLEN AND GENE SHALIT

Joe Allen's restaurant is on Forty-sixth Street between Eighth and Ninth avenues, a subsidewalk establishment of brick walls and theatre posters. It has been a favorite haunt of theatrical people for a quarter of a century (which sounds more impressive than twenty-six years). It was here that Joe Allen, proprietor, talked with a customer, Gene Shalit of NBC.

GS: How come the theatre posters on the wall are all flops and failures?
JA: It started with *Kelly* in the mid-1960s, a monumental flop that cost something over half a million dollars. Originally, to make it to the wall, a show had to cost over half a million and run less than a week. With inflation, the numbers no longer matter; it's how much attention a show gets.

GS: How do your customers feel about being on the wall?
JA: When a poster goes up, someone with the show will initially be miffed if not terribly offended. But with the passage of time I see them coming in with friends and pointing to it with glee. It's a kind of heroic battle scar. Our latest addition is *Nick & Nora.* The cast came in for a closing-night party and presented us with the poster, which is being framed as we speak.

GS: Have theatre people come here from the start?
JA: We opened in May 1965, and the first show whose cast came in with some regularity was *Half a Sixpence.* Because of the way theatre people are, the restaurant had almost instant tradition. In 1970, *Applause* with Lauren Bacall recreated this restaurant on the stage for a big production number. All the people in the number were customers, so after a while they didn't know if they were onstage or really here.

GS: Most of your waiters and waitresses have acting ambitions. How do they get along with customers who've made it?

JA: The illustrious Sylvia Miles was in here one night and was being waited on by a waiter named Bobby Freeman, who happens to be black. She ordered a cup of coffee, and he said, "How would you like your coffee?" She looked up at him and said, "I like my coffee like my men." To which Bobby replied, "We don't have any gay coffee."

GS: Your bar has no opening, so the bartender can't slip away unseen for a break. He has to climb over the top of the bar, which is quite a production.

JA: Ralph Waite was tending bar one night when he got a phone call from his agent, and he took off his apron and jumped over the bar and brushed his hands and said, "That's it." He had just gotten "The Waltons." Never to be seen again. [*Laughs*] Not a lot of notice.

GS: Since actors and actresses are out of work more often than they're *in* work, have you ever "carried" them?

JA: Both voluntarily and involuntarily. But in fact their reputation as credit risks is not true. For the most part they're at least as creditworthy as the rest of the population and perhaps a little more so. Some will say, "Look, I've run up this bill and I don't have a job, but as soon as I do, I'll pay it," and I say, "That's fine." It goes with the gig. If you have to have a roomful of *any*thing, better a roomful of actors than a roomful of accountants. At least they're amusing.

CURTAIN

Joe Allen Gene Shalit

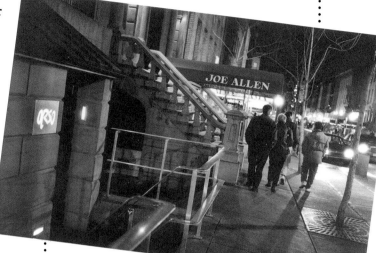

Inside *(opposite)* and outside Joe Allen restaurant on West Forty-sixth Street—Broadway's "Restaurant Row."

Photo *(opposite)* by William Gibson

Photo *(above)* by Frank Franca

YACEK SAMOTUS

JAY BRADY

YACEK SAMOTUS

YACEK SAMOTUS

JAY BRADY

The Grand Auction at the Broadway Flea Market in Shubert Alley *(top, left)*; the company of *Les Misérables* pull the winners of their grand raffle backstage at the Imperial Theatre *(top, right)*; Daisy Eagan outside *The Secret Garden* boutique on West Forty-fourth Street *(center)*; the Stage Managers Association's table at the Broadway Flea Market *(bottom, left)*; the company of the Third Annual Gypsy of the Year Competition in the alley behind the St. James Theatre *(bottom, right)*. Colleen Dewhurst *(opposite)* signing and selling her autograph at the Broadway Flea Market.

EPILOGUE

The essays and photographs in this book illustrate but a small portion of the artistry and industry that make up Broadway. We are a diverse and highly competitive lot working against formidable odds in a hand-crafted but high-tech, multimillion-dollar business. Other than a few year-end award shows, we seldom come together publicly in a united response to anything. But for a generation of theatrical professionals, there has been one compelling exception: AIDS.

Without a doubt, the American entertainment industry's response to AIDS has been led by the theatre community. Long before it was professionally "safe" to do so, and years before many dared even to wear a red ribbon, stars such as Leonard Bernstein, Brad Davis, Colleen Dewhurst, Harvey Fierstein, Whoopi Goldberg, Bill Hoffman, Larry Kramer, Patti LuPone, Bette Midler, Joe Papp, Chita Rivera, Susan Sarandon, Tommy Tune, and a handful of others declared to a skeptical public that AIDS affects us all—men and women, people of all ages, races and religions, lesbian, gay, and straight. Leadership, not denial, is the appropriate political response; compassion, they said, not judgment, the responsible course of action.

Few listened, but soon among our own, the heart and muscle of the industry—actors, singers and dancers, stage managers and technicians, writers, publicists, producers, designers, ushers, musicians, and others—joined these first courageous few in a groundswell of fund-raising and political activity that brought AIDS out of the shadows and before a national audience. Millions of dollars were raised, thousands of PWA's (people with AIDS) assisted, and a breach was made in the wall of fear that paralyzes so many others.

JOSEPH MARZULLO

Still we face a fundamental and bigoted silence from many in positions of leadership and power. Until our federal government is forced to make AIDS a national priority, our only hope, our salvation, is in individual acts of kindness and courage. Just a few of the thousands of these acts that have come from the American theatre community are represented by the photographs on these four pages. But it's this kind of commitment that makes it possible for us to bring you the other 284.

Recently, on a crisp Saturday morning, West Forty-ninth Street between Broadway and Eighth Avenue was filled with activity hours before the weekly matinee crowd was due to arrive. At the Eugene O'Neill Theatre half a dozen workmen scampered up and down scaffolding, hoisting into place the bright red, blue, and yellow neon marquee for

Cameron Mackintosh's *Five Guys Named Moe.* Across the street, a much larger, more somber group of theatrical professionals gathered on the sidewalk of St. Malachy's ("the actors' chapel"), oblivious, for the moment, to the familiar opening-night preparations across the street. Another all-too-familiar scene was about to be played. AIDS had taken one more, and yet another memorial service was set to begin. Since then too many others have followed.

This needless suffering and dying must end. We urge you, as you read this book, to remember *why* we present it. We implore you to do whatever you can to bring about a meaningful response to this plague. Join us, open your heart, extend a hand, write a check, vote, volunteer, and fight back. But, above all, *do not be silent.*

What we do together makes a difference. Imagine, demand, and work for a cure.

Tom Viola Rodger McFarlane

JAY BRADY

JAY BRADY

LINDA COLER

WILLIAM GIBSON

The company of *Once on This Island* at the Third Annual Gypsy of the Year Competition *(top, left);* B. D. Wong at the benefit reading of Truman Capote's "A Christmas Memory" *(bottom, left);* company members of *Miss Saigon* and *The Secret Garden,* Gypsy of the Year award winners *(middle);* Anne Runolfsson and "horse head" at the Gypsy of the Year Competition *(top, right);* Jack Kenny and the company of *Fiddler on the Roof* autographing posters *(bottom, right).*

Glenn Close, Gwen Verdon, and the company of the Sixth Annual Easter Bonnet Competition *(top, left* and *right)*; Alix Korey in "Help Is on the Way" at the Late-Night Cabaret Series at Steve McGraw's *(bottom, left)*; *The Secret Garden*'s boutique outside the St. James Theatre; *Cats*'s John Leggio at the Winter Garden Theatre.

BIOGRAPHIES OF CONTRIBUTORS

JANE ALEXANDER first received acclaim in *The Great White Hope,* for which she won a Tony Award. She was also nominated for her performances in *6 Rooms Riv Vu, Find Your Way Home,* and *First Monday in October.* For her performance in the film of *The Great White Hope* she was nominated for an Academy Award, as well as for *All the President's Men, Kramer vs. Kramer,* and *Testament.* She won an Emmy Award for her work in "Playing for Time," and also for television she played Eleanor Roosevelt in the much-heralded "Franklin and Eleanor" and Georgia O'Keeffe in "Portrait of a Marriage." Recent New York appearances include *Shadowlands* and the Roundabout Theatre's revival of *The Visit.* She is married to director Edwin Sherin.

JOE ALLEN is owner of the restaurants here and abroad that bear his name and are favorites with theatre personalities.

LUCIE ARNAZ made her Broadway debut in the musical *They're Playing Our Song.* She has gone on to appear in productions of *Cabaret, Vanities, Annie Get Your Gun,* the national tour of *Seesaw,* and Broadway's *Lost in Yonkers.* She is married to actor Laurence Luckinbill.

EILEEN ATKINS most recently appeared in New York in her solo performance as Virginia Woolf in *A Room of One's Own.* Previously she appeared at Manhattan Theatre Club in *Prin.* She made her New York debut in *The Killing of Sister George* in a role she originated in her native Great Britain, and she later played here as Elizabeth I in *Vivat! Vivat Regina!* Some of her other roles include *Exit the King, Heartbreak House, Hedda Gabler,* and *Mountain Language.* She can be seen in the films *Equus, Oliver Twist,* and *The Dresser.* Among her many television appearances, she played with Alec Guinness in "Smiley's People," and with her longtime friend Jean Marsh she created the series "Upstairs, Downstairs."

EMANUEL AZENBERG has produced all of Neil Simon's plays since *The Sunshine Boys.* Among them are *The Good Doctor, Chapter Two, California Suite, Brighton Beach Memoirs, Biloxi Blues, Broadway Bound,* and *Lost in Yonkers.* His other presentations include *The Lion in Winter, Scapino, Ain't Misbehavin', Whose Life Is It Anyway?, Children of a Lesser God, Master Harold . . . and the Boys, Sunday in the Park with George,* and *The Real Thing.* His work has earned him numerous Tony, Drama Desk, New York Drama Critics Circle, and Outer Critics Circle awards.

KATHY BATES began her career at The Actors' Theatre of Louisville, where one of her roles was in the original production of Marsha Norman's *'night, Mother.* She repeated her performance in the Broadway presentation. Earlier she made her New York debut in *Vanities* and also played in the off-Broadway success *Frankie and Johnny in the Clair de Lune.* She has gone on to win an Academy Award for her work in *Misery.*

HINTON BATTLE has won Tony Awards for his work in *Sophisticated Ladies, The Tap Dance Kid,* and *Miss Saigon.* He debuted on Broadway at sixteen, creating the role of the Scarecrow in *The Wiz.* Other Broadway credits include *Dreamgirls* and *Dancin'.* He played *Ain't Misbehavin'* in Las Vegas and *Stardust* at the Kennedy Center. He has choreographed for several pop stars, created music videos, hosted his own video dance show, and performed in concert for sold-out audiences in Japan.

ROBERT BILLIG is a musical supervisor for *Miss Saigon.* He was musical director of the original Broadway production of *Les Misérables* and serves as production musical supervisor for all North American companies of that show. He was also musical supervisor and vocal arranger for all first-class productions of *The Best Little Whorehouse in Texas* and *Little Shop of Horrors* in the U.S. On Broadway he conducted *Song & Dance* with Bernadette Peters, *Singin' in the Rain, The Magic Show,* and Tommy Tune's *My One and Only.* He conducted national tours of *No, No, Nanette, Seesaw,* and *Barnum,* and created vocal arrangements for the film of *Little Shop of Horrors.*

KEN BILLINGTON has designed lighting on and off Broadway, in regional theatres, for tours and major opera companies. His Broadway credits include *On the Twentieth Century, Working, Sweeney Todd, Foxfire, Shirley MacLaine on Broadway,* and *End of the World.* He has received numerous citations and awards for his designs.

KELLY BISHOP helped create *A Chorus Line* in her role as the original Sheila. She received a Tony Award for her performance. She has appeared in the films *An Unmarried Woman* and *Dirty Dancing,* as well as on television. Recently she performed in the renowned Lincoln Center production of *Six Degrees of Separation.*

BARRY BROWN is a producer. His first show, the premiere of *Gypsy* in London, starred Angela Lansbury. The production then toured the United States before opening at Broadway's Winter Garden Theatre. With his late partner, Fritz Holt, he went on to present the Tony Award–winning revival of *The Royal Family,* Bette Midler in *Clams on the Half Shell Revue,* Franco Zeffirelli's *Saturday Sunday Monday,* and *La Cage aux Folles.* He produced the star-studded *The Best of the Best* at the Metropolitan Opera House, which was the first major AIDS benefit in the United States, and has since presented an average of three such benefits internationally per year, raising more than $10 million for research and patient care.

ROSCOE LEE BROWNE was an internationally acclaimed track-and-field star before becoming an actor. When his running career ended after an injury, he spent ten years working as a national sales representative, speaking chiefly on the after-dinner circuit. The day he decided to become an actor he auditioned for and was cast in *Julius Caesar,* produced by a then unknown Joseph Papp. He has not stopped acting since, having appeared in theatre, films, and on television in musicals, comedies, Shakespeare, Brecht, Genet, and O'Neill. He has recently performed in August Wilson's *Two Trains Running,* and is also an accomplished poet and short-story writer.

BETTY BUCKLEY made her Broadway debut as Martha Jefferson in *1776*. She went on to play in *Pippin, The Mystery of Edwin Drood,* and *Song and Dance*. She originated the role of Grizabella in the New York production of *Cats,* for which she won a Tony Award. She can be seen in the films *Carrie* and *Tender Mercies* and in several television films. On television she also starred in the long-running series, "Eight Is Enough."

ELLEN BURSTYN received a Tony Award for *Same Time, Next Year* and an Academy Award for *Alice Doesn't Live Here Anymore* in the same season. She appeared in the film version of *Same Time, Next Year* as well as *The Last Picture Show, The Exorcist,* and *Resurrection,* all of which earned her Academy Award nominations. She recently played in *Shirley Valentine* on Broadway and on national tour. Upon Lee Strasberg's death, she became co-artistic director of the Actors' Studio in New York. She became the first woman president of Actors' Equity Association in 1982.

CHARLES BUSCH most recently wrote and starred in *Red Scare on Sunset*. He is a co-founder of Theatre-in-Limbo, for which he also wrote and acted in *Vampire Lesbians of Sodom, Psycho Beach Party, Times Square Angel,* and *The Lady in Question*. He has written an adaptation of Truman Capote's book for the musical *House of Flowers* for Patti LaBelle and a new libretto for the musical *Ankles Aweigh,* produced by the Goodspeed Opera House.

ZOE CALDWELL has worked with some of the great talents in the theatre—Dame Judith Anderson, Charles Laughton, Dame Edith Evans, Paul Robeson, Sir Tyrone Guthrie, and Harold Clurman among them. A native Australian, she received the Order of the British Empire from Queen Elizabeth II. She won Tony Awards for her performances in *Slapstick Tragedy, The Prime of Miss Jean Brodie,* and *Medea*. Off-Broadway she played in *Colette*. On television her portrayals have included Sarah Bernhardt, Medea, Carlotta Monterey, and Madame Arkadina in *The Seagull*. As well as having performed throughout the English-speaking world, she has directed extensively. Among her directing credits are James Earl Jones and Christopher Plummer in *Othello,* Colleen Dewhurst in *An Almost Perfect Person,* and recently Broadway's *Park Your Car in Harvard Yard* with Judith Ivey and Jason Robards. She is married to producer Robert Whitehead.

CAROL CHANNING made Broadway history as Dolly Levi in *Hello, Dolly!,* winning a Tony Award along the way. She made her first sensation on Broadway playing Lorelei Lee in *Gentlemen Prefer Blondes*—a role she reprised in *Lorelei*. Other stage appearances have been in *Wonderful Town, Pygmalion, The Vamp, Jerry's Girls,* and *Legends,* opposite Mary Martin. She has appeared often on television and in film, winning an Oscar nomination for *Thoroughly Modern Millie*.

BETTY COMDEN & ADOLPH GREEN have collaborated since the 1940s on musical lyrics and books. They won Tony Awards for their books for *Applause* and *On the Twentieth Century* and were awarded as lyricists for *Wonderful Town, Hallelujah, Baby!,* and *The Will Rogers Follies*. Their other shows include *On the Town* and *Bells Are Ringing*. They wrote screenplays and lyrics at MGM during the "golden age" of movie musicals, including such classics as *Singin' in the Rain* and *The Band Wagon*. They have been nominated for several Academy Awards for their movie work.

BARBARA COOK originated roles in the musicals *Flahooley, Plain and Fancy, Candide, The Music Man, She Loves Me,* and *The Grass Harp*. She was awarded a Tony for her performance in *The Music Man*. She also starred in much-acclaimed revivals of *Oklahoma, Carousel, Show Boat,* and *The King and I*. After giving up her work as an actress, she embarked on a concert/recording career. She can be heard on several new recordings of musicals including *"Follies" in Concert*. Her solo albums range from studio to live concert recordings.

MICHAEL CRAWFORD won a Tony Award as the Phantom in Andrew Lloyd Webber's *The Phantom of the Opera,* a role he originated in London earning an Olivier Award—England's equivalent to the Tony. He also won an Olivier for his performance in *Barnum* and in London played in *Same Time, Next Year, Billy, Flowers for Algernon,* and *No Sex Please, We're British*. He can be seen in the films *Hello, Dolly!, A Funny Thing Happened on the Way to the Forum, The Knack, How I Won the War, Hello and Goodbye,* and *Alice in Wonderland*. He has recorded two albums of songs and recently toured the United States in the concert *The Music of Andrew Lloyd Webber*.

JOHN CULLUM received Tony Awards for his performances in *Shenandoah* and *On the Twentieth Century*. He has also appeared on Broadway in *On a Clear Day You Can See Forever, 1776, Vivat! Vivat Regina!, Deathtrap, Private Lives,* and *Doubles*. He has also worked in regional theatre, films, and television.

CRAIG DAWSON was an actor before becoming maître d' at Charlie's Restaurant and now, at the same address, Sam's Restaurant. He has been with the two establishments for fifteen years. Sam's has become one of the more popular meeting places in the theatre district known for its informal, fun atmosphere.

HENRIETTA DERASMO has been an usher in Broadway theatres for over thirty years and is the chief usher at the Palace Theatre.

CHRISTOPHER DURANG is a playwright and director who trained at the Yale School of Drama. His plays have included *The Marriage of Bette and Boo, Sister Mary Ignatius Explains It All for You,* and *The Actor's Nightmare*. His cabaret work includes "Das *Luisitania* Songspiel," which he performed with Sigourney Weaver.

ALAN EISENBERG has been executive secretary of Actors' Equity Association since October 1981. He is a graduate of the University of Michigan and New York University School of Law. He practiced labor law for many years before joining Equity. He has been a visiting professor at the Yale School of Drama since 1982. He lives in New York with his wife and two daughters.

HARVEY FIERSTEIN is a playwright and actor who received Tony Awards for best play and director for *Torch Song Trilogy*. He went on to re-create his role in the film version of the play. He wrote the books for the Broadway musicals *La Cage aux Folles* and *Legs Diamond*.

WILLIAM FINN has written and composed *March of the Falsettos* and *Falsettoland,* which have recently been combined into one evening and brought to Broadway under the title *Falsettos,* which won him Tonys for both original score and book. He has also written and composed *In Trousers* and provided lyrics for *Tango Apa-*

sionado and *The Winter's Tale.* His musical *Romance in Hard Times* was presented at the New York Shakespeare Festival.

VICTOR GARBER began his career in his native Canada. He made his New York debut in a highly praised performance as Oswald in *Ghosts.* His work has included everything from Shakespeare to musical comedy. Some productions he has appeared in on Broadway and in regional theatre are *Deathtrap, Little Me, As You Like It, Tartuffe, Sweeney Todd, They're Playing Our Song, The Miser, Noises Off, Assassins,* and *Two Shakespearean Actors.*

LARRY GELBART is a writer and producer. His television series "M*A*S*H" has become a classic of the medium. For the theatre he wrote the books for Broadway's *A Funny Thing Happened on the Way to the Forum* and *City of Angels* and the play *Mastergate.* His screenplays include *Oh, God* and an Oscar-winning script for *Tootsie.*

PAUL GEMIGNANI has most recently served as musical director for Broadway's *Crazy for You.* Some of the more than twenty Broadway shows he has been musical director of include *A Little Night Music, Follies, Pacific Overtures, Sweeney Todd, Evita, Dreamgirls, Merrily We Roll Along, Jerome Robbins' Broadway, Sunday in the Park with George,* and *Into the Woods.* Original-cast recordings he has conducted include *Assassins, "Follies" in Concert, Man of La Mancha* with Placido Domingo, and *Kismet* with Samuel Ramey.

JOHN GIELGUD was born into a theatrical family that included his aunt Ellen Terry. His career has spanned seven decades. He has acted in all forms of drama from Oscar Wilde and Chekhov to Pinter and David Storey. He is best remembered for his work in Shakespeare and is considered the definitive Hamlet of his generation. He toured widely with his *Ages of Man,* a performance based on Shakespeare's writings, the recording of which is a standard for vocal interpretation of the playwright's verse. As a director he presented the classic revival of Wilde's *The Importance of Being Earnest,* in which he starred opposite Dame Edith Evans, and the controversial, modern-dress *Hamlet* with Richard Burton on Broadway. He has worked extensively in film and television and has won major acting awards. He was knighted for his lifelong commitment to the theatre.

ALYCE GILBERT was wardrobe supervisor for *A Chorus Line* from its premiere at The Public Theatre to the end of its run at Broadway's Shubert Theatre. Her other Broadway credits include *Ballroom, Dreamgirls, Chess, Welcome to the Club, Grand Hotel,* and *The Will Rogers Follies.* Off-Broadway she worked on many productions for The New York Shakespeare Festival and at Theatre de Lys, The New Theatre, and East Side Playhouse.

FRANK D. GILROY won both a Tony Award and a Pulitzer Prize for his play *The Subject Was Roses,* which he also adapted for film. He wrote the novel and screenplay for *Desperate Characters.* In the early days of T.V. he scripted dramas for all of the major live shows including "Omnibus," "Playhouse 90," "U.S. Steel Hour," and "Kraft Theatre." He also originated the T.V. series "Burke's Law." Some of his other plays are *That Summer—That Fall, The Only Game in Town,* and *Last Licks.*

JOANNA GLEASON won a Tony for her work as the baker's wife in *Into the Woods.* She made her debut in *I Love My Wife* and went on to receive much praise for her performance in *A Day in the Death of Joe Egg.* She has also acted in *It's Only a Play, Social Security, The Real Thing,* and *Nick & Nora.*

JACK GOLDSTEIN is a founding board member of Save the Theatres and has served as its executive director since its inception. He was instrumental in the campaign to have Broadway theatres landmarked after the demolition of the Morosco, Helen Hayes, and two other theatres. Previously he served five years on the President's Advisory Council on Historic Preservation and currently works as a consultant specializing in public policy and the arts.

JOEL GREY created the role of the MC in *Cabaret,* winning a Tony Award, and an Oscar for the film version. He returned to the role when it was revived on tour and on Broadway. He also starred in the Broadway musicals *George M!, Good Time Charlie,* and *The Grand Tour.* He has appeared in many films and on T.V.

JONATHAN HADARY has appeared on Broadway as Herbie in *Gypsy* opposite Tyne Daly, in *As Is, Torch Song Trilogy,* and *Gemini.* At Playwrights Horizons he played in Stephen Sondheim's *Assassins* and can be heard on the original-cast recording. His other off-Broadway credits include *Wenceslas Square, Tomfoolery, Scrambled Feet, El Grande de Coca-Cola,* and *Lips Together, Teeth Apart.* He re-created his role in *As Is* for cable T.V. and has made appearances in that medium in "Law and Order," "Miami Vice," "Love, Sidney," and "Another World." For the past three years he has hosted the Broadway Cares/Equity Fights AIDS *Gypsy of the Year* show at the St. James Theatre.

UTA HAGEN made her professional debut at age eighteen as Ophelia in Eva LeGallienne's production of *Hamlet.* In that same year she appeared on Broadway as Nina in *The Seagull* with the Lunts. With her then-husband Jose Ferrer she played opposite Paul Muni in *Key Largo,* in *Vicki, Angel Street,* and as Desdemona in Paul Robeson's production of *Othello.* She won her first Tony in Clifford Odets's *The Country Girl.* She played opposite Anthony Quinn as Blanche DuBois in the first national tour of *A Streetcar Named Desire* and later succeeded Jessica Tandy in the Broadway run. She created the role of Martha in *Who's Afraid of Virginia Woolf?,* winning a second Tony Award. For forty-five years she has been on the faculty of the Herbert Berghof Studio, where she has trained many of the theatre's outstanding actors. She later married Mr. Berghof and appeared with him many times on the stage. The recipient of three honorary doctorates, she has also been inducted into the Theatre Hall of Fame. Among her several books are *Respect for Acting* and *The Challenge of the Actor.*

SHELDON HARNICK has written lyrics to his partner Jerry Bock's scores for some of the most popular Broadway musicals. They include *Fiorello!, She Loves Me, Fiddler on the Roof,* and *The Rothschilds.* He won Tony Awards for both *Fiorello!*—which also won him a Pulitzer Prize—and *Fiddler on the Roof.* Previously he made contributions to several renowned revues such as *Two's Company, New Faces of 1952,* and *John Murray Anderson's Almanac.*

JULIE HARRIS emerged as one of the foremost actresses in the American theatre with her performance as Frankie Adams in *The Member of the Wedding,* a role she re-created on film. She won Tony Awards for her performances in *I*

Am a Camera, The Lark, Forty Carats, The Last of Mrs. Lincoln, and *The Belle of Amherst*—a record number of awards for a dramatic actress. She has toured throughout the United States with her solo performances playing such historical figures as Emily Dickinson, Charlotte Brontë, and recently Isak Dinesen in *Lucifer's Child.* She has played in many films, including *East of Eden* opposite James Dean. On television she was seen for several seasons on "Knots Landing." She recently starred in the national tour of *Lettice & Lovage.*

HELEN HAYES is considered to be the First Lady of the American Theatre. She began her career as a child and went on to become the most popular actress of her day in such plays as *What Every Woman Knows, Coquette, Mary of Scotland, Victoria Regina, Harriet,* and *Mrs. McThing.* She was the recipient of the first Tony Award presented to an actress, for her work in *Happy Birthday,* and she won a second for *Time Remembered.* She was also one of the first actresses to win an Academy Award, with her performance in *The Sin of Madelon Claudet.* In film she also starred opposite Gary Cooper in *A Farewell to Arms.* Upon her retirement from the stage she returned to films and scored a great success in *Airport,* winning another Oscar almost fifty years after her first. Her husband was the late playwright Charles MacArthur. She has written several memoirs, the most recent being *My Life in Three Acts.* She has been inducted into the Theatre Hall of Fame.

GREGORY HINES recently won a Tony Award for his performance in *Jelly's Last Jam.* His other Broadway appearances have been in *Sophisticated Ladies, Eubie,* and *Comin' Uptown,* all of which earned him Tony nominations. He began his career as a tap dancer when not even three years old, as one of the Hines Kids. That duo became the Hines Brothers, and when they were later joined by their father they were renowned as Hines, Hines, and Dad. His many films include *White Nights, The Cotton Club, A Rage in Harlem, Tap, Off Limits,* and *Running Scared.* His PBS television special, "Gregory Hines: Tapdance in America," was rewarded with an Emmy Award.

AL HIRSCHFELD studied art in Paris, London, and New York. His caricatures of Broadway shows and their stars began appearing in *The New York Times* over forty years ago and have become a visual metaphor of the New York stage. His work has been collected in several volumes of books, and he is the recipient of many honors, including Doctor of Fine Arts from the University of Hartford.

WILLIAM M. HOFFMAN is the author of *As Is,* one of the first plays to tackle the subject of AIDS. His other plays include *The Children's Crusade, Gulliver's Travels,* and *A Book of Etiquette. The Ghosts of Versailles,* an opera for which he wrote the libretto for John Corigliano's score, was commissioned by and premiered at The Metropolitan Opera in New York for its 100th anniversary and was taped for television.

STUART HOWARD is a casting director whose Broadway credits include *Cat on a Hot Tin Roof, Fiddler on the Roof, La Cage aux Folles, Gypsy,* and *Nick & Nora.* National tours he has cast are *Bye Bye, Birdie* starring Tommy Tune, *The King and I* with Rudolf Nureyev, and *Six Degrees of Separation.* He has also cast for regional theatre, television, film, and the London production of *Carmen Jones* directed by Simon Callow at the Old Vic.

TINA HOWE is a playwright whose *Coastal Disturbances* was nominated for a Tony. Her other works include *The Art of Dining, Museum,* and *Painting Churches.*

DAVID HENRY HWANG wrote *M Butterfly,* which played on Broadway, national tour, and in Los Angeles. It won the Tony Award for best play. His works, including *F.O.B.,* have been read and seen at the Eugene O'Neill Theatre Center's National Playwrights Conference, the New York Shakespeare Festival, Second Stage, and the Actors' Theatre of Louisville.

BILL IRWIN is an actor, dancer, clown, and writer. He trained at the Ringling Brothers Barnum and Bailey Clown College and with Herbert Blau. He appeared on Broadway in *Largely/New York* and was recently seen with Liza Minnelli in the film *Stepping Out.* He is the recipient of Guggenheim and MacArthur Foundation fellowships.

DANA IVEY was nominated for two Tonys in the same year for *Sunday in the Park with George* and *Heartbreak House.* She has appeared on Broadway and off, in regional theatre, in films, and on T.V. She created the role of Daisy in *Driving Miss Daisy* off-Broadway. She has played in *Quartermaine's Terms, Beggars in the House of Plenty,* and The Roundabout Theatre's revival of *The Subject Was Roses.* She was Gertrude to Kevin Kline's Hamlet at the New York Shakespeare Festival and on T.V.

JUDITH IVEY won Tony Awards for her performances in *Steaming* and *Hurlyburly.* Other theatre work includes roles in *Piaf, Mourning Becomes Electra, Design for Living, Whose Life Is It Anyway?, Much Ado About Nothing,* and recently in Zoe Caldwell's staging of *Park Your Car in Harvard Yard* opposite Jason Robards. She can be seen in the films *The Woman in Red, Compromising Positions, Brighton Beach Memoirs,* and *Miles from Home.*

BERNARD B. JACOBS is president of the Shubert Organization in charge of the firm's wide range of theatre productions, presentations, and operations. He is also president of The Shubert Foundation, Inc., which is dedicated to the advancement of performing arts in America as well as many charitable causes. His other appointments include serving as a vice-president of The League of American Theatres and Producers, visiting professor at the Yale School of Drama, adjunct professor of theatre at Columbia School of the Arts, and as a trustee of the Actors' Fund of America. A graduate of New York University and Columbia School of Law, he practiced law for many years before turning all of his energies to the Shubert Organization.

JAMES EARL JONES triumphed on Broadway in *The Great White Hope,* winning a Tony Award and later repeating his performance in the film version. He went on to play in *Othello* with Christopher Plummer, *Bloodknot, King Lear, Of Mice and Men, Master Harold . . . and the Boys,* and August Wilson's *Fences,* winning a second Tony. He has made many films, including *Claudine, The Empire Strikes Back, Matewan,* and *Gardens of Stone.* His television appearances are numerous, and he was awarded an Emmy for his work in "Gabriel's Fire."

JUDY KAYE made her Broadway debut as Rizzo in *Grease.* She went on to play in *On the Twentieth Century* and *The Phantom of the Opera,* for which she received a Tony Award. She has worked extensively in regional theatre and has frequently appeared in concert and revues.

HOWARD KISSEL is the theatre critic of the New York *Daily News.*

DON KOEHLER is commissioner of the Broadway Show League, which organizes softball games played between teams made up from the various Broadway companies. He also works the stage door at the Booth Theatre.

ROCCO LANDESMAN is president of Jujamcyn Theatres, producers of *The Secret Garden, M Butterfly, Gypsy, City of Angels, Grand Hotel,* and *The Grapes of Wrath.* Prior to joining Jujamcyn, he co-produced the Broadway musicals *Big River* and *Into the Woods.* He has taught dramatic literature and criticism at the Yale School of Drama and written articles for several publications. He is married to set designer and producer Heidi Landesman.

NATHAN LANE has most recently been seen in New York in the Broadway revival of *Guys and Dolls* and opposite George C. Scott in *On Borrowed Time.* Other stage appearances include *Lips Together, Teeth Apart, Some Americans Abroad, Bad Habits, Broadway Bound, Present Laughter, Merlin,* and *The Wind in the Willows.* He has acted in the films *Frankie and Johnny, He Said, She Said, Ironweed,* and *Joe Versus the Volcano.*

ANGELA LANSBURY trained for the theatre in her native England and New York City before going to Hollywood while still a teenager. At MGM Studios she was featured in a host of films including *Gaslight, National Velvet, The Picture of Dorian Gray, The Harvey Girls,* and *State of the Union.* She made her debut in musical theatre in Stephen Sondheim's *Anyone Can Whistle* and from there became the toast of Broadway in *Mame,* earning her first Tony. She went on to win Tonys for her performances in *Dear World, Gypsy,* and *Sweeney Todd.* Her revival of *Gypsy,* which premiered in London, was the first performance of the musical in Great Britain. At London's National Theatre she played Gertrude in *Hamlet,* and at the Royal Shakespeare Company she played in Albee's *All Over.* She has worked extensively in television, and her portrayal of the much-beloved Jessica Fletcher in "Murder, She Wrote" has won her several Emmy and Golden Globe awards. She has been inducted into the Theatre Hall of Fame.

ARTHUR LAURENTS is a writer and director. He wrote the books for the musicals *West Side Story* and *Gypsy,* as well as the plays *The Time of the Cuckoo, Home of the Brave,* and *Invitation to a March.* He won Tony Awards for his book for *Hallelujah, Baby!* and for his direction of *La Cage aux Folles.* He has directed several productions of *Gypsy* and recently wrote the book for and directed Broadway's *Nick & Nora.* He wrote the novels *The Way We Were* and *The Turning Point,* both of which he adapted for the screen.

PETER LAWRENCE is production manager for Emanuel Azenberg/Iron Mountain Productions. As a production stage manager he has worked on more than fifteen Broadway shows and has directed the national tours of *Rumors, Social Security,* and *Broadway Bound.* He has been associate producer for the ABC/TV series "The Thorns" and of Mike Nichols's Broadway production of *Death and the Maiden.*

DOROTHY LOUDON is a singer and an actress who began her career in cabaret. She won a Tony Award as Miss Hannigan in Broadway's *Annie.* She starred in Michael Bennett's production of *Ballroom,* and also in *Sweeney Todd, Noises Off,* the revival of *The Women,* and with Katharine Hepburn in *West Side Waltz.* She has worked in cabaret and concerts throughout the years and has recently recorded several highly acclaimed, award-winning records.

PATTI LuPONE began her career with The Acting Company after graduating from the Juilliard School of Music and Drama. She appeared in *The Robber Bridegroom, The Water Engine, The Cradle Will Rock, Working,* and in a Tony-winning performance playing the title role in *Evita.* She appeared in the London production of *Les Misérables* and played Reno Sweeney in the Lincoln Center revival of *Anything Goes.* On television she can be seen in the drama "Life Goes On."

CAMERON MACKINTOSH began his producing career in London with productions that included *Godspell, Side by Side by Sondheim,* and *Oliver!* He has gone on to produce over 250 productions including *Cats, Song and Dance, Little Shop of Horrors, Les Misérables, The Phantom of the Opera, Miss Saigon,* and *Five Guys Named Moe.* With offices in London and New York, his productions have played in cities throughout the world and in dozens of foreign languages. He is currently preparing to produce the film version of *Les Misérables.*

KEN MARSOLAIS produced the Eugene O'Neill centennial revivals of *Long Day's Journey into Night* and *Ah, Wilderness!,* starring Colleen Dewhurst and Jason Robards. He also presented the revival of *You Can't Take It with You* with the same acting team, and the Edward Albee–directed revival of *Who's Afraid of Virginia Woolf?* with Colleen Dewhurst and Ben Gazzara. His other productions include *The Skin of Our Teeth, Poor Murderer, The Shadow Box, The Queen and the Rebels,* and *Ned and Jack.* He produced the film *An American Original,* a documentary on Philip Curtis's life and works. Recently, he presented the concert "Celebrating Sondheim" at Carnegie Hall.

BARBARA MATERA was born in Great Britain, where she worked in the costume shops at the Old Vic and Covent Garden. She then opened her own small costume shop in London, which she operated until emigrating to the United States in 1960. She founded Barbara Matera Ltd. in New York with her husband, Arthur, where they make costumes for theatre, film, television, and ballet.

ELIZABETH IRELAND McCANN has produced works that have garnered sixty-four Tony nominations with twenty wins. Her more notable productions are *Dracula, The Elephant Man, The Dresser, Amadeus, Home, Orpheus Descending,* and *Nick & Nora,* plus eight New York presentations of the Royal Shakespeare Company. Off-Broadway she has produced *Painting Churches* and *Pacific Overtures.* She has also presented a Broadway season of Pilobolus Dance Theatre and two season tours of the D'Oyly Carte Company. She served as executive director of The Big Apple Circus, and is on the board of City Center of Music and Dance, Manhattan Theatre Club, and INTAR.

RODGER McFARLANE, one of America's leading AIDS activists and fund-raisers, is former executive director of Gay Men's Health Crisis (GMHC), the nation's first and largest AIDS service organization. His benefit production credits include the landmark 1983 SRO performance of Ringling Brothers and Barnum & Bailey Circus at Madison Square Garden; "The Best of the Best," featuring Bette Midler, at the Metropolitan Opera House in 1985; BRAVO Cable Network's annual telecast of "Unfinished Stories: Artists & AIDS"; and literally hundreds more. The recipient of many honors for public service, he accepted a 1991 Outer Critics Circle Award and 1992 Drama Desk Award on behalf of Broadway Cares/Equity Fights AIDS, which he has served as executive director since 1989.

IAN McKELLEN won a Tony Award for his performance as Salieri in *Amadeus.* Other New York appearances include *The Promise, Acting Shakespeare,* and *Wild Honey.* Though he is known for his work in the classical repertory, especially Shakespeare, his versatility as an actor has also led to appearances in plays by Alan Ayckborn, Tom Stoppard, and in the West End production of *Bent.* He has been strongly associated with London's Royal National Theatre, where he played in a highly acclaimed production of *Richard III,* which subsequently toured the world. He was recently knighted for his work in the theatre.

TERRENCE McNALLY is a playwright whose many works include *Bad Habits, It's Only a Play, The Rink, The Ritz, Lisbon Traviata, Frankie and Johnny in the Clair de Lune,* and *Lips Together, Teeth Apart.* He has long been associated with Manhattan Theatre Club, where many of his plays have premiered. His has also written the screenplay for the film *Frankie and Johnny,* based on his play.

ROBERT MORSE created the Tony Award–winning role of Finch in *How to Succeed in Business Without Really Trying.* He re-created his role in the film version of the musical. He also starred in the musical *Sugar* and has appeared in theatre throughout the country as well as in films and on television. His metamorphosis into Truman Capote in *Tru,* a one-man theatrical portrait of the writer, won him much acclaim, including a second Tony Award.

KATE NELLIGAN trained for the stage in London, where she went on to appear with the Royal Shakespeare Company, the National Theatre, the Old Vic, the Bristol Old Vic, and in the West End. In this country, she made her Broadway debut in *Plenty* and has played in *Serious Money, Spoils of War,* and *A Moon for the Misbegotten.* Her film work includes *Eye of the Needle, Eleni,* and her Oscar-nominated performance in *Prince of Tides.*

PETER NEUFELD has been general manager for a score of Broadway shows and tours including *No, No, Nanette, Annie, Working, Timbuktu!, Sweeney Todd, Evita, Talley's Folly, March of the Falsettos,* and *Cats.* He was a co-producer for both *Evita* and *Cats.* With his partner R. Tyler Gatchell, he formed Gatchell & Neufeld, Ltd., in 1969, a theatrical management and production organization.

MANDY PATINKIN is a singer and actor who made his Broadway debut in *Evita,* winning a Tony for his portrayal of Ché Guevara. He was also nominated for his work in *Sunday in the Park with George.* Recently he appeared on Broadway in *The Secret Garden.* His films include *Maxie, Yentl, Ragtime, The House on Carroll Street,* and *The Doctor.* He's recorded two albums of songs, many of which he's performed in his highly praised sold-out concerts throughout the U.S.

FAITH PRINCE won a Tony for her performance as Miss Adelaide in *Guys and Dolls.* Other Broadway appearances have been in *Jerome Robbins' Broadway* and *Nick & Nora.* She originated the role of Trina in the musical *Falsettoland.* Other New York credits include *Bad Habits, Urban Blight, Little Shop of Horrors,* and *Scrambled Feet.* She co-starred in the feature film *The Last Dragon.*

HAROLD PRINCE is a producer and director who has presented many of the classics of American musical theatre. He started his career as an assistant to George Abbott and went on to produce *Fiddler on the Roof, A Funny Thing Happened on the Way to the Forum, Pajama Game,* and *Damn Yankees.* He produced and directed *Cabaret, Zorba, Company, Follies, A Little Night Music, Pacific Overtures,* and *Sweeney Todd.* After years of producing, he turned his energies exclusively to directing such productions as *On the Twentieth Century, Evita, The Phantom of the Opera,* and *Kiss of the Spiderwoman.* He has also directed in opera and film and has won many Tony Awards for his contributions to the theatre.

LYNN REDGRAVE began her career in the classics at London's National Theatre with Laurence Olivier and in the West End. She achieved international prominence in the film *Georgy Girl.* After settling in the United States, she has done extensive work in the New York theatre and on television. She starred on Broadway in *My Fat Friend,* played opposite Ruth Gordon in Shaw's *Mrs. Warren's Profession* at Lincoln Center, and appeared in *A Little Hotel on the Side* and *The Master Builder* for the National Actors' Theatre. Her memoir is titled *This Is Living.*

CHARLES NELSON REILLY won a Tony Award for his performance in *How to Succeed in Business Without Really Trying.* Other Broadway appearances have been in *Bye Bye, Birdie, Hello, Dolly!, and Skyscraper.* He has also appeared often on television and was nominated for an Emmy for his work in "The Ghost and Mrs. Muir." In his second career as a director he helped guide Julie Harris toward a Tony for her solo portrait of Emily Dickinson in *The Belle of Amherst.*

FRANK RICH is drama critic of *The New York Times.* He first saw Broadway in 1957, when his mother took him to see *Bells Are Ringing* at the Shubert Theatre.

LLOYD RICHARDS was for many years director of the Yale Repertory Theatre and dean of the Yale School of Drama. He is also the artistic director of The National Playwrights Conference at the Eugene O'Neill Theatre Center. He directed the original production of *A Raisin in the Sun* and all of August Wilson's plays from *Ma Rainey's Black Bottom* to *Two Trains Running,* winning a Tony for his work on *Fences.* He is also on the board of directors for Theatre Communications Group.

JASON ROBARDS first achieved prominence in Eugene O'Neill's *The Iceman Cometh* and then played in the American premiere of his *Long Day's Journey into Night* opposite Fredric March and Florence Eldridge. He has become a major interpreter of O'Neill's characters, playing in *Hughie, A Touch of the Poet,* and opposite Colleen Dewhurst in *A Moon for the Misbegotten, Ah, Wilderness!,* and again in *Long Day's Journey into Night.* He won a Tony Award for *The Disenchanted* and also played in *Toys in the Attic, A Thousand Clowns, After the Fall,* and recently *Park Your Car in Harvard Yard.* His many films include Oscar-winning performances in *All the President's Men* and *Julia.* He has starred in several television films, among which are "The Day After," "Sakharov," "Haywire," and in an Emmy-winning performance, "Inherit the Wind."

GLORIA ROSENTHAL became interested in the Gypsy Robes when researching an article for Playbill magazine and has since become the Gypsy Robe historian. Her Gypsy Robe articles and photographic material have appeared in several periodicals and books. As a free-lance writer and author, she has been published in a wide variety of national publications.

FRANCIS RUIVIVAR has appeared on Broadway in *Chess, Starlight Express,* and *Shogun: The Musical.* He rejoined *Miss Saigon* as the Engineer after having performed the role during Jonathan Pryce's vacation. He toured nationally in *Cats* and internationally with *Evita,* and has acted in regional theatre and on television.

MICHAEL RUPERT won both a Tony Award and Drama Desk Award for his work in the revival of *Sweet Charity.* He created the role of Marvin in *March of the Falsettos* and *Falsettoland.* Other Broadway appearances have been in *The Happy Time, Pippin,* and *City of Angels.* Regionally he has played in *Damn Yankees, Troupers, Working,* and Leonard Bernstein's *Mass.* He made his debut as a composer with *3 Guys Naked from the Waist Down.* He wrote the score and starred in the musical *Mail* at the Pasadena Playhouse, the Kennedy Center, and on Broadway.

VINCENT SARDI owns and operates the famous "theatrical" restaurant that bears his family name—Sardi's. It has been a much-beloved, vital part of the Broadway community for more than forty years. The classic caricatures of theatre notables that cover its walls are a panorama of the personalities that have made Broadway what it is. They have recently been highlighted and reproduced in a book titled *Off the Wall.*

GENE SHALIT has been an integral part of NBC T.V.'s "Today" show for the past twenty years and is one of the most prominent film critics and interviewers in the country. He has conducted T.V. interviews with most of the major personalities in film, T.V., theatre, and music. On NBC Radio his voice has been heard coast to coast as the "Man About Everything." He recently published the book *Laughing Matters: A Celebration of American Humor.*

CAROLE SHELLEY was one of the original Pigeon sisters in Neil Simons's *The Odd Couple,* playing Gwendolyn on Broadway, in the film, and on television. She was born in London and trained for the stage there. She won a Tony for her performance as the actress Madge Kendal in *The Elephant Man* and is well known for her work in the plays of Noël Coward and George Bernard Shaw. Some of her other New York appearances have been in *The Norman Conquests, Noises Off,* and *Stepping Out.* She acted in the national companies of *Noises Off, Broadway Bound,* and *The Royal Family.*

WOODY SHELP has made hats for such Broadway shows as *Funny Girl, Follies, A Chorus Line, The Secret Garden,* and *The Will Rogers Follies.* He has also worked in film and television.

LIZ SMITH is one of the most widely read and quoted journalists in the country. Her column regularly appears in *New York Newsday, The Los Angeles Times,* and is syndicated in sixty other newspapers in major cities around the United States. She also appears as a commentator on Fox Television.

STEPHEN SONDHEIM began his career as a lyricist writing the words for *West Side Story, Gypsy,* and the Richard Rodgers score of *Do I Hear a Waltz.* He wrote both lyrics and music for *A Funny Thing Happened on the Way to the Forum* and went on to write *Anyone Can Whistle, Company, Follies, A Little Night Music, Pacific Overtures, Sweeney Todd, Merrily We Roll Along,* the Pulitzer Prize–winning *Sunday in the Park with George, Into the Woods,* and *Assassins.* He has won five Tony Awards. For film he has written the score for *Stavisky,* music for *Reds,* and the songs for *Dick Tracy* —one of which won an Oscar as Best Song.

FRANCES STERNHAGEN has played in all forms of theatre on Broadway, off-Broadway, and in regional roles ranging from Restoration drama to musicals. Some productions she has appeared in include *The Country Wife, Blithe Spirit, The Skin of Our Teeth, The Cocktail Party, The Good Doctor, Equus, On Golden Pond,* and *Driving Miss Daisy.* She has acted extensively on T.V. and has appeared in the films *Fedora, Outland, Romantic Comedy, Bright Lights, Big City,* and *Misery,* among others.

ELAINE STRITCH studied theatre with Erwin Piscator at the New School for Social Research. She has appeared on Broadway in *Pal Joey, Bus Stop, Sail Away, Who's Afraid of Virginia Woolf?,* and *Company.* Later, she lived and worked for many years in London, where she starred in the hit T.V. series "Two's Company." Some of the many films she has been seen in are *A Farewell to Arms, Three Violent People, Providence, September,* and *Cocoon II.* Since returning to this country she has resumed her work in cabaret as well as theatre, film, and T.V., and was featured in the concert, documentary, and recording of *"Follies" in Concert.* She received an Academy Award nomination for Best Supporting Actress for her work in Woody Allen's *September.*

SUSAN STROMAN most recently choreographed Broadway's *Crazy for You,* which earned her a Tony. She co-conceived and choreographed the off-Broadway Kander and Ebb revue *And the World Goes 'Round.* She also created the dances for the revival of Kander and Ebb's *Flora the Red Menace.* She choreographed *Liza Minnelli—Stepping Out at Radio City Music Hall.* At New York City Opera she choreographed for Harold Prince's production of *Don Giovanni* and that company's revival of *A Little Night Music.*

LYNNE THIGPEN has played on Broadway in *The Magic Show, Tintypes, A Month of Sundays,* and *Fences.* Her films include *Godspell, The Warriors,* and *Tootsie.* She was a regular on television's "Love, Sidney," makes frequent appearances on "L.A. Law," and has been seen in a number of television films.

ALFRED UHRY came to New York to become a lyricist and was a protégé of the late Frank Loesser. He wrote the book and lyrics for *The Robber Bridegroom.* Other musicals include *Here's Where I Belong, Swing, America's Sweetheart,* and five reconstructions of period musicals for the Goodspeed Opera House. His first play, *Driving Miss Daisy,* won a Pulitzer Prize for drama.

GWEN VERDON epitomizes the dancing Broadway star. She was also the leading exponent of the late Bob Fosse's choreographic style and starred in many of his musical theatre creations, which he tailored to her unique talents and charms. She won Tony Awards for her performances in *Can-Can, Damn Yankees, New Girl in Town,* and *Redhead.* Other Broadway shows she starred in are *Sweet Charity* and *Chicago.* She has worked as a dance mistress for movie musicals and staged the second company of Fosse's *Dancin'*. She works often in T.V. and in such films as *Damn Yankees, Cocoon,* and Woody Allen's *Alice*. She has been a major contributor to preserving the legacy of Bob Fosse.

TOM VIOLA is the Managing Director of Broadway Cares/Equity Fights AIDS, for which he accepted a 1992 Drama Desk Award. He has written more than sixty articles for a variety of national and regional magazines. In 1988, as Actors' Equity Special Projects Coordinator, he produced the Union's 75th Anniversary events, including its 75th Anniversary Gala. For three years following, as Administrative Director of Equity Fights AIDS, he co-produced the Annual Gypsy of the Year Competitions, the 1991 Broadway Flea Market, and facilitated the production of scores of other EFA events nationwide, helping to raise over $2,900,000 for EFA. He is co-producer of the off-Broadway show *The Night Larry Kramer Kissed Me,* and is currently completing Colleen Dewhurst's autobiography *Why Am I Laughing?,* a project on which he worked for a year and a half while serving as Ms. Dewhurst's assistant at Equity.

ROBIN WAGNER was rewarded with Tonys for his set designs for *On the Twentieth Century* and *City of Angels*. His most recent creations have been seen in Broadway's *Crazy for You* and *Jelly's Last Jam*. Other works include *Jerome Robbins' Broadway, Chess, A Chorus Line, Dreamgirls, 42nd Street, Lenny, Promises, Promises, The Great White Hope,* and *Hair*. He has worked off-Broadway, in regional theatre, and for opera companies throughout the world. He teaches theatre arts at Columbia University, is a trustee for the New York Shakespeare Festival, and is senior vice president of The Design Edge.

ELI WALLACH trained for the theatre under Sanford Meisner at the Neighborhood Playhouse. He has established himself as one of America's foremost actors with his performances in such works as *Mr. Roberts, The Rose Tattoo* (which won him a Tony Award), *Camino Real, Rhinoceros,* and *Luv*. His many movie appearances include *The Misfits, Lord Jim, Cinderella Liberty,* and *Nuts*. He has acted in many national tours, in regional theatre, and T.V. films. He is an original member of the Actors' Studio and often acts with his wife, Anne Jackson.

TONY WALTON is a designer who has created sets for *Pippin, The Good Doctor, Chicago,* Bette Midler's *Clams on the Half Shell Revue, The House of Blue Leaves, Anything Goes, Lend Me a Tenor, Six Degrees of Separation, Grand Hotel,* and *The Will Rogers Follies*. He won Tony Awards for his scenic designs for *Pippin, The House of Blue Leaves,* and *Guys and Dolls*. His designs for the films *Mary Poppins* and *Murder on the Orient Express* won him Oscars, and he also designed *All That Jazz, The Wiz,* and *Regarding Henry*. He won an Emmy for the television version of Dustin Hoffman's *Death of a Salesman*.

WENDY WASSERSTEIN won both the Tony Award and the Pulitzer Prize for drama for *The Heidi Chronicles*. Her first playwriting success was *Uncommon Women and Others*. She has also written *Isn't It Romantic* and the television play "Drive, She Said."

LILLIAS WHITE has played on Broadway in *Cats, Once on This Island, Dreamgirls, Rock 'n' Roll: The First 5,000 Years,* and *Barnum*. She won an Obie Award for her work in William Finn's *Romance in Hard Times* and was recently seen in Cy Coleman's *The Life*. She is currently a regular on T.V.'s "Sesame Street."

ROBERT WHITEHEAD has, in more than forty years of work on Broadway, produced or co-produced some of the most notable plays in the American theatre. His first production was *Medea* with Dame Judith Anderson, which he revived in recent years with his wife, Zoe Caldwell, in the title role and Judith Anderson returning as the Nurse. Some of his other presentations include *The Member of the Wedding* with Julie Harris and Ethel Waters, *The Visit* starring Alfred Lunt and Lynn Fontanne, *Bus Stop* with Kim Stanley, *The Skin of Our Teeth,* and the original production of Eugene O'Neill's *A Touch of the Poet,* both starring Helen Hayes, *A Matter of Gravity* and *West Side Waltz,* both with Katharine Hepburn, and *No Man's Land* with Sir John Gielgud and Sir Ralph Richardson. He has produced several plays by Arthur Miller, including the revival of *Death of a Salesman*. Recently he presented *A Few Good Men* and *Park Your Car in Harvard Yard*. A creative force behind the forming of the Broadway Alliance, he produced its first offering, *Speed of Darkness*.

AUGUST WILSON established himself as one of the foremost writers of contemporary American drama with his play *Ma Rainey's Black Bottom*. He continued his cycle of plays about Afro-American life, each set in a different decade of the twentieth century, with *Fences,* which won the Tony for best play, and was followed by *Joe Turner's Come and Gone* and *The Piano Lesson*. Both *Fences* and *The Piano Lesson* won the Pulitzer Prize for drama. His most recent work is *Two Trains Running*.

JULIE WILSON has become known as a premier interpreter of the songs of Cole Porter, Harold Arlen, Kurt Weill, Irving Berlin, and Stephen Sondheim. She has had a diverse career including Broadway, films, nightclubs, cabaret, and recordings. Her nightclub work has taken her throughout the world. On the London stage and in national tours she has played in such musicals as *Company, Kismet, Gypsy, Pajama Game,* and *Bells Are Ringing*.

ALEX WITCHEL is a reporter for *The New York Times*. Previously, she was house manager for *Dreamgirls* at the Imperial Theatre and *A Chorus Line* at the Shubert.

B. D. WONG made his Broadway debut with his acclaimed performance as Song Liling in *M Butterfly,* for which he won a Tony Award. He has appeared on T.V., in films, and played in the first Asian American production of *A Chorus Line,* presented by the East/West Players.

Written and compiled by Stefan Fitterman

INDEX

(Page numbers in **boldface** refer to photo captions.)